The rise of the modern educational system

This book is published as part of the joint publishing agreement established in 1977
between the Fondation de la Maison des Sciences de l'Homme and the Press
Syndicate of the University of Cambridge. Titles published under this arrangement
may appear in any European language or, in the case of volumes of collected essays,
in several languages.

New books will appear either as individual titles or in one of the series which the
Maison des Sciences de l'Homme and the Cambridge University Press have jointly
agreed to publish. All books published jointly by the Maison des Sciences de
l'Homme and the Cambridge University Press will be distributed by the Press
throughout the world.

Cet ouvrage est publié dans le cadre de l'accord de co-édition passé en 1977 entre la
Fondation de la Maison des Sciences de l'Homme et le Press Syndicate of the
University of Cambridge. Toutes les langues européennes sont admises pour les
titres couverts par cet accord, et les ouvrages collectifs peuvent paraître–plusieurs
langues.

Les ouvrages paraissent soit isolément, soit dans l'une des séries que la Maison des
Sciences de l'Homme et Cambridge University Press ont convenu de publier
ensemble. La distribution dans le monde entier des titres ainsi publiés conjointement
par les deux établissements est assurée par Cambridge University Press.

The rise of the modern educational system:

Structural change and social reproduction 1870–1920

DETLEF K. MÜLLER
Ruhr-University Bochum

FRITZ RINGER
University of Pittsburgh

BRIAN SIMON
University of Leicester

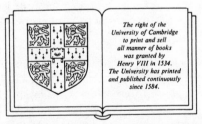

The right of the
University of Cambridge
to print and sell
all manner of books
was granted by
Henry VIII in 1534.
The University has printed
and published continuously
since 1584.

CAMBRIDGE UNIVERSITY PRESS
Cambridge
New York   New Rochelle   Melbourne   Sydney

EDITIONS DE
LA MAISON DES SCIENCES DE L'HOMME
Paris

Published by the Press Syndicate of the University of Cambridge
The Pitt Building, Trumpington Street, Cambridge CB2 1RP
32 East 57th Street, New York, NY 10022, USA
10 Stamford Road, Oakleigh, Melbourne 3166, Australia
and Editions de la Maison des Sciences de l'Homme
54 Boulevard Raspail, 75270 Paris Cedex 06

First published 1987
Reprinted 1988 (Twice)

Printed in Great Britain at the University Press, Cambridge

British Library cataloguing in publication data

The Rise of the modern educational system:
structural change and social reproduction
1870–1920.
1. Education – History – 19th century
2. Education – History – 20th century
I. Müller, Detlef K.   II. Ringer, Fritz
III. Simon, Brian
370'.9'034   LA126

Library of Congress cataloging in publication data

The Rise of the modern educational system.
Bibliography.
Includes index.
1. Education – Great Britain – History – 19th century.
2. Education – France – History – 19th century.
3. Education – Germany – History – 19th century.
I. Müller, Detlef K.   II. Ringer, Fritz K., 1934–
III. Simon, Brian.
LA631.7.R57   1987   370'.941   86–17601

ISBN 0 521 33001 7
ISBN 2 7351 0168 1 (France only)

Contents

Part I: Concepts and hypotheses

vi   *Contents*

Part II: Structural change and social reproduction in England

Part III: Debate and concluding discussion

Tables and figures

Contributors

James Albisetti: Associate Professor, Honors Program and History Department, University of Kentucky. Author of *Secondary School Reform in Imperial Germany* (Princeton, 1983) and of articles on women's education in Imperial Germany.

Klaus Harney: Professor of Education, J. W. Goethe-Universität, Frankfurt. Author of *Die preussische Fortbildungsschule* (Weinheim, 1980) and of articles on adult and vocational education.

John Honey: Until 1985 Professor and Dean of the Faculty of Education, Leicester Polytechnic. Author of *Tom Brown's Universe: The Development of the Victorian Public School* (London, 1977) and of articles on the 'public' schools in England.

Roy Lowe: Senior Lecturer in the Faculty of Education, University of Birmingham. Co-author of *The English School: Its Architecture and Organisation* (London, 1977) and author of articles on aspects of English education during the nineteenth and twentieth centuries.

Detlef K. Müller: Professor of the Social History of Education at the Institut für Pädagogik, Ruhr-Universität Bochum. Director of the research project on 'Knowledge and Society in the Nineteenth Century'. Author of *Sozialstruktur und Schulsystem: Aspekte zum Strukturwandel des Schulwesens im 19. Jahrhundert* (Göttingen, 1977) and of articles on the social history of German secondary education.

David Reeder: Senior Lecturer in Education and Urban Studies, University of Leicester. Editor of *Urban Education in the Nineteenth Century* (London, 1977) and of *Educating our Masters* (Leicester, 1980). Author of articles on the history of education and, as an urban historian, on aspects of urban development in England in the nineteenth century.

Fritz Ringer: Mellon Professor of History at the University of Pittsburgh. Author of *The Decline of the German Mandarins: The German Academic Community, 1890–1933* (Cambridge, Mass., 1969), of *Education and Society in Modern Europe* (Bloomington and London, 1979) and of articles on French and German social and intellectual history.

Jürgen Schriewer: Professor of Comparative Education, J. W. Goethe-Universität, Frankfurt. Author of *Die französischen Universitäten, 1945–1968* (Bad Heilbrunn, 1972) and of *Schulreform und Bildungspolitik in Frankreich* (Bad Heilbrunn, 1974). Co-editor of *Geschichte der Pädagogik und systematische Erziehungswissenschaft* (Stuttgart, 1975). Author of articles on theories and methods in comparative education, on the French educational system and on the history of educational thought.

Brian Simon: Emeritus Professor of Education, University of Leicester. Author of *The Two Nations and the Educational Structure, 1780–1870* (London, 1960), of *Education and the Labour Movement, 1870–1920* (London, 1965), of *The Politics of Educational Reform, 1920–1940* (London, 1974) and of other works on contemporary educational issues and psychology.

Hilary Steedman: Research Officer, National Institute of Economic and Social Research, London. Author of articles in *Comparative Education, Compare* and *European Journal of Education.*

Heinz-Elmar Tenorth: Professor of History and Philosophy of Education, J. W. Goethe-Universität, Frankfurt. Author of *Zur deutschen Bildungsgeschichte 1918 bis 1945* (Cologne and Vienna, 1985), and of articles on the history of teachers in Prussia and on the philosophy of education.

Preface

The original discussion which finally led to the publication of this volume took place at an international seminar held in 1979 at the Ruhr-University Bochum. This was organised by Detlef Müller under the auspices of a wider Research Project on Knowledge and Society in the Nineteenth Century (Sonderforschungsbereich Wissen und Gesellschaft im 19. Jahrhundert), which was financed by the Deutsche Forschungsgemeinschaft (DFG) of the Federal Republic of Germany. After papers were exchanged and fully discussed, two additional conferences were held at Leicester and at Bochum to complete plans for the present volume and to discuss further the major concepts and hypotheses.*

From the beginning we directed our attention to underlying similarities or patterns that could be detected amid the welter of specific national differences in the development of English, French and German secondary and higher education. In place of *ad hoc* descriptions of particular institutions, and of strictly national narratives, we favoured socio-historical and comparative approaches to educational *systems*. Indeed, we aimed at a systematic interpretation of structural change during what we came to regard as a decisive period in the history of European secondary and higher education. We agreed that this formative period extended from about 1870 to the First World War or shortly thereafter, although certain key processes in England in fact originated as early as the 1850s.

We also agreed that the structural changes that took place in education

* The editors wish to express their gratitude to the DFG, to the University of Bochum, to the Sonderforschungsbereich and to the Social Science Research Council in England for support under the SSRC–DFG exchange scheme, which assisted in the planning of the international seminar. Thanks are due also to Ingrid Bickmann and Gisa Schaefer for the typing of the manuscript, and to Helma Aschenbach and Roy Lowe for help with proofreading.

during this period were not shaped by anything like the objective 'needs' of industrial–technical economies. Instead, the three national systems of education that emerged resembled each other primarily *in their social effects*, and this despite apparent dissimilarities in specific institutional forms. Thus the role played by the state and by centralised public administration differed markedly in English, French and German education, and yet the institutional patterns that emerged were not nearly as dissimilar as has sometimes been thought. In all three nations the processes we studied resulted in hierarchical systems of education that tended to reproduce and to fortify the class and status structures of society.

How this end result came about is not easy to say in a few words. There were important *interactions* between the educational system and the occupational system, and between established educational traditions and institutions on the one hand, and new social pressures on the other. But far from being mere effects of altered conditions outside the educational system, the dynamics of change within that system had a logic and force of their own. In this sense the structural transformation of secondary education during this period was a relatively autonomous, and indeed partly causal, element within the larger process of social change. As in that larger process, moreover, outcomes in education were often partly or wholly inconsistent with the intentions of at least some of the agents who helped to bring them about, and this increased our dissatisfaction with purely intentional accounts of educational change.

On the other hand, we were also agreed on the need for detailed empirical and *historical* work. We therefore continually checked and rechecked our interpretive concepts and hypotheses against our own historical knowledge and against that of expert colleagues who participated fruitfully in our discussions, though not all of them ultimately became contributors to this volume. Among the concepts and hypotheses we discussed, the model of 'systematisation' was initially proposed by Detlef Müller. The notion of 'segmentation' was introduced by Fritz Ringer, while Hilary Steedman offered the concept of 'defining institutions'. Brian Simon sought, within a Marxist framework of analysis, to develop a coherent alternative to the sort of simplification that would make the educational system a mere adjunct of the economy.

The Introduction that follows is intended to present an initial survey of the main analytical issues to be addressed and debated. Then, in Part I of the book, each of the three editors presents his own preferred analytical scheme. In Chapter 1 Detlef Müller describes the process of systematisation and illustrates it with a summary account of structural change in German secondary education between 1870 and 1920. In Chapter 2 Fritz Ringer writes about the concept of segmentation and applies it primarily to the history of French secondary education from the 1860s to the end of the First

World War. In Chapter 3 Brian Simon focuses on England, especially secondary education after 1850, and considers the analytical relevance of 'systematisation', of 'segmentation', and of other promising approaches to the social history of English education. He also thereby introduces Part II of the book, which is entirely devoted to the English system, again with a predominant emphasis on secondary education.

The decision to devote the central Part II of the volume to England owed something to the strength of the 'English delegation' at our conferences, as well as to related practical issues. But we also came to the conclusion that it was wise to concentrate our efforts on a single national case, in particular its secondary school system, for this has been particularly important in its impact on twentieth-century social structures. It seemed to us particularly interesting and suggestive, moreover, that analytical models derived from the study of Continental systems proved largely applicable to the English experience.

Part II appropriately begins with Hilary Steedman's account of systematisation in the history of the endowed grammar schools (Chapter 4). David Reeder then discusses the reconstruction of secondary education in England from 1869 to 1920 (Chapter 5), and John Honey analyses the culture of the English 'public' schools in 'The Sinews of Society' (Chapter 6). Finally, Roy Lowe offers an account of structural change in English higher education (Chapter 7), which was of course closely related to parallel processes at the secondary level. The fact that secondary education for women is not included in Part II reflects our sense that the codification of systematic structures in this field did not take place until after the systematisation of boys' secondary education.

The concluding Part III of the book is intended to preserve and convey key portions of the very lively debates that took place at our conferences. Thus James Albisetti defends the view that the stated intentions and proposals of major participants in the education debates of the late nineteenth century should be taken seriously, while also highlighting a series of remarkable parallels between the French and German versions of these debates (Chapter 8). Klaus Harney and Jürgen Schriewer then undertake an even broader critique of the main comparative and analytical approaches presented in this volume (Chapter 9). James Albisetti and Elmar Tenorth more specifically assess the concepts of systematisation and of segmentation, respectively (Chapters 10 and 11), and Detlef Müller and Fritz Ringer then offer separate rejoinders and concluding comments.

It is worth noting in this connection that our conferences and the work on this volume gradually brought its editors, as well as some of its other contributors, closer together in their views than they had been at the outset. Nevertheless, important differences in approach and interpretation certainly remain. This book is therefore offered not as a single, co-ordinated and completed theory of change in education during our period, but as an attempt to stimulate scholarly discussion and perhaps to raise somewhat the level of debate in the field.

Detlef K. Müller
Fritz Ringer
January 1986   Brian Simon

Introduction

FRITZ RINGER

In England, as in France and Germany during the later nineteenth century, educational institutions were transformed by interrelated structural changes that set the decisive patterns for subsequent developments in education right up to the present day. One way to describe the transformations of this critical period is to point out that they brought secondary and higher education into closer interaction with the occupational system of the high industrial era. Primarily involved on the side of the educational system were certain younger and less prestigious institutions and curricula that were considered 'modern', 'technical' or 'applied' and thus potentially fruitful contributors to economic and technological progress. Primarily affected on the side of the occupational system was a range of younger professions that had come to be more educated than their early industrial precursors and whose expertise was arguably more relevant to commerce and industry than that of the older liberal and learned professions. The *partial* and *sectoral convergence* between the educational and the occupational systems that began in this way during the late nineteenth century has continued, through recurrent crises, ever since.

Economic functionalists have understandably been tempted to interpret this phenomenon of convergence as an adjustment of the educational system to the technological requirements of high industrial and late industrial economies. After all, contemporary societies do indeed have to equip large numbers of people with competences that early industrial societies could neglect. Thus Robert Locke has plausibly argued that high rates of economic development in Germany toward the end of the nineteenth century were due in large measure to the quantity and quality of training offered at the German technical institutes, which were both larger and more practically oriented than the Ecole Polytechnique in Paris, and yet more scientific in their approach to knowledge than the French *écoles nationales d'arts et métiers*.[1] Moreover, there certainly were scientists, technical experts, business leaders and educational reformers during the later nineteenth century who actively urged the modernisation of educational institutions in the light of newly emerging technical and economic 'needs'. When such new educational options as the French *enseignement spécial* and the German *Realgymnasium* first became available, they attracted enrolments quickly enough to suggest a positive 'market' or 'demand' for such options among parents from certain social groups.

Nevertheless, the economic functionalist approach to educational change is seriously flawed in several respects. To begin with, no one has ever succeeded in specifying the functionalist case by demonstrating the usefulness of *particular* curricula for *particular* technical or business positions. Thus Locke merely asserts that the abstractly theoretical bent of the Ecole Polytechnique spoiled its graduates for practical technical work. But even if we accept this judgement as generally reasonable, we may find it harder to concede Locke's simultaneous claim that the *écoles nationales d'arts et métiers* offered *too little* in the way of systematic science and technology, a claim that conflicts with Rodney Day's persuasive evidence to the contrary.[2] While also giving little attention to the qualitative character and quantitative significance of practically oriented programmes in French science faculties and related institutions, Locke simply tells us that the German technical institutes, and they alone, offered the *right sort* of education in the *right quantity* for optimal economic growth. But how does he know that? Could he specify the 'needs' of industry with comparable exactitude even for today? Were there enough places in industry even for the engineers and technicians that France did produce? Might Germany not have drawn more economic benefit from its highly developed system of primary and post-primary schooling, or from a surviving apprenticeship system and an emerging vocational school programme, than from its universities and technical institutes? And are we not beginning to wonder nowadays whether general forms of higher education may be more useful, even from the viewpoint of economic productivity, than highly articulated systems of specific technical qualifications? To raise such issues is just to indicate that the economic functionalist account of educational change (and the educationalist account of economic growth) must be questioned in detail, even though it seems initially plausible when stated at a very high level of generality.

A further difficulty with the economic functionalist case is more immediately apparent in the historical sources themselves. We can read what was written during the public debates over the future of secondary education in England, France and Germany, for example, and we can certainly find a few single-minded spokesmen for scientific and technical education among the participants in those debates. Yet we cannot help but notice as well that most recommendations made in those discussions aimed not only at economic benefits, but also and even primarily at a certain structure of social roles and ranks, in which those with 'applied', or 'merely practical' or 'technical', schooling typically ranked very low indeed. Even when established business leaders pointed to the needs of the economy, they often in fact explicitly or implicitly directed their most 'practical' advice to students from the middle and lower levels of the social hierarchy, while associating themselves, or perhaps their sons, with the more 'elevated' objectives of the traditionally most prestigious institutions and curricula.

It is therefore appropriate, we would argue, to look at the educational transformations of the later nineteenth and early twentieth centuries primarily in terms of their *social effects*, rather than primarily in terms of their *economic causes*. The educational systems that emerged from the structural changes of that crucial period, it seems to us, ended by perpetuating and reinforcing the hierarchic organisation of their societies, and we really want to ask just how this came about.

There has been a tendency to assume that the enlargement of access to secondary schools and university-level institutions that began in the late nineteenth century was a kind of opening of the educational system to new sectors of the population, a 'democratisation', or an improvement in the access chances of the less advantaged social groups. But recent research has thrown considerable doubt on the hypothesis that increased enrolments resulted in a significantly more equal distribution of *relative* educational opportunities. More students from the lower middle and working classes did indeed reach the universities, but so did larger numbers of students from the propertied upper middle classes. The resulting *relative* gains achieved by the working classes long remained virtually insignificant, and even the advances made by the lower middle classes were neither great nor easy to assess in view of rapidly changing socio-occupational categories and of the growing complexity and *hierarchical* differentiation of educational institutions. In becoming more widely available, moreover, educational qualifications tended to lose some of their value in the 'job market'. The old assumption that educational expansion has meant 'democratisation' in the sense of increased individual *socio-occupational mobility* has thus lost most of its credibility. As a matter of fact, individual mobility may be highly overrated as a historical issue – and as a species of 'democracy' – in education as in other fields. In any case, one must begin to seek alternative conceptions of the significance of education for social stratification.

The French sociologist Pierre Bourdieu's concept of social reproduction struck several of us as potentially useful in this connection because it provides an alternative to economic functionalist views of education and because it focuses more on relatively stable class and status relationships than it does on individual mobility. Social reproduction as conceived by Bourdieu entails the re-creation of hierarchic social relationships over time, or from parental to filial generations.[3] Bourdieu distinguishes between economic, social and cultural capital. Social capital consists of familial 'connections' and the like. Cultural capital in one of its forms is cultural 'background', a relationship to the dominant culture that is passed along by the family. If those who inherit this form of cultural capital enter the school system, they have a very high chance of obtaining valuable credentials, which in turn will give them access to favourable occupational and social positions. Thus educational credentials largely confirm and certify family background; but they also constitute a new and highly convertible form of cultural capital. In describing contemporary French society, Bourdieu has stressed the bimodal shape of the social hierarchy, the fact that the distribution curves for economic and cultural capital are typically somewhat separated, as if by an axis of symmetry. He has also called attention to the phenomenon of 'conversion' (*reconversion*), that is to changes in the reproductive strategies of dominant social groups that have affected the relationship of partial interconvertibility between economic and cultural capital in post-war France.

In a simple form of social reproduction, the distribution of the three types of capital within a parental generation would be reincarnated in an essentially similar distribution within the following generation. The children of the highly educated would end up with educational advantages comparable to those of their parents. But this is *not* to say that most university students would necessarily be the children of university graduates. After all, university-educated parents might also have been joined at the universities by less favoured social groups. Their success in passing on their cultural capital would have to be considered perfect if all their children reached universities, even if the children had to share this advantage as much as, but no more than, the parents shared it. Indeed, what is reproduced, according to Bourdieu, is always a set of *relative* advantages and disadvantages, positions in a set of class *relationships*, not absolute quantities of economic, social or cultural capital.

Nor is social reproduction typically as simple as the examples of the last two paragraphs. In a certain context, even the widening of access to advanced education might help to reproduce the prevailing class relationships by improving the legitimating capacity of the educational system. More routinely, absolute assets might be increased to maintain relative advantages, or exchanged for more promising relative advantages in another realm. Or as has already been suggested, there might be significant changes in the relationships among the several forms of capital, or in their interconvertibility. Thus important social groups might find it necessary or advantageous to rely more heavily than in the past on education as a means of maintaining their social positions. Something along those lines apparently happened in connection with the structural changes of our period. Increasingly articulated educational systems came to play more central roles in perpetuating social hierarchies, and it is this development we have tried to understand under the heading of education and social reproduction.

The main difficulty we have had with Bourdieu's model is that it is rather unhistorical. Despite the flexibility introduced by the idea of possible changes in the relationships among the several species of capital, Bourdieu's educational system seems timelessly and almost too perfectly to fulfil its reproductive function. But I suspect that the degree of separation or incongruity between the distributions of economic and cultural capital has varied historically and from country to country, that it was greater during the early nineteenth century than it is today, and that it has in fact been attenuated by the convergence between education and occupation since about 1870. In any case, all of us have been interested in dynamic processes of structural *change*, and we are convinced that these processes profoundly altered the role played by the educational system within the larger society. More specifically, we believe that modern educational systems as we know them only really emerged during our period, together with that capacity to define and perpetuate social distances that Bourdieu rightly ascribes to them.

That is why most of us were fascinated by the work of Detlef Müller, and particularly by his emphasis upon processes of change *within* the educational system, and upon the impact of educational qualifications upon the socio-occupational hierarchy. According to Müller, the Prussian *Gymnasium* of the early nineteenth century enrolled a good many students who did *not* prepare for university entry, but left school after a few years to pursue a variety of non-graduate occupational paths. The *Gymnasium* thus functioned almost as a common school, with a socially diverse pattern of recruitment that was closely linked and effectively sustained by an equally diverse 'output' of academically oriented graduates *and* non-academically oriented early leavers. In its social effects this pattern was at least potentially 'democratic', to the extent that students entering the *Gymnasium* from relatively humble backgrounds might be encouraged by academic success and by the prompting of teachers to alter their perspectives from those of early leavers to those of graduates and university entrants. The more this happened, however, the greater the academically and socially conservative pressures became to transform the *Gymnasium* into a purely university-preparatory institution and in effect to channel potential early leavers away from the *Gymnasium* into the *Realschulen, Realgymnasien* and *Oberrealschulen* of the later nineteenth century. While these less fully accredited institutions ultimately managed to send many of their graduates to the universities as well, they long in effect prevented their pupils from competing effectively for access to the universities and to the academic professions. The overall process, according to Müller, was thus one of exclusion, not one of expansion and democratisation.

With this in mind Müller developed the concept of systematisation, which really launched the whole discussion that produced this book. An initially diverse collection of vaguely defined schools, Müller argues, was gradually transformed into a highly structured *system* of precisely delimited and functionally interrelated educational institutions in Prussia, and possibly elsewhere, during the late nineteenth and early twentieth centuries. In a sense the Prussian educational system became *more systematic*: the boundaries between different types of secondary institutions were more sharply drawn; curricula and graduate qualifications were meticulously specified; and the functional relationships among the different parts of the total system were fully articulated. Partly, the process was one of bureaucratic rationalisation. Government officials extracted fixed and explicit rules from previously implicit patterns of practice; in pursuit of a rational division of labour, they fully specified institutional roles. At the same time, the system thus created was a socially hierarchical one, and the whole process of systematisation was also a conflict-ridden exercise in social demarcation. Powerful interest groups intervened in decisive ways at a time of socially conservative reaction to the great depression of the late nineteenth century. What emerged from the systematisation of Prussian secondary schooling between 1870 and 1920, according to Müller, was therefore a rigorously stratified or 'class' system of education that has since been extended and modified but by no means replaced.

It is worth noting that the process of systematisation proceeded from the top of the academic hierarchy downwards. Thus in Prussia, beginning in the early nineteenth century, Latin schools that met certain standards were officially designated *Gymnasien*, while the remaining schools fell into a residual category of institutions that were both incompletely accredited and incompletely defined. From 1860 on, the later so-called *Realgymnasien* began to take shape, while the even less favoured *Oberrealschulen* did not emerge until 1878. At each step of the process new academic and social territories were thus in effect charted or colonised. More recently organised programmes were initially defined primarily by the boundary that separated them from the older and more established institutions. But as even remoter lands were opened up, further academic and social distinctions were discovered or invented. The decades around 1900 witnessed a critical stage in this downward advance of systematisation, in England and France as well as in Germany, as an essentially binary pattern of elite and popular schooling was superseded by an essentially triadic structure of elite second-ary, non-elite secondary, and higher primary education.

Of course educational systems have always been to some degree systematic, in the sense that their parts have been interrelated and interactive. Yet in Europe during our period the major systems certainly became more systematic than ever before. They seemed to evolve *as if* all particular institutions and arrangements were being adjusted to a unified overall plan. As complete hierarchies of school types were elaborated, the rank order of qualifications they offered came to define a corresponding hierarchy of occupations. This was particularly clear in late nineteenth-century Prussia, where educational qualifications were used to set civil service ranks, which in turn structured the wider occupational system. Certainly in France, and probably elsewhere as well, educational qualifications had a similarly defining impact upon the structure of occupations, so that the sectoral convergence between the educational and occupational systems during these crucial decades was a *genuinely interactive one*. With little exaggeration, one can speak of an 'educationalisation of the occupational system', not an industrialisation of education or a functional adjustment of the educational system to the economy. And this adds force to the concept of the relative autonomy of the educational system within the larger society.

My own contributions to our discussion have focused on the concept of 'segmentation' and on the idea of the 'generalist shift'. The term 'segmentation' is essentially descriptive. It refers to the division of educational systems into parallel segments or 'tracks', which differ both in their curricula and in the social origins of their pupils. Statistical measures of segmentation report the degree to which particular secondary programmes or schools, for example, deviate from the norm for the secondary system as a whole in their students' social origins. Curricular differentiation alone does not constitute segmentation; clear social differences must be involved as well. What matters is the *conjunction* between social and curricular differences, for such a conjunction will invest curricular differences with socially hierarchical meanings, which in turn will define the social status of graduates. It is only through the wedding of traditional cultural models to social distinctions that educational systems have come to play so powerful a role in social reproduction.

What I call the 'generalist shift' is the observable tendency of newly established 'practical' or 'applied' educational programmes and institutions to take on a more generalist and academic character, largely in response to the socio-cultural aspirations of teachers and parents.[4] The idea of the generalist shift has seemed to me particularly suited to the history of French 'special' and 'modern' secondary schooling from the 1860s to the turn of the century, but it may also help to account for the process of systematisation as a whole.

Simplifying a little, one can picture the European educational systems of the mid-nineteenth century as defining an academic and social scale. Primary schools for the lower classes made up the lower end of this scale. At the upper end highly accredited secondary schools trained their graduates for the universities and for the traditionally learned professions, while also schooling non-graduate pupils for other middle-class occupations. Driven along partly by enrolment pressure and competition for credentials, the process of systematisation was a filling-in of the intervening positions along this academic and social scale. Whether already in existence or newly created, intermediate institutions tended to move upwards, imitating and approaching the traditionally prestigious secondary schools. The latter, meantime, defined and asserted their distinctiveness with increasing vigour, as did less favoured institutions with respect to rivals even lower on the scale.

The result was that lines in the middle ranges of the scale were sharply debated and ever more precisely drawn. Forms of segmentation had existed earlier; but they now became more significant for certain sectors of the occupational system, as well as more finely articulated, and much more systematic in character. Indeed, the public discussions between educational reformers and social conservatives in France and elsewhere during the late nineteenth and early twentieth centuries become much more comprehensible if one reads them as conflicts over the precise social meanings and statuses to be assigned to older and younger programmes conceived of as more or less *generally* educative, as against those conceived of as partly or wholly 'applied' or vocational in character.

Hilary Steedman has suggested the concept of 'defining institutions' in place of the 'generalist shift'. Her point is that certain distinctive characteristics of the most prestigious school types were non-curricular, at least in England. Since the generalist shift, by my own account, is essentially an imitation of the dominant institutions, one need not prejudge whether the aspect imitated was curricular or not. In addition to curriculum, the ethos and organisation of defining institutions were in fact emulated, at least in England.

These certainly are cogent arguments. On the other hand, curricular differences seem particularly capable of investing social distances with cultural meanings, thus legitimating and perpetuating them. Indeed, as I have suggested elsewhere, the English system of the twentieth century may have been unusually flexible precisely because social differences between schools had not been thoroughly linked to curricular ones.[5] More generally, too, it is hard to imagine a non-curricular difference that would acquire the symbolic force of the distinction between, on the one hand, pure or theoretical and, on the other, practical or applied knowledge, or between 'disinterested' and utilitarian learning.

Of course curricular divergences did not acquire such meanings by force of logic, just as the classical curriculum was not inherently or necessarily less modern than the modern one. Bourdieu has rightly described the contents of a dominant culture as arbitrary, in the sense that they are neither logically nor biologically necessary. And yet there is nothing truly accidental about such linkages as that between Latin and an inherited past, Latin and disinterested culture, or Latin and social distinction. These associations had *historical* origins, and they proved extraordinarily forceful and enduring. That is why they continue to require our special attention.

Let me repeat at this point that my concept of segmentation is primarily descriptive, and that it does not in itself offer a theory of educational change. It does focus attention, however, upon the way in which curricular and cultural alternatives acquire socially hierarchical meanings, and here it is firmly linked to a historical theory, or a theory of tradition. The wedding of curricular patterns to social meanings takes place in an essentially historical process, for the curriculum offered by the traditional forms of elite education is unconsciously supposed to confer qualities upon the student that enrich him personally – and thus indirectly elevate him socially as well. But the qualities involved are clearly products of historical traditions; most typically, they are idealisations of qualities ascribed to the social and cultural elites of former days: the English gentleman, the *honnête homme*, the Humboldtian idealist of *Bildung*. Thus historical traditions confer meanings upon curricular contents, meanings that become important symbolic assets – and defining elements in the hierarchy of education.

My enthusiasm for the sociology of Max Weber, as a matter of fact, is largely due to the place of history in his analysis.[6] Crucial to this aspect of his theory is his distinction of status position from class position, and his definition of status in terms of life-style and social honour. History was brought into his explanatory models because he recognised that status conventions were bound to change more slowly than the realities of class. The past is therefore always present in the symbolic contents of favoured life-styles; the signs of educational distinction are historical compromises in an almost Freudian sense, and the whole status system need never be fully congruent with the hierarchy of wealth and economic power. The rank order of educational institutions and curricula translates a pre-existent social hierarchy into the language of academic prestige, whether in the idiom of cultivation or in that of merit. Once established and vested with a certain autonomy, the educational hierarchy then acts back upon the social hierarchy, primarily to legitimate and reinforce it, but also to supplement and complicate it by the reintroduction of partly incongruent status traditions. The potential tensions and conflicts between the class and status orders, I would argue, became particularly sharp and visible during the crisis of the late nineteenth century precisely because the earlier separateness of the educational hierarchy was being eroded by the increased interaction between education and occupation.

Bourdieu has by no means neglected these relationships. Usually leaving social capital out of account, he has distinguished cultural from economic capital, much as Weber distinguished status from class. Moreover, he has given more searching attention to the symbolic contents of educational traditions, and to social categories and meanings more generally, than any other social theorist since Weber. His account of cultural reproduction derives much of its force from his awareness that hierarchic social relationships are not only expressed but also sustained by such categories and meanings, and that educational systems contribute significantly to their perpetuation. His conception of social reproduction is thus linked to a theory of legitimation – of ideology as symbolic domination, rather than as mere reflex and epiphenomenon.

These dimensions of Bourdieu's work are indispensable for the social historian of education and of knowledge. On the other hand, Bourdieu's 'cultural capital' is not explicitly and fully enough linked to the past; its distribution seems as immediately variable as the distribution of economic capital. Here again, Bourdieu might give more attention to genuine change over time, to historical contingency and variability, and thereby also to the social and ideological incongruities induced by the presence of the past. In other respects Bourdieu has developed aspects of Weber's theories well beyond their original formulations. With respect to status, tradition and history, however, it is Weber's approach that still appears more fruitful.

Despite a certain convergence of viewpoints, as the attentive reader will discover in the chapters that follow, the contributors to this volume continue to disagree about several issues, at least in emphasis. Thus Müller interprets the evolution of Prussian secondary schooling over the course of the nineteenth century primarily as a process of *exclusion*, and his analysis is based on rigorous research at the local and regional level. My own summary sketch of Prussian secondary enrolments in Chapter 2 is intended to challenge Müller's interpretation, or at least to qualify it; but I focus on *net* and *long-term* quantitative changes *in all of Prussia*. Of course, one has to expect a divergence between local, short-term processes on the one hand, and their aggregate effects on the other. My suggestion is only that the exclusionary dynamic must *somewhere* and *sometime* have been accompanied by a countervailing process of expansion. In Prussia as in France, I would argue, there certainly *was* a dynamic of exclusion along the lines charted by Müller; but there was also a process of expansion in the non-elite or 'modern' sector. Over the long run and in the aggregate, these two *countervailing* dynamics produced the net effect of quantitative stability in the traditional secondary sector, along with moderate expansion in the newer and less highly accredited programmes, especially at the non-graduate level. What we may really need, therefore, is a set of explanatory models that will account for the simultaneous presence of *exclusion and expansion*, and for the *interactive* relationship between them.

A further difference between Müller and myself appears to be largely a matter of perspective. Müller's concept of systematisation focuses on the way in which the fuller articulation of European educational systems after 1870 contributed to the emergence of a highly stratified society. It thus tends to stress the *modernity* of educational systematisation and its role in the establishment and maintenance of a *class* society. My account of segmentation, by contrast, looks more to the past. It emphasises the importance of inherited meanings, and it thus leaves open the possibility of incongruities between the status hierarchy of cultivation on the one hand, and the emerging high industrial class structure on the other. But again it may be desirable to combine the two viewpoints. For there surely was a process of systematisation in the sense intended by Müller; but there was also a somewhat paradoxical activation of *traditional* meanings in the hierarchical structure of the *modern* educational systems that emerged.

That brings me, in conclusion, to an even broader tension and an even more difficult problem of mediation that ran through all our discussions. I mean the tension between the narrative history of particular actions and the analysis of structural change, which is also the difference between the intentional choices of individual agents and groups on the one hand, and systematic outcomes on the other. Certain of Müller's critics found particularly his early accounts of systematisation problematic because they interpreted them as narratives in which 'the system' functioned as a mysterious sort of agent. Or they challenged what they took to be a teleological element in his analysis; they asked how the system could aim at becoming what it ultimately became. In reality, as Müller certainly recognises, systematisation was a real historical process, not a self-adjusting automatic device, and the ultimate consequences of structural change were hardly ever aimed at, whether by individual agents, by social groups or by 'the system'.

In an effort to clarify this facet of our discussion, I have given particular attention to the role of conflicting and contradictory intentions, and to outcomes that were not fully intended by any of the parties involved in the process of change. At least in the French context, even the dominant groups in the conflict over the future of secondary education were occasionally forced to modify their original objectives. Together with weaker adversaries, they then produced compromises that differed from both parties' initial intentions. The actual institution of a new curriculum or school type, too, could alter the original purposes of its sponsors. There was an effect of 'feedback' or trial-and-error that made for a gap between early intentions and ultimate outcomes.

The generalist shift also particularly interested me because it perfectly exemplified this possible gap between intentions and outcomes. Of course the social groups and interests affecting the process were diverse indeed. But their motives and objectives not only conflicted with each other; they also often bore very indirect and even contradictory relationships to the effects they produced. Thus headmasters of non-traditional schools might simply want their institutions to prosper and teachers to obtain better salaries; yet they often proceeded by imitating the traditional schools and programmes, whose prestige they thus unintentionally reinforced. And what about parents and pupils who rebelled against the instrumental instruction offered them and who wanted at least a smattering of 'general culture' as traditionally defined? Did not their legitimate objection to a form of symbolic domination also tend to confirm it? One simply has to keep in mind that agents, whether individuals or groups, act and think in institutional contexts, as well as in fields of knowledge and belief, that typically limit their choices and very often distort the results of their actions. On the other hand, we also encountered sequences in which outcomes were largely or wholly consistent with the intentions of major agents. The leadership exerted by reformist officials in the French Ministry of Education fell at least partly into this category. But the work of the Taunton Commission as described by Brian Simon was a particularly remarkable experiment in planned change. A whole system of institutional arrangements was here almost 'invented' by a group of influential individuals who were in an institutional position to set down general objectives and thus largely to shape subsequent developments. Paradoxically, it was in England, not in France or in Prussia, that an agency of the state, a Royal Commission, played so decisive a role so early in the process of systematisation. The traditional contrast between English and Continental patterns of change in education might have led us to expect the reverse.

Altogether, we would not be surprised if the kind of work represented in this volume were ultimately to encourage a new and more careful look at *differences* between national systems of education. For the present, however, we have focused primarily on the underlying structural *similarities*. Our general aim has been to strengthen the case for comparative studies, and for systematic structural analysis, as against narrative institutional history. We have sought to uncover patterns of change that were broader and more persistent than the intentions of particular agents – and the specific innovations usually celebrated in our textbooks.

In conclusion, a word of caution may be in order. As has already been suggested, there has been a certain convergence of viewpoints among the participants in this volume. Several of us somewhat changed our positions, or at least our emphases, as our discussions proceeded. As a consequence, papers written in response to a participant's earliest formulations may no longer be fully appropriate to the latest form of his argument. The reader is asked to excuse the occasional indirections that inevitably result when a continuous debate, particularly one held at long distance and over a considerable time interval, is represented as a single, simultaneous confrontration of fixed positions.

Part I
Concepts and hypotheses

1. The process of systematisation: the case of German secondary education*

DETLEF K. MÜLLER

Comparative analysis in the history of education must be based on complex regional or national investigations, which in turn must be guided by a research strategy that from the beginning encompasses comparative perspectives and thus escapes regional or national isolation. Systematic comparison cannot rely upon traditional works for individual countries; it cannot simply relate the Paulsens and Liards to each other.[1] The questions pursued in these traditional accounts were so narrow that reference to the educational institutions of other countries was virtually excluded. Comparative analyses that merely confront and compare school forms or describe the relevant political and pedagogical discussions can at best achieve a clear overview of different national structures, but they cannot produce new hypotheses or adequately specified research results.

To move from the national or regional to the comparative level of analysis, one has to fix the place and weight of individual school types within their respective national systems; one must compare the role of higher-grade schools and 'public' schools within the English system as a whole with the role of lower-level and full-scale *Gymnasien* in Germany, or with that of French provincial *collèges* and Parisian *lycées*. Seen in comparative perspective, for example, the German *Gymnasien* lose their integral and homogeneous aspect and become a plurality of types, the highest-ranking of which correspond to the English 'public' schools and to the Parisian *lycées*, even while many others only attained the level of the English higher-grade schools or of the French provincial *collèges*.

In his *Education and Society in Modern Europe* Fritz Ringer has developed an analytical conception that is expanded and specified in the present

* Translated and edited by Fritz Ringer.

publication.[2] His concept of segmentation makes comparative historical analysis possible, particularly with respect to social mobility within the educational system and the social function of institutional differentiation. My own approach takes Ringer's as a point of departure, but focuses especially upon the conditions in which the educational system originates and develops, and upon the impact of changes within that system upon the structure of society.

Fundamental to my own analytical model is the distinction between the process in which the educational system originates and the systematic structure that is reached only at a certain point in time. The concept of the 'educational system' in my scheme is not used loosely, but is precisely defined.[3] Only when the various school forms or educational institutions are interconnected, when the parts of the system are related to each other and their functions interdefined, should one have recourse to the concept of a system. Among German historians of education, the terms *Schulwesen* (the set of all schools) and *Schulsystem* (the system of schools) have until now been used synonymously, as have *Bildungswesen* (set of educational institutions) and *Bildungssystem* (system of educational institutions). But these concepts can be used to characterise different phases in the development of schools and educational institutions. One can speak of a *set* of educational institutions where these institutions have not yet been systematised, but the concept of 'educational system' presupposes the integration of the various educational options available within a national territory.

From the seventeenth century on, the Jesuit order had constructed a virtually perfect educational system, in which all institutions and processes were exactly regulated. But while this 'system' transcended national boundaries and encompassed all of continental Europe, it remained unrelated to the national and regional forms of education that were present as well. The contemporaneous educational institutions of the Protestant towns were organised individually and separately by each town, in complete isolation from each other or from any common objective; privately supported schools followed only the programmes of their founders. The availability of schools, their curricular programmes and the qualifications of their teachers were dependent upon the accidents of regional development; school attendance and choice of school were left to parents alone. Only the organisation of educational institutions by the states since the second half of the eighteenth century was able to transcend confessional characteristics and regional particularities in a long-term process, and thus to lay the foundations for the development of such nation-wide, internally differentiated and functionally articulated educational organisations as the English, French and German systems of the late nineteenth century.

At the same time, the consequences of state intervention must not be overestimated. The actions of states made the institutionalisation of the modern educational system possible: they established frameworks and they increasingly ordered and controlled the process of educational development. But they did not determine that process. One has to abandon the image of a state-controlled organisation that encompassed all educational institutions, shaped them according to plans, supervised them in conformity with legal norms and regulated them in pursuit of social and political aims, just as one has to give up the notion that the various English school forms were unique in character and neither structurally nor functionally comparable. In the whole history of modern educational developments in all states, new school forms were not in actual fact created; rather, existing institutions were reorganised and reclassified. In their clients and sponsors, their confessional characteristics, their housing, their division into grades, their curricula, their teachers and students, institutions adhered to inherited patterns that could be overcome only in a lengthy and conflictual process, which differed for each institution and which led to divergent results.

To specify the structural changes that transformed modern national educational institutions in the nineteenth and twentieth centuries, and to discern and delimit the factors determining these changes in their full complexity, I propose to picture the overall process as an increasing *systematisation* of schools, universities and career paths. The educational institutions of the West European states, which were very incompletely institutionalised at the beginning of the nineteenth century, were gradually transformed during the course of that century into state-wide educational systems, with increasingly codified and organised relationships among the school types (school system), among the university courses of study (university system), and between these two levels and occupational careers (occupational system).

The process of systematisation encompasses three phases: (i) the term 'system emergence' refers to as yet unrelated developments in initially autonomous areas (individual school types, for example) that anticipate the later system; (ii) the 'constitution of the system' refers to the integral organisation of all parts of the system, their functional articulation and classification; (iii) the term 'system complementation' refers to the rounding-out of the constituted system through modification of existing forms, through integration of areas not yet codifiable at the time of the system's constitution, or through the establishment of new institutions in pursuit of objectives unforeseen at the time of the system's constitution. To use and distinguish the terms 'system constitution' and 'system complementation' in a meaningful way, one has to postulate that fundamental organisational and structural principles, as well as functional classifications and distinctions, are laid down in the educational system during the phase of system constitution and that they cannot be removed or circumvented in subsequent developments. After the constitution of the system further changes are largely shaped by the autonomous dynamics of the system, while new educational demands are met predominantly by means internal to the system.[4]

Systematisation in Prussia: the major hypotheses

The educational reforms in the German states at the beginning of the nineteenth century initiated a development in which collections of diverse school types and vocationally oriented institutions were transformed into an educational system that has become paradigmatic for modern industrial societies.[5] Drawing on the American sociologist Talcott Parsons' characterisation of decisive phases in the development of modern social systems as the industrial, the democratic and the educational revolutions, one can argue that in Germany, in contrast to other West European countries and the United States, the educational revolution preceded the democratic revolution.[6]

The German system of public administration, as compared with the English system of administration by a hereditary elite, entailed selection on the basis of achievement and knowledge, as against social origins, tradition and economically grounded influence. In France attendance at a few selected *lycées* or exclusive private schools opened the way to elite institutions for the training of higher civil servants. In England attendance at certain 'public' and selected grammar schools led to the elite universities of Oxford and Cambridge. In Germany, by contrast, a broad spectrum of *Gymnasien*, distributed over the entire country and of equivalent standing regardless of region, awarded the *Abitur* and thus the right to attend the universities, which again were widely distributed and which differed in the quality of individual faculties and in the social origins of students, but not in the standing of their examinations and degrees.

The process of systematisation in Prussia began with the establishment of modern educational institutions at the beginning of the nineteenth century. For the boys' schools the process was largely complete by the end of the century; right up to the present the fundamental structures established have only been modified. The Prussian primary and secondary boys' schools became the systematic core of the modern German school system. Girls' secondary schools and certain of the vocational schools were not integrated into the existing school system, or into the system of civil service careers, until the beginning of the twentieth century.[7]

The establishment of the standardised *Abitur* examination and certificate (1810), the granting of partial exemption from compulsory military service to upper-division secondary pupils who became *Einjährige* (one-year volunteers) (1810), the introduction of university-level state examinations (1804–30) and of qualifying standards for secondary teachers (1812) gradually transformed distinctive regional educational structures into comparable units. A great variety of curricular stipulations and of administrative decrees had the effect of turning only marginally specialised schools into increasingly integrated, clearly delimited school types and thus, by the end of the century, bringing about a functionally differentiated definition of the total system. In the first half of the nineteenth century the highly diverse regulations for particular institutions and school types were brought together only in collections of administrative decrees. They were initially classified only by administrative department and date of regulation, regardless of their occasion, their importance and their pertinence to specific school types. The next step was a subdivision by field, but a classification by type of school and grade level followed only gradually from the middle of the century on.

Beginning in the 1870s, higher officials within the educational administration systematically ordered the existing decrees by subject matter and thus created an integrated and comprehensive regulatory scheme, to which they attributed the character of a public educational regulatory scheme. Highly diverse individual decrees were no longer restricted to particular cases (e.g. an order on the exemption of pupils from instruction in Greek at the *Gymnasium* in X), but were integrated with the few decrees that originally had a generally compulsory character (e.g. the *Abitur* regulation), thus acquiring an increased range of application as well as a more imperative character. Permissive regulations (e.g. 'the school in town X *may* . . .') became injunctions and finally fixed orders for all institutions of a certain type in all of Prussia. Thus in the phase of system emergence, an increasingly autonomous, internally directed, differentiated and comprehensive apparatus of educational administration succeeded in enforcing the implementation of such generally compulsory traits of the system as the structure of sequential age groups in place of flexible criteria of school attendance and promotion – and the standardisation of courses of study into nine-year and six-year sequences.

The increasing differentiation of the educational system was initially guided primarily by the attempt to integrate unique school forms, which had their own specific curricula and teaching personnel, into the overall system. The structural and functional transformation of the school system at the state-wide, Prussian level was no mere addition of essentially parallel regional processes. Given chronologically and structurally dissimilar regional forms of organisation, the process of system emergence can be adequately described only if regional developments in education are investigated in relation to such larger social changes as population growth, urbanisation, economic development and social structure.

The Prussian humanistic *Gymnasium* has usually been regarded as a full-term, academically and socially homogeneous institution; but this is to misjudge its nineteenth-century structure and function. Until around 1860 and 1870 the *Gymnasium* had in fact more similarities with the modern comprehensive school, which is internally differentiated to offer divergent course programmes and to suit divergent levels of academic performance, than it had with its later successor. Until the 1840s the *Gymnasium* theoretically encompassed only the three highest secondary grades (4–6), while the lower secondary grades made up what was known as the 'school'. Three-year secondary 'schools' and five- to six-year *Gymnasien* were only gradually transformed into nine-year institutions oriented towards the *Abitur*. In the larger towns the lower secondary 'schools' also served a majority of the urban population as a means of their completing the compulsory years of schooling. A course of study ending after the second or third secondary grade at the age of 13 or 14 (after six or seven years of primary and secondary schooling) was provided for in the overall curriculum and acknowledged by teachers as an educational unit. The majority of secondary pupils left school early to enter an artisanal or mercantile occupation. Only a small fraction became *Gymnasium* graduates (*Abiturienten*), completing the eight- or nine-year secondary course with a successful *Abitur* examination. Among Berlin pupils in the third secondary grade in 1865, for example, barely 24 per cent completed the *Abitur*.

On the other hand, some of the children of the higher social strata were educated in private schools or by tutors before entering the *Gymnasium* proper. Such delayed entries into the *Gymnasium* emphasised the 'low' character of the secondary 'school'. The elementary grades (for ages 6–9/10) that preceded the 'school' were appropriately called 'pre-schools' (*Vorschulen*). Together the 'pre-schools' and 'schools' enrolled children during the years of compulsory schooling. The term 'pre-school' lost its original meaning only after the lower secondary grades were fully integrated into the *Gymnasium*. Thus in the last third of the nineteenth century the *Vorschulen* increasingly became fee-paying elementary schools attached to the several secondary school types and patronised by the higher social strata. The name *Vorschule* survived because the term *Progymnasium*, which would have suited the later function of the *Vorschule*, was appropriated in the first half of the nineteenth century by institutions that could not be developed into full-term *Gymnasien* because they were located in small towns. *Progymnasien* encompassed only two to four grades beyond the lowest three (beyond the 'school'), they had few pupils, and these often intended to transfer to the upper grades of a nine-year secondary institution in another town.

The wide regional distribution of the *Gymnasien* and schools was initially necessitated by the decentralised structure of Prussian public administration (judges and higher officials living in small towns), by the divergent traditions of newly integrated provinces, by the educational needs of Protestant pastors, teachers and officials, and by the economic situation of the middle classes. Limited financial resources and modest salaries did not permit the Prussian middle classes to invest much in the education of their children. Yet the attainment of advanced secondary qualifications (*Einjährige, Abitur*) was required to preserve the social position of the educated upper middle class (*Bildungsbürgertum*). Those few pupils within a given town or district who intended to prepare for university study required the establishment of a *Gymnasium* encompassing the upper grades, and they would live at home until they attained the *Einjährige* or the *Abitur*. But these upper grades were costly and could be financed only out of the fees paid by the more numerous students in the middle and lower grades who left before completing the *Abitur*. These early leavers, the majority of secondary students until the last third of the nineteenth century, earned the right of entry into the lower and intermediate grades of the civil service and, during the last third of the century, into lower, intermediate and higher white-collar positions in banking, commerce and industry as well.

The multifunctional structure of the *Gymnasium* and of the other secondary schools was thus a precondition of their existence during the first half of the nineteenth century. Even when financial resources are adequate, student–teacher ratios in public education cannot fall below a certain limit. Apart from a few elite institutions, the majority of Prussian *Gymnasien* and secondary schools depended upon the early leavers, and the premature establishment of a differentiated set of primary, higher primary and modern secondary schools (*Realschulen*) would have put the survival of most *Gymnasien* in doubt. Thus the delayed industrialisation of Prussia, as compared to England and France, made possible the socially open character of the early *Gymnasium*.

After the middle of the nineteenth century, during the era of high industrialisation, of population increase, of urbanisation and of high social mobility, this socially open character of the *Gymnasium* and of the other secondary schools led in the 1880s and 1890s to a large oversupply of 'one year volunteers', *Abiturienten*, university students and candidates for the academic professions. Hence the slogan 'academic proletariat', which figured in the political debates of those years.

For the majority of *Gymnasium* students the duration of school attendance was defined by occupational expectations, which in turn were predetermined by the occupations, social positions and education of the parents. Pupils and teachers largely conformed to the existing status conventions. The school was thus not initially confronted by a demand for social mobility. But a large proportion of the early leavers acquired increased educational and occupational expectations for their children, expectations which were bound to alter the established social equilibrium even if the duration of school attendance increased by only one year. Social tensions arose when increased social and geographical mobility, along with low employment prospects in some sectors, raised the occupational expectations of parents and pupils and thus the duration of school attendance, and when prolonged schooling became necessary even to maintain the family's social position.

During the phase of system constitution the multifunctional (comprehensive school) character of the existing secondary schools was replaced by a vertical differentiation. The newly articulated and hierarchic system of school types encompassed primary schools, upper primary and higher primary schools, with or without secondary transfer options, six-year *Realschulen* and nine-year *Oberrealschulen* without Latin, six-year *Realprogymnasien* and nine-year *Realgymnasien* with extensive Latin and Greek. This range of institutions seemed to correspond to the diversity of social needs, to pedagogical realities (course durations dictating the contents and sequence of teaching units) and to differences of individual aptitude. An apparent rationality of organisation created the false impression that the several subsystems were functional and that the educational system was simply replacing familial and vocational forms of education. The apparent rationality of the school system as a whole made possible its 'relative autonomy', since the curricula of the several school types, together with the corresponding qualifications, were established *within* that system.[8]

During the phase of system emergence an occupational differentiation developed that ran parallel with the differentiation of school types. In the Prussian postal service of the late nineteenth century, for example, educational qualifications were linked to bureaucratic ranks in a system of six grades:

1. *Workers without permanent positions:* School leavers from undifferentiated primary schools, or early leavers from eight-year primary schools (dirty jobs, hard physical labour).
2. *Lower grades:* Primary school leavers with good grades who qualified as 'military aspirants' after 12 years of military service as NCOs, or early leavers from secondary schools (skilled workers with permanent positions, postmen, conductors).
3. *Lower intermediate grades:* 'Military aspirants', or secondary school students who completed all but the highest three grades (post office assistants, senior assistants, postmasters).
4. *Intermediate grades:* Secondary school qualifications from the one-year military exemption to the *Abitur* (postal candidates, secretaries, postmasters, senior secretaries, bookkeepers, accountants).
5. *Lower upper grades: Abiturienten* (postal candidates, secretaries, inspectors, postal directors at the head of small post offices).
6. *Upper grades:* University study, state examination, legal proba-

tioners (postal councillor, senior postal councillor, senior postal directors at the head of larger post offices).[9]

Because of the close link between educational qualifications and occupational rank, schooling in Prussia also determined the degree of social mobility, fixing both the beginning level of a career and its upper limits. This applied initially to the civil service alone; but after the middle of the nineteenth century it also affected rank levels and salary groupings in commerce and industry, which were modelled on civil service equivalents. Educational qualifications thus became the primary goals of secondary schooling, and levels of education became the primary criteria of social differentiation in the bureaucracy and in society as a whole.

The structural relationships established within the formalised hierarchy of qualifications and occupational ranks can be analysed as preconditions of social reproduction. The relevant properties of the Prussian educational system developed during the phase of system emergence. They were (i) a high degree of institutionalisation in all parts of the system, (ii) a rigorous coupling of the various levels of the socio-occupational structure to secondary and university-level courses and qualifications, (iii) an increasing differentiation and codification of internally homogeneous educational options, manifested in a system of structurally interrelated school types, courses and occupational qualifications, and (iv) an ever more complex rationalisation and legitimation of the school types, and of the relationships among them, in educational theory.

As these conditions developed during the course of the nineteenth century, structural change in education became a consequence of the interconnections between social reproduction, the constitution of the educational system, and the development of educational theory. To analyse such a system of educational paths and its genesis adequately, one has to see particular institutions in their relationships to the overall structure of the system. Organisational or curricular changes in individual school types, and their theoretical justifications, can no longer be assigned a random significance, or added up *ad hoc* into histories of particular school types or intellectual issues, but must be understood in their significance within the process of system emergence and system constitution. Since any modification of a particular school type, course of study, or occupational qualification altered the weight of all other elements in the structure, the historical and sociological significance of any such modification can be assessed only in an analysis that encompasses the overall context, that does not ignore the patent autonomy of the educational system, and that integrates the internal with the external relations of particular measures and structures.

Historical analysis reveals that school courses and qualifications did not stem from economic needs, that they were not simply fixed by an already established structure of required qualifications. Rather, qualifications, as well as the examinations and courses on which they were based, had the function of converting the occupational requirements of public administration, commerce and industry into educational qualifications, of sorting them by occupation, and of ordering them in a horizontal as well as a vertical typology. Course plans did not follow from economic and occupational demands; rather, the internal differentiation and hierarchical ordering of qualifications within the school system made possible the differentiation and hierarchical ordering of the occupational structure.

System formation with its accompanying social consequences, however, was not the result of strategic conservative planning by the dominant social strata or bureaucracies, but the result of an overall development within a set of educational institutions. This overall development – the process of systematisation with its phases of system emergence, system constitution and system complementation – was conditioned *not only* by the fact that modern educational administration requires generally accepted and comparable standards of course completion, the adjustment of regional differences, and the codification of legal frameworks, *but also* by the interaction between the occupational structure and the educational system, and by the divergent social interests of teachers and of the propertied and educated middle classes. The analysis of systematisation requires both the abandonment of immediate and superficial causal ascriptions and the consistently integrated treatment of the educational system and of the factors affecting it in their full complexity.

The emergence of the system, 1800–80

In the Prussian General Code of 1794 schools and universities were declared state institutions. Schools that maintained the minimum course durations and the minimum educational standard stipulated in the laws on obligatory schooling, as well as institutions that offered general education or vocational instruction, were subject to state inspection as 'public' educational institutions.[10]

The General School Regulation of 1763 made school attendance formally compulsory in Prussia for seven to eight years. The introduction of compulsory schooling necessitated an expansion in the supply of public education, as well as the supervision, classification and curricular delimitation of the existing educational institutions, which ranked from rural elementary grades attended only in the winter months to municipal Latin schools whose upper grades were meant to prepare for university entry as well. At the end of the eighteenth century the quality of a given school depended only upon the characteristics of its teachers and students. Neither teachers nor pupils were offered social or material incentives to teach or to attend. Among directors of Protestant municipal schools the majority held primary positions as pastors; most teachers were young theologians who had not yet obtained parish assignments and who supported themselves on the modest remuneration of their instructional work. Like the Brothers who taught at the schools of the various Catholic orders, Protestant theologians concentrated upon those parts of their own theological studies that could be transmitted to pupils aged 8–16, namely Latin, Greek and religion. A Latin school, as distinct from a rural or urban elementary school, was an institution at which at least one teacher had begun or completed a university course in theology, and that teacher taught Latin.

Enrolment in a Latin school brought no formal qualifications for entry into stipulated occupations, and the universities either accepted anyone interested in attending or gave examinations of their own. For the majority of students educational and occupational expectations were limited to the priesthood or pastorate, the latter preceded by long years of poorly paid school teaching or harried domestic tutoring. The propertied middle class and the nobility did not send their children to Latin schools, but had them instructed and educated by tutors. The majority of Latin school pupils had to earn their living by running messages or by singing as 'choristers' at funerals and weddings. The names assumed by Latin schools mislead modern scholars about their original structures and functions, such names as *Gymnasium*, *Gymnasium illustre*, *Pädagogikum*, *Lyceum*, *Collegium* and cathedral school (*Domschule*) having been chosen more or less at random.

The educational reforms at the beginning of the nineteenth century could not have been expected to realise greater quality of educational and social opportunity. To raise the standards of schools and universities, teachers with higher qualifications had to be employed; to prevent their transfer to parish positions, higher salaries had to be paid. But higher salaries implied higher student fees. The poorest children thus had to be replaced by children from the more prosperous social strata.

An educational administration independent of the Churches was established in Prussia for the first time in 1787 with the creation of the School Council (*Oberschulkollegium*), composed of legal administrators, university professors, and rectors of Latin schools in the larger towns. The measures taken by the School Council initially focused upon a reform of the universities and of the larger Latin schools. To prevent the incipient dissolution of the universities into professional schools of theology, law and medicine, and to halt the decline of the old faculty of philosophy, the latter was freed from the function of providing a general education merely in preparation for professional studies and was placed beside the three 'upper' faculties as an equal fourth faculty. The four faculties were held together as parts of universities and as such were granted important rights and privileges. Small universities, which could not be fully developed in this way, were closed or demoted to the level of Latin schools or seminaries.

The task of general preparation that had been performed by the old philosophical faculties was transferred to the upper grades of the larger Latin schools. The introduction of a secondary leaving examination (*Abitur*) as the sole prerequisite for university entry sharply separated the universities from the Latin schools, which were thus assigned the decisions on university admission. At the same time, at least three years of university study and a concluding examination were required for all civil service positions based on completed university courses (e.g. the pastorate and the judiciary). The study of theology was no longer a prerequisite for anyone entering the teaching profession. Secondary teaching at a Latin school was raised to the level of an independent academic profession, with three years of study at a philosophical faculty, a state examination and civil service status. Like the other three faculties, the faculty of philosophy acquired a clientele orientated exclusively to its course offerings: the candidates for secondary teaching positions. Students in the faculty of philosophy acquired professional prospects in teaching that gave them a status equal to that of students of theology, law and medicine. These future secondary teachers made possible the great expansion and internal differentiation of the faculties of philosophy during the nineteenth century and determined the high standards of the human and natural sciences in the German universities.

Beginning in the 1820s, only university-educated teachers could be employed at schools that sent 'students to the university', or at institutions that prepared for the second or third secondary grades of those schools. Excluded from this regulation were 'primary and lower secondary schools' (*niedere Bürgerschulen*) that conveyed *only* elementary knowledge ('reading', 'writing', 'simple quantitative relations and measures', and 'first teachings of religion') and did not go beyond the curriculum of ordinary municipal schools set down in a regulation of 1831. The 1831 decree on examination standards distinguished the qualification to teach in the 'lower' and 'intermediate' grades of a secondary school – without specification of school type – from the qualification to teach in the 'upper grades of the *Gymnasium*'; the distinction was less between school forms than between grade levels. Only the upper grades of Latin schools were especially protected and reserved for teaching-candidates with high qualifications. Institutions that could pay for university-trained teachers and carry out *Abitur* examinations were officially recognised as university preparatory schools and given the name *Gymnasium*.

The guidelines for the *Abitur* examination and for the state examination for secondary teachers were at first the only official frameworks for the structure of the *Gymnasium*. The instructions issued by the educational administration to *Gymnasium* headmasters during the years 1824–39 left 'suitable teaching arrangements' and the 'timetabling of lessons' to the heads and teachers of individual institutions, who were 'carefully to consider' the 'unique qualities of their teachers and of their resources' and their 'own particular orientation' in deciding 'how to approach their goals in the most appropriate way'.[11] In the first statistical handbook for German *Gymnasien* (1837) the authors, Brauns and Theobald, cited the 1827 *Programme of the Stralsund Gymnasium* as representative of 'normal' *Gymnasien*:

Our institution, like most *Gymnasien*, is composed of six main grades. The Sixth (*Sexta*) and Fifth (*Quinta*) make up the lower division and prepare for the lower trades as well as for further study; the Fourth (*Quarta*) and Third (*Tertia*, generally a two-year sequence) make up the intermediate division and prepare as well for the higher occupations of merchants, farmers, artists, etc. To accomplish this even better, a so-called modern class (*Realklasse*) at the level of the Fourth and Third is provided for students not planning on university study; they participate in most of the regular classes of those grades (including Latin, from which no one is exempted), but are instructed in French, English, advanced practical calculation, proper handwriting, and mathematical and practical drawing, this in place of Greek in both grades, [and] of Mathematics in Third . . . The Second (*Sekunda*, two years) and First (*Prima*, two years) make up the upper division and are devoted to the real preparation for the academic professions (*den Gelehrtenstand*).[12]

The *Gymnasium* that was distinguished amid the variety of existing school forms initially encompassed only the upper division. During the first half of the nineteenth century only a few *Gymnasien* were able to extend the academic objectives of their upper divisions – preparation for university study – to their intermediate and lower divisions, a change which at the very least required (i) adequate financial resources from public funds or from income sources of their own, (ii) the self-sufficiency of a boarding school and a rigorous, state-wide selection of pupils, and (iii) location in a large municipality with additional, varied instructional offerings, or in a town with a high proportion of high officials and members of the liberal professions. Until the 1880s few towns possessed more than one *Gymnasium*; they therefore could not set apart one institution for special distinction and high funding.

In Table 1.1 I have charted the Prussian localities in which more than one *Gymnasium* or more than one secondary school existed in 1880. Though there were 246 *Gymnasien* in the State of Prussia at that time, only five towns had more than three *Gymnasien* and only two additional towns had more than two *Gymnasien*. From a total of 488 secondary schools, 283 were *Gymnasien* and *Progymnasien* (incomplete *Gymnasien*), 183 were modern secondary schools (*Realschulen*) with Latin (which in 1882 became

Table 1.1. Secondary school locations in Prussia, 1880, in order of importance (towns with at least 3 secondary schools or 2 Gymnasien)

School location	Province	Administrative rank	Population (×1000)	No. of secondary schools			Rank among all Prussian towns		
				Gymnasien	Mod. with Latin	Mod. without Latin	By population	By no. of Gymnasien	By no. of all secondary schools
Berlin	Brandenburg	Capital	1122	16	7	2	1	1	1
Breslau	Silesia	District	273	5	2	3	2	2	2
Königsberg	E. Prussia	District	141	4	3	–	4	3	3
Köln	Rhineland	District	145	4	2	–	3	3	4
Frankfurt/Main	Hessen	Mun. circle	137	1	1	4	5	16	5
Hanover	Hanover	District	123	3	1	1	6	5	6
Danzig	W. Prussia	District	109	2	2	–	7	6	7
Magdeburg	Saxony	District	98	2	1	1	8	6	8
Stettin	Pomerania	District	92	2	1	1	13	6	8
Hildesheim	Hanover	District	26	2	1	1	50	6	8
Halle/Saale	Saxony	Mun. circle	71	2	1	–	17	6	11
Posen	Posen	District	66	2	1	–	19	6	11
Osnabrück	Hanover	District	33	2	1	–	35	6	11
Brandenburg	Brandenburg	Mun. circle	29	1	2	–	45	6	11
Aachen	Rhineland	District	86	1	2	–	15	16	17
Barmen	Rhineland	Mun. circle	96	1	1	1	9	16	18
Düsseldorf	Rhineland	District	95	1	1	1	10	16	18
Dortmund	Westphalia	Mun. circle	67	1	1	1	18	16	18
Kassel	Hessen	District	58	1	1	1	20	16	18
Wiesbaden	Hessen	District	50	1	1	1	25	16	18
Liegnitz	Silesia	District	37	2	–	–	31	6	15
Glogau	Silesia	Town	19	2	–	–	83	6	15

Source: Detlef K. Müller, Datenhandbuch zur deutschen Bildungsgeschichte (Göttingen, forthcoming).

Realgymnasien and *Realprogymnasien*), and 22 were modern secondary schools (*Realschulen*) without Latin (which in 1882 became *Oberrealschulen* and six-year *Realschulen*). Yet all three school types were simultaneously available in only 12 Prussian towns, and only in these towns could parents and students choose between the two 'humanistic' and the strictly 'modern' curricular options.

Only one Prussian boarding school offering the *Gymnasium* curriculum could truly be called an elite institution. This was Pforta County School (*Landesschule Pforta*), which began only at the level of the Third and which was able to select its 200 students, including almost 75 per cent on scholarships, according to a high standard of academic achievement.[13] A large share of Pforta graduates reached outstanding positions in society; in 1856–77, during one headmaster's term of office alone, more than 30 became full professors at German universities. It was this elite institution that provided many apologists and critics of the *Gymnasium* with what was often their only school experience. Thus Nietzsche, Wilamowitz and Paulsen were Pfortians who projected their educational experiences there upon the generality of Prussian *Gymnasien*, although the majority of these differed more from Pforta than Pforta differed from an English 'public' school.

Until the 1860s, with few exceptions, the lower and intermediate divisions of Prussian *Gymnasien* remained in the same situation as the other secondary schools, which scarcely went beyond the course offerings of fully developed primary and higher primary schools, and this reality contrasted sharply with the ideology of *Gymnasium* teachers. At the end of the nineteenth century, numerous *Gymnasien* and *Progymnasien* tried, through expansive festivities and imposing publications, to lay claim to the elite status of university-preparatory schools with a tradition of centuries. Yet despite such historical inventions these institutions were little more in the first half of the century than municipal primary schools with optional instruction in the ancient and modern foreign languages.

An 1831 decree of the Prussian Ministry of Culture emphasised this role of the *Gymnasium* as a comprehensive school:

It is wrong to assume that the instructional programme of the *Gymnasium* is intended only for pupils who want later to devote themselves to university study and is not suited to the development of every intellectual ability. The materials taught in the *Gymnasium*, and the sequence and proportion in which they are taught in the various grades, make up the foundations of any higher general education. The experience of centuries . . . testifies that precisely the subjects taken up in the instructional programme of the *Gymnasium* are particularly educative, in that all the intellectual potentials and capacities of youth can be developed and strengthened in and through them.

'Higher general education' as used in this passage did not imply the later distinction between academic (*wissenschaftlich*) and popular education, but was meant to set general education apart from specialised instruction. Highly educated, in this perspective, was not the secondary graduate who had mastered two foreign languages, but the adult who could read and write and who was capable of supporting himself. Socially, the decree that has been cited excluded only the marginal groups within the urban population: 'The education of human beings in all conditions of life, however different, would be in a lamentable state if everyone always wanted to learn only what he needed to pursue his trade and earn his daily bread.'[14]

In explanation of the curricular programme of 1837, revised in 1856, the Ministry officially confirmed the comprehensive school function of the *Gymnasium* as late as 1862: 'Many pupils move from the intermediate grades into civil life. The *Gymnasium* best takes care of such pupils if it develops their ability to think as much as possible, and equips them with a sure competence in the elementary foundations of oral and written expression.'[15] In a teaching plan for instruction in drawing at *Gymnasien* and *Realschulen* that was conveyed to the Provincial School Councils in late 1863, the Minister of Culture considered the interests of early leavers: 'In our experience, most *Gymnasium* pupils leave as early as the Fourth or Third in order to devote themselves to some occupation; the teaching programme, taking this into account, is organised so that such pupils too will have had practice in linear drawing as well as in free sketching.'[16]

Out of consideration for the majority of pupils, Greek was not made obligatory at the *Gymnasium* and Latin was not evaluated for pupils who wanted to leave school after a lower or intermediate grade. The official promptings to make Greek and Latin compulsory that are frequently cited by historians of education pertained only to students preparing for the *Abitur* and university entry. In 1856, for the first time, a ministerial decree permitted the exemption of pupils from Greek only at *Gymnasien* in which 'a modern school (*höhere Bürger-oder Realschule*) exists in addition to the *Gymnasium*', so that 'the *Gymnasium* must also meet the needs of those not preparing either for university study or for an occupation for which a *Gymnasium* education is required, but who are seeking to acquire the general education necessary for a middle-class occupation at a secondary school'.[17] In fact, these grounds for exemption still applied to the majority of *Gymnasium* students.

In the first volume of his historical–statistical description of Prussian secondary education (1864), Ludwig Wiese, the official responsible for secondary education within the Prussian Ministry of Culture, pointed again and again to the schematic and more classificatory than normative character of the curricular plans and timetables he was publishing for the various school types: 'The regime of secondary schools portrayed is not to be regarded as a barrier against flexibility; it permits a great variety of distinctive arrangements.' Wiese described the secondary schools as set off from 'primary schools' by 'instruction that reaches beyond immediate needs', from 'vocational schools (*Fachschulen*)' by the aim of general intellectual education, and from the universities by the introductory character of secondary instruction. The secondary schools were not to focus upon the small minority of future academics (members of the university-educated professions), but were to include all students who sought instruction beyond the confines of immediate, elementary needs. The multifunctionality of the *Gymnasien* was confirmed at the highest ministerial level in 1864 by Wiese's emphasis on the diversity within the general framework of the *Gymnasium*. 'Provincial *Gymnasien*' in particular, according to Wiese, were to give appropriate consideration in the intermediate grades to the needs of a large number of pupils who leave after these grades.[18]

It was only the full development of the modern secondary schools and the associated codification of qualifications after 1860 that required a gradual narrowing and delimitation of educational objectives and of school types. The modern secondary schools (*Realschulen*) had developed separately from the *Gymnasien*. Originally, at the beginning of the nineteenth century, they consisted of all Latin schools that had not been recognised as *Gymnasien*, and of municipal or town schools (*Stadtschulen*) newly founded in the 1830s.[19] The majority of pupils subject to compulsory schooling in the Prussian towns at the beginning of the nineteenth century were enrolled in primary schools maintained by the Protestant or Catholic Churches, or in private schools. In place of these institutions, public 'town schools' (*Stadtschulen*) were created for children whose parents could pay at least part of the school costs themselves. These town schools were to function as municipal primary schools, while also preparing for the intermediate grades of the *Gymnasium*. Latin was offered privately by town school teachers. In addition to the town schools, free 'paupers' schools' (*Armenschulen*) were established for children whose parents lived on public assistance. These 'paupers' primarily included small farmers, servants and agricultural labourers who had emigrated into the towns and who had not yet found work. The paupers' schools were institutions of public assistance, in which the children were to be more supervised than instructed. As soon as the parents could earn their own income, the children were to transfer to the town schools. In Berlin at the beginning of the nineteenth century, for example, some 20 per cent of pupils subject to compulsory schooling were assigned to paupers' schools.[20] (In the countryside, the 'rural primary schools' had to combine the objectives of the town and paupers' schools. Until the middle of the nineteenth century, therefore, primary schools in the countryside cannot be compared with those in the towns.)

The poverty of most Prussian towns in the first half of the nineteenth century severely limited their investments in education. At the beginning of the century the Prussian state transferred to the municipalities the financial burdens resulting from the lost war against France, while also imposing – without the agreement of the partly autonomous municipal councils – such expensive obligations as road construction, public health care, public assistance and schooling. In many towns, until the middle of the century, the costs of financing the war debt exceeded all other budgetary allocations.[21]

This financial situation retarded the development of the town schools and encouraged their transformation from municipal primary into secondary schools. Such a transformation was especially supported by town school teachers who had passed the state examination for secondary teachers but had failed to find a position in a *Gymnasium*. The town schools competed for fee-paying pupils with the lower and intermediate grades of the *Gymnasien*. In these circumstances the town school teachers attributed a function to the *Gymnasium* that their successors, the *Realschule* teachers of the 1860s, were to contest: the function of an elite institution preparing solely for university study. According to this notion the town schools were to prepare for middle-class occupations (artisans, commerce, the lower and intermediate civil service), as well as for transfer into the upper division of the *Gymnasium*. Essentially, the *Gymnasium* was to be limited to its upper division. (In Bavaria this scheme had been put into practice and it survived until about 1870: a five-year 'Latin school' was followed by a four-year upper division of the *Gymnasium* type, and the term *Gymnasium* was applied exclusively to this upper division.)[22]

Population growth, increased social differentiation and especially the expansion of public administration and of the mercantile and technical occupations led to increased aspirations to social mobility among parents.[23] Available spaces in *Gymnasien* and town schools stagnated or increased only slowly, while private schools actually shrank in numbers. The resulting changes in the educational market encouraged the town schools to expand their curricular offering, while socially narrowing their field of recruitment. The battle of the modern secondary schools for privileges approaching those of the *Gymnasien*, as described by historians of the modern schools, obscures this process. The qualifications associated with the completion of the various *Gymnasium* grades (e.g. completion of the Third for entry into the intermediate grades of the civil service) were used by town school teachers both to enlarge the curricular programmes of their institutions and to enhance their own standing by the claim that levels of academic achievement equal to those of the *Gymnasium* grades should also lead to equal levels of certification. In this process these teachers totally ignored the social prospects and occupational expectations of the majority of their pupils.

In a decree of 1859 those town schools that had developed during the first half of the nineteenth century into institutions comparable to the *Gymnasien* were set apart from the rest of the town schools, renamed 'modern secondary schools' (*Realschulen*) and assigned a curriculum of their own that officially confirmed their structural transformation into modern-language *Gymnasien*, and that encouraged their further development. Fourteen years after the decree of 1859 the participants in the first General Conference of German Modern School Teachers (*Realschulmänner*) in Gera demanded the formal establishment of a new type of intermediate school.[24] They sought unrestricted access to the universities and to the state examinations for their institutions. Nine-year modern secondary schools were to rank as modern-language *Gymnasien* at the side of the ancient-language *Gymnasien* and be assigned the typological name *Realgymnasien*. The model was a secondary school in Berlin that had been recognised as a *Realgymnasium* since 1827, that had always been ranked equal with the *Gymnasien* in class durations and qualifications, and whose typological name had been altered to *Gymnasium* in 1868.[25]

The moving forces in support of the *Realgymnasium* were the rectors and teachers at a few particularly well-developed and well-endowed modern secondary schools in the large Rhenish towns of Prussia. Here modern secondary institutions under town patronage had become the elite schools of the Protestant middle class, who had become successful in commerce and industry and dominant in the municipal councils. In their facilities, teachers' salaries and fee rates, these schools had quite deliberately been placed in opposition to the Catholic *Gymnasien* and *Progymnasien*, which occasionally charged no fees and whose scholarship pupils were regarded with smiling condescension as potential priests and officials. (In 1864 the fees charged by some of the Rhenish modern secondary schools exceeded even the highest rates charged by the most elite and expensive Prussian *Gymnasien*.)[26] But even while the modern secondary schools were thus upgraded, the Prussian *Gymnasien* reached so high a standing, and *Gymnasium* education became so important as a sign of social status, that the Rhenish middle class, too, adopted the *Gymnasium* as its preferred school, leaving the *Realschulen* to the sons of tradesmen and to scholarship students driven out of the *Gymnasien*. For the teachers at modern secondary schools, this made it all the more important that their schools be officially recognised as accredited secondary.[27]

In addition to the modern secondary schools *with Latin*, secondary schools *without Latin* developed in Prussia. In county towns from 1830 on vocational or trade schools (*Provinzialgewerbeschulen*) were founded that, after compulsory schooling had been completed, prepared for certain trades (artisans to specialised workers) and offered the option of going on to the 'trades institute' (*Gerwerbeinstitut*), a central school in Berlin that trained pupils for specialised occupations.[28] In parallel with the structural transformation of the *Gymnasien* and modern secondary schools, this trades institute (oriented more towards secondary than towards trade school students) raised its entrance requirements and curricular objectives (it was elevated to become a *Gerwerbeakademie* in 1866) and thereby indirectly shaped the programme and influenced the attitudes of potential pupils of the trade or vocational schools. The reorganisation of the Prussian trade schools in 1870 raised the entrance requirements and made transfers from preparatory classes with a generalised curriculum possible. This opened the way to the creation of a full-term school. The preparatory classes became the lower and intermediate grades of the full-term institution; they were given names corresponding to those in use at *Gymnasien* and *Realschulen* (the Sixth to the Third). The original trade school – now the upper division with a Second and a Third – lost all its links with occupational training. The curricular plan of the whole institution now encompassed only generally educative subjects; every link to apprenticeship training was erased, and transfers from municipal and rural primary schools were excluded. At the end of the 1870s these new full-term institutions were renamed *Oberrealschulen* (nine-year modern secondary schools without Latin) and classified as secondary. At the same time, the 'academy of trades' (*Gewerbeakademie*) was upgraded to 'technical college' (*technische Hochschule* – the term *Hochschule* implying the university level). The graduates (*Abiturienten*) of modern secondary schools without Latin were to go on primarily to such technical colleges; general admission to the universities was not yet granted them.

The structural transformation of the *Gymnasien*, of the town or modern secondary schools, and of the trade schools necessitated a reform of municipal schooling for those pupils who wanted to leave school after completing their compulsory schooling, in order to enter an apprenticeship for an occupation. From the mid-1850s on the paupers' schools were further developed, renamed 'community schools' (*Gemeindeschulen*) or 'town schools' and offered as a substitute for the lower and intermediate grades of the *Gymnasien* and of the former town schools.[29] The paupers' schools were raised to the level of ordinary schools for children of compulsory school age; they became 'primary schools' (*Volksschulen*), and by the end of the century gave to the majority of school-age children their only form of general education. For the majority of pupils access to the secondary schools had thus been closed. At the same time, the teaching programme of the new *Volksschulen* was raised sharply above that of the old paupers' schools and adjusted to the former level of the *Realschulen* and of the lower *Gymnasium* grades. The new primary schools were internally articulated, divided in the large towns into a lower, an intermediate and an upper division of two grades each (from the end of the nineteenth century on into eight grades in all) and supplemented with select classes for students with good achievement levels. Pupils who could not meet the normal demands were relegated to special schools for the learning-deficient. Some of the *Volksschulen* in the

Prussian towns in fact attained an academic level fully equal to that of the corresponding secondary school grades, except that they offered no foreign languages.[30]

The constitution of the system, 1880–1900

The curricular and examination regulations of 1882 and 1892 applied, for the first time in the nineteenth century, to the whole range of Prussian secondary schools.[31] Whereas earlier regulations only pertained to individual school types, the measures of 1882 and 1892 ordered the structures and functions of all schools and qualifications in a coherent way. *Gymnasien* and *Pro-gymnasien* remained unchanged in their outward structures, but the curricula of the individual grades were exclusively determined by the ultimate goal of the *Abitur*. Early leaving was excluded in principle. The nine-year modern secondary school with Latin became the *Realgymnasium*, whose teaching programme from the Sixth to the Fourth was made identical with that of the *Gymnasium*. Modern secondary schools with Latin in which upper divisions could not be developed became *Realprogymnasien*. Modern secondary schools without Latin became *Oberrealschulen*; those without upper divisions became *Realschulen*. Until the end of the century only graduates of the *Gymnasium* had unrestricted access to the universities; graduates of the *Realgymnasium* were fully admitted to the universities only for the study of modern foreign languages, while graduates of the *Oberreal-schule* remained formally excluded from the universities.

In 1900 all three types of Prussian secondary schools were declared equal in principle, either as full-term institutions with nine-year durations and *Abitur* examinations (*Gymnasium, Realgymnasium, Oberrealschule*) or as preparatory institutions with six-year durations and leaving examinations (*Progymnasium, Realprogymnasium, Realschule*). Foreign languages missed (i.e. Greek for graduates of the *Realgymnasium*, Latin for graduates of the *Oberrealschule*) could be made up and certified through supplementary examinations at the universities.[32]

In the whole field of boys' secondary education the developments that have been outlined resulted in an internally differentiated school system whose parts were functionally related to each other. Transfers among the school types were excluded in principle, or were restricted to the lowest two grades. Decisions about which school to attend, and thus also about future academic and occupational options, had to be made at the time of entry into the lowest secondary grades, at the age of nine or ten. What factors determined the structural changes that have been described? And what pedagogical and social consequences followed from the constitution of the school system?

I have discussed the wide regional distribution of the Prussian *Gymnasien*, as well as the structural transformation of the modern secondary schools and provincial trade schools. The upgrading of these institutions and the extension of their programme durations (from the level of the Third to that of the *Abitur*) were rarely dictated by the existing demands for schooling. Thus intermediate and upper divisions of modern secondary schools were instituted and expanded even when there was room in the lower and intermediate grades of local or nearby *Gymnasien*. During the late 1860s and the 1870s the transformation of existing schools was supplemented by waves of new school foundations. The towns had by this time paid off their debts and were increasingly assigned a share of the income from indirect taxes and from the profits of the Austro-Prussian and Franco-Prussian wars. Having been forced gradually to relinquish their control of the *Gymnasien* to the state during the first half of the nineteenth century, the towns now sought to compensate by upgrading and expanding a school type that the state had left in their hands: the modern secondary school with Latin (*Realgymnasium*). Municipal and central educational policies entered into a competition that practically ensured the establishment of new *Gymnasien* as state institutions and of new *Realgymnasien* as municipal ones.[33] (The modern secondary schools without Latin, most of which evolved from state-founded county trade schools, were primarily state institutions.)

The resulting expansion of secondary education was sustained by an enlarged social demand for secondary and university graduates, which was partly created by the educational system itself. The extension of secondary programmes and the foundation of new schools led to a sharp increase in secondary teaching positions, which could be filled only by raising the number of secondary and university graduates.[34] An immediate increase in secondary graduates was encouraged within the schools themselves, as teachers recommended the completion of the *Abitur* and university study to students who would previously have left school early for economic reasons, or because of their parents' limited occupational expectations. This raising of student expectations coincided with an ever higher valuation of academic qualifications for the higher-ranking occupations, a development which further motivated pupils to surpass their parents' educational and occupational expectations. The enlarged demand for graduates fostered the impression that university or *Gymnasium* qualifications generally assured higher incomes or more secure social positions than lower levels of schooling.

The public campaign via the press, led by associations of teachers at non-*Gymnasium* institutions (e.g. *Realschul-männer-verein*), for the upgrading of their school forms lent additional social weight to the entitlements being demanded, which further enhanced the expectations of parents and pupils and encouraged ever longer school attendance.[35] At the same time, increased prosperity enabled ever larger groups of parents to bear the financial burden of schooling their children and to risk long-term educational and career plans.

During the first half of the nineteenth century, in addition to the *Gymnasium* and to the modern secondary schools, there were many schools that were not officially secondary, but which had taken over the teaching programme of the lower secondary grades. The borderlines between the various school forms were unclear; differences were minimal between the lower grades of *Gymnasien*, of modern secondary schools and of schools not administratively classed as secondary. Foreign languages not offered by a given school could usually be taken privately, made up or waived. The *Gymnasium* was a pre-university school only from the Lower Second on, that is in the highest four grades. The regulations of the Ministry of Education applied primarily to the upper divisions and to the *Abitur* examination. The gradual extension of administrative directives to the lower and intermediate grades, along with the bureaucratic preference for encompassing and consistent regulations, increasingly distinguished the *Gymnasium*, the most developed school type, from the other school forms, assigning it the educational objectives of a full-term academic institution, one clearly set apart from the other schools and internally articulated in a functional way. The multifunctionality of the lower and intermediate grades was replaced, at least in the official definitions, with an early and exclusive orientation towards the *Abitur*. The remaining school forms had to accommodate to this process, either by augmenting their durations and curricula, or by filling gaps in the 'market' for which their programmes seemed suitable. The debate over curricula (*Humanismus–Realismus*) became a competition for shares of the student market and for monopolies of entitlements.

Throughout much of the nineteenth century Prussian educational institutions encouraged social mobility; but their structural characteristics also engendered a crisis of academic unemployment that began in the 1880s.[36] During the 1860s and 1870s Prussian civil service positions in public administration, in central and local government, in the legal system, in educational institutions and in the state postal and railway services had been markedly increased and filled with young personnel. Simultaneously, there had been a strong demand created by the need to replace officials who had entered the state services during their founding period in the 1830s and who had now reached retirement age. By the early 1880s, therefore, posts in the intermediate and higher civil service were occupied by men who still had another thirty to forty years in office. The long-term economic crisis that began in the 1870s (the Great Depression) slowed the expansion of the public service and thus the demand for new personnel for a long time, while also reducing the chances of alternative employment in the higher-ranking industrial and commercial positions.[37]

For those in office – and therein lies the paradox of this crisis – these developments led to the positions that they held being upgraded and made secure; for the succeeding generations of secondary and university graduates, however, they led to a progressive devaluation and restriction of earned qualifications and entitlements. (As late as 1870, for example, one could become a postal inspector after completing the Third at a *Gymnasium*, whereas the same position ten years later required the *Abitur*. The holder of a position based on the completion of the Third was retroactively raised to the status of a secondary graduate, whereas the student leaving after the Third in the 1880s reached a secretarial position at best.)[38] Thus students were forced to lengthen their schooling. The completion of a lower or intermediate secondary grade became worthless. But the further a pupil advanced in the grade sequence of a secondary school, the more likely he was to aim at the highest possible goal within a given school form, namely the *Abitur*. This dynamic particularly affected children from social strata that had earlier attended secondary schools with limited aims, and who had excluded the *Abitur* and university study from their expectations. The educated upper middle class (*Bildungsbürgertum*), which reproduced its social position primarily by way of the *Abitur* and the universities, experienced this process as a threat to its existence.[39] Against the background of serious recessionary crises from the 1870s on, of increasing threats to the intermediate and upper ranks of the propertied and educated classes, and of a steadily increasing number of unemployed secondary and university graduates, conservative social and educational policies found increasing support among the same social strata that had supported liberal policies in the 1870s. (A typical slogan in the debates of the late nineteenth century was that of 'academic proletariat'.)[40]

The policies of the Prussian Ministry of Culture in the 1880s were especially designed to reduce secondary school attendance by children from the lower and intermediate social strata.[41] Since more difficult examinations and increased fees offered only limited means of control (neither the children nor the incomes of the university-educated civil servants could be excessively strained), intra-systemic means of channelling students had to be instituted, the social effects of which had to be veiled for those affected. The rapid development of educational institutions through the 1870s, and the school administration's increasing effort, from the 1850s on, to codify the various school types and to regulate curricula and examinations according to uniform principles, provided conservative policy makers with an opportunity to reinterpret the administrative classification of the various school forms in the light of a social and educational functionalism. Bureaucratic categories thus took on social and educational meanings that had not initially been present or intended. The multifunctionality of the various school types was officially abrogated, and this changed the ranks and the potential clienteles of particular school types within an increasingly stabilised total system.[42]

The Ministry of Culture did not construct a system, or invent new school forms, in order to limit the students' expectations and prospects, or to reduce or divert them. But it did ascribe to the existing school forms a functional position in relation to the other school forms, and it ordered all these schools in a social and educational hierarchy of curricula and credentials. The imprecision in the definition of existing schools, the variety of their social and educational goals, the flexibility of their curricula and course durations, were replaced with precise regulations for each school type. The duration and worth of particular school forms, and their academic and social positions within the educational system, were deduced from the diversity of individual aptitudes and from the society's need for a variety of qualifications and styles of socialisation.

The policy goal of protecting the educated upper middle class from aspirations to mobility among the intermediate and lower middle classes by way of a hierarchical structuring of school types was hidden behind arguments that appeared to be guided only by principles of purposive rationality and by functional requirements. (It is sometimes difficult to decide whether educational policy makers and teachers' associations themselves believed in their arguments, or used them in a merely tactical way.) 'General education' was reduced to the ability of individuals to construct 'intellectual worlds' that were 'suitable' for the positions in which their aptitudes and social origins had placed them. Society became a neutral agent in the allocation of educational opportunities; the division of labour and the social articulation that had developed within it were to determine the differentiation of school forms as well. The three main functions in the social division of labour – the intellectual (creative and guiding), the managerial (arranging) and the motor – were to define the school types: the academic type (humanistic education), the (productive) middle-class type (modern or 'realistic' education) and the popular education type, each of which was to be further subdivided in a functional way (e.g. schools for the mentally deficient were to be separated from regular *Volksschulen*, and modern language *Gymnasien* to be distinguished from the classical ones).[43]

The constitution of the school system initiated in the curricular regulations of 1882, coupled with the established structure of credentials, made possible a separation of formal qualifications from substantive curricular demands. The *Gymnasium* was to strive to guarantee and legitimate the social reproduction of the university-educated professions and of the higher social strata, while school types offering lesser qualifications or none were lined up lower down in an institutionalised hierarchy characterised by stable distances between types. Regulated through formal entitlements, these distances between school types provided not only for the required flexibility in curricula and qualifications, but also for a now institutionalised channelling of social ascent. At the same time, these distances protected the children of the educated upper middle class from the pressure of academic competition with the children of parents without university education. Children of 'academically' educated parents came to predominate more and more in the *Gymnasien*; children from the lower and intermediate (productive) middle classes were increasingly concentrated in the modern secondary schools, so that they were subjected to a more rigorous academic selection if they wished to move up through the hierarchy.

The occupational chances of students were not to be determined by their academic achievements *within* a school type, but by the degree to which their parents were informed and motivated about the choice *among* school types. In a vertically segmented school system, the allocation of formal qualifications became independent of substantive curricular demands on students. The *Volksschule* for the majority of the population could adjust its curriculum and teaching methods to changing occupational and social requirements, without having to raise the level of the credentials it offered. The careers and prospects of adults were determined not only by their knowledge and attitudes as students, but also by the school forms they had attended. Despite the high standards of instruction in the *Volksschulen*, the graduates of these schools had no prospect of entering occupational fields that had been functionally assigned to the secondary schools.

Before the constitution of the school system, successful attendance in the lower grades of a *Gymnasium* had subdivided the occupational expectations of the lower and intermediate social strata (journeymen to middle-level employees, small independent producers and tradesmen, master artisans). Early leavers from the *Gymnasium* had better prospects than the graduates of the *Volksschulen*; they had been partly integrated into the upper middle class and had thus developed wider frameworks of action; they had been informed about school qualifications by their own experience and they had – proudly – acquired a sense of their relationship to a *Gymnasium*. (The category of former pupils encompassed not only students from the upper division, but those from the Sixth and Fifth as well.) Even when they entered professions like those typically filled by graduates from country or municipal *Volksschulen*, the early leavers had shown an increased propensity to send their own children in turn to a *Gymnasium*, and to support them for a longer attendance there, if possible.

The constitution of the system of school types led to more and more of the early leavers withdrawing from the higher-ranking schools, especially from the *Gymnasium*, and thereby delayed or prevented intra- or inter-generational processes of mobility that had earlier been possible. Educational and occupational paths no longer led from a father's completion of a *Gymnasium* Fourth to the son's completion of a *Gymnasium* Second, but remained confined within an internally differentiated set of *Volksschule* courses. But while the completion of the *Gymnasium* Fourth as an educational investment increased in value for those already employed, even as it was devalued for those just leaving school, the value of completing a *Volksschule* course steadily decreased. This led to economic and social restrictions that made *Volksschule* students and parents less concerned about schooling, and thus reduced their aspirations to mobility through education. By contrast, the accumulation of educational capital by the early leavers (i.e. the increase in the value of the courses they had completed) had earlier encouraged them to invest more highly in the education of their children.

As compared with the majority of early leavers from the *Gymnasium*, *Volksschule* graduates, and to some extent modern secondary graduates as well, had a lower propensity to choose a *Gymnasium* for their children. In assessing their children's options, evaluating their aptitudes, and estimating the role of education and of credentials in occupational success, as well as the significance of educational qualifications for the quality of life, they drew on patterns of motivation that had been negatively affected by their own familial and school socialisation. Just a few years of attendance at a *Gymnasium* would have been good protection against either overestimating that school's academic demands and standards or underestimating the value of even its non-graduate credentials. School socialisation at a *Gymnasium* did not reinforce the limitations of familial socialisation, but reduced their impact.

Potential early leavers from a *Gymnasium* or from less accredited secondary schools, too, could respond without difficulty to the devaluation of the credentials that had earlier been associated with early leaving simply by extending their time in school; children from the lower and intermediate social strata that had been diverted to the primary schools, by contrast, had no such chance for a positive reaction to the devaluation of primary school completion as a credential. The possibility of transferring from a primary school to a *Gymnasium* was almost totally eliminated and erased from the expectations of parents and pupils, precisely by the differentiation of school types.

The complementation of the system

The systematisation of boys' secondary education by administrative decree in the 1880s and 1890s was difficult to enforce at the local level. The structural openness and flexibility that had been administratively conceded to the *Gymnasien* and modern secondary schools during the first half of the nineteenth century had allowed local school authorities and school headmasters to deviate from the general rules where necessary, and thus to adjust the structures of their institutions to local needs and to the educational objectives of teachers and pupils. The Ministry of Culture and the county school councils tolerated such deviations; but a deepening conflict ensued between the bureaucracy's demand for systematisation on the one hand, and the wishes of local school authorities, teachers and pupils on the other, a conflict that was ultimately decided in favour of the educational administration.

The new system of boys' secondary schooling, which precisely fixed the place and rank of the several school types, was particularly difficult to apply in the numerous towns that had only one local school. The majority of small and middle-sized towns were forced to limit themselves to one school type. A combination of small populations and a broad range of educational backgrounds within these populations required great flexibility in the schooling provided. In the face of these realities the claims of secondary teachers and educational policy makers about the suitability of specific secondary school types for particular, internally homogeneous population groups degenerated to the level of ideology. Since the multifunctionality of the *Gymnasien* and modern secondary schools had been officially abrogated, the educational administration was continually forced to permit exceptional arrangements so as to allow schools to survive.

These concessions became so numerous that they in turn had to be integrated into a bureaucratic scheme. The multifunctionality of all schools that had been officially abrogated was, paradoxically, now made the special objective of a new school type: the so-called 'reformed institutions' (*Reformanstalten*). A *Reformanstalt* was permitted to combine several school forms; a *Reformrealgymnasium*, for example, was a combination of *Realgymnasium* and *Oberrealschule*. From the beginning of the twentieth century on, the new 'reformed' school type became the preferred model for newly founded schools in small municipalities and in the expanding industrial towns. Through a variety of combinations (e.g. two six-year types with the addition of different options), even small communities were able, in most cases with relatively little expense, to accommodate the increasingly dominant ideology of distinctive, internally homogeneous school types, while at the same time achieving a high degree of conformity to the credentials system and to the educational aims of parents and students.

As universities required certification in Latin (*Latinum*) for most fields of study, Latin remained an essential subject even in the reformed institutions; but since the combination of *Realgymnasium* and *Oberrealschule* was particularly common, Latin at these schools was taught as a second foreign language, after either English or French. Latin was begun in the Fourth, not in the Sixth (the lowest grade) as it was in the *Realgymnasien*. The offer of Latin in the reformed institutions forced the *Oberrealschulen* in turn to make Latin available as an option, while the *Realgymnasien* tended to replace Latin with English or French as a first foreign language. The old communality between the *Gymnasium* and the *Realgymnasium*, which had both begun with Latin in the lowest grades until the end of the nineteenth century, was dissolved. The *Realgymnasium* and the *Oberrealschule* moved nearer to each other via the model of the reformed institutions, tending to form a single new school type at the side of the *Gymnasium*. From schools that did not begin Latin until the third year, transfers to a *Gymnasium* were excluded. To their own pupils, on the other hand, the majority of *Gymnasien* permitted the replacement of Greek with a modern foreign language.

The National Socialists drew the consequence of these developments within the system; *Realgymnasien*, *Oberrealschulen* and *Reformanstalten* were consolidated into a single school type, the 'high school (*Oberschule*) for boys', which became the secondary school for the majority of pupils. English began in the lowest secondary grade, Latin in the third lowest grade; the upper division was divided into a languages and a sciences branch. The only remaining institutions without Latin were secondary schools without lower divisions (*Aufbauschulen*), which followed directly upon the upper grades of *Volksschulen*. The *Gymnasien* were retained as a special school form.[44]

The reforms that followed after the constitution of the system did not lead to genuine structural changes; they simply drew the policy consequences of conditions given in the constituted system. In addition to the modifications that have been outlined, two complementary developments consolidated and stabilised the established system: (i) the integration of girls' secondary schools early in the twentieth century, and (ii) the introduction of the common four-year elementary school in the 1920s.

From the beginning of the nineteenth century on, girls' schooling was subject to the same formal regulations as boys' schooling: seven to eight years of compulsory school attendance. Municipal or country *Volksschulen* had to be provided for girls as well as for boys. Secondary education for girls was at first left to private initiative or to the headmasters of boys' secondary schools. Girls' schools (*höhere Töchterschulen*) had been affiliated with many *Gymnasien* and boys' modern secondary schools: *Gymnasium* teachers had given courses at these schools; the girls had been able to attend classes at *Gymnasien* or modern secondary schools. It was only the structural changes in boys' secondary education during the second half of the nineteenth century that broke up these affiliations. The towns established girls' secondary and higher primary ('middle') schools; like the *Gymnasien* and modern secondary schools of the first half of the nineteenth century, these schools were flexible and multifunctional in their curricula, sequence of grades, and educational objectives. The vertical segmentation of the boys' school system, especially the sharp divide between primary and secondary schools, made the flexibility and multifunctionality of the girls' schools seem dysfunctional and socially inferior, comparable to the *Volks-schulen*.[45]

The girls' secondary and higher primary schools in their traditional form could still meet the educational needs of girls from the higher and intermediate social strata; but they could no longer satisfy their social self-image. Since the segmentation of the boys' secondary school system had been 'deduced' from the differentiation of society, and since the distribution of secondary students among the school types had been legitimated through theories of academic aptitude, girls from the higher and intermediate social strata were increasingly put at a disadvantage by the self-image of the boys' secondary schools. To resolve this problem, the girls' schools had to be organised as a distinctive system patterned after that of the boys' schools. Girls and boys were physically separated; but after the beginning of the twentieth century they were instructed in equivalent school forms. This integration also extended to girls' education the entitlement regulations of the boys' school system and thereby opened occupational prospects to the graduates of girls' secondary schools that had not originally been anticipated even in the most radical arguments of the women's movement during the second half of the nineteenth century. Thus the logic of the boys' school system determined the development of the girls' schools.

The Constitution (Article 146) of the Weimar Republic in 1920 prescribed a 'common elementary school' (*gemeinsame Grundschule*) for all children. The elementary grades of secondary schools (*Vorschulen*) were dissolved. Transfer to a higher primary or secondary school had to be preceded by four years of elementary instruction in a *Grundschule*. The institution of the compulsory elementary school thoroughly obscured the social objectives that had led to the constitution of the school system. Seemingly rational arguments could now be used to link educational differentiation entirely to functional and educational requirements. The apparently direct and harmonious correspondence of educational institutions to the aptitudes of pupils, as well as to the functional needs of society, made the educational system seem autonomous and free of social conflict in the eyes of the public. Success or failure within the educational system could be ascribed to the aptitude, motivation and resilience of the individual. Occupational prospects became mere conditions of school success or failure. The self-image of the school forms as generally educative institutions, the theory of general education, and the examinations given and entitlements offered by the various school types, made social privileges seem individual achievements, particularly to the social groups consigned to the *Volksschulen*.[46]

The changing structure of enrolments

Fritz Ringer and I agree in our assessments of systematisation and of its social and educational consequences. 'The defenders of the *Gymnasium*', as he writes in Chapter 2, 'won a qualified victory in the battle of the schools' (p. 66). These defenders included university-educated parents, the associations of 'academic' professions, *Gymnasium* teachers and the socially more exclusive part of the propertied upper middle class.

Within the process of systematisation, however, Ringer attributes to the *Gymnasium* a more stable role and character than I do:

Apparently, the *Gymnasium* enrolment pyramid had been even narrower at the top, in relation to the base, during the early nineteenth century. Yet, for the period 1870–1911 and for Prussia as a whole, the net change in the shape of the *Gymnasium* was rather slight. What really happened in Prussia during the high industrial period, therefore, was a significant addition to the modern segments of the secondary system, most notably at the lower secondary level (pp. 65–6).

In contrast to this view, my thesis is that the *Gymnasium* began the process of structural transformation as a municipal comprehensive school within a school system that was highly progressive and only mildly segmented or systematic in Ringer's sense of 'rigorously defined and codified'. The emergence and constitution of the system then led to a vertical segmentation *within* the secondary system. In principle, if not quite in practical reality, the upper middle class in possession of cultural and economic capital (the university-educated upper middle class, entrepreneurs and large landowners) were separated from the proletariat. The structure and ideology of the school system as constituted led parents who had not themselves been educated at universities or *Gymnasien* to eliminate themselves as clients of the *Gymnasium*. This social self-elimination could be represented as an educational selection and used to legitimate the *Gymnasium*: the *Gymnasium* became the school for the most highly talented students within the overall system of secondary education.

In what follows, I want to elucidate the process of systematisation, and especially the structural transformation of the *Gymnasium*, by way of a statistical analysis. Thus Table 1.2 reports on all Prussian boys' schools that can be considered secondary during the period from 1832 to 1939, on total enrolments in these schools, and on the distribution of the totals for all schools over the three main types of (i) *Gymnasien, Progymnasien* and curricular equivalents, (ii) modern secondary schools with Latin, including *Realgymnasien, Realprogymnasien* and curricular equivalents, and (iii) modern secondary schools without Latin, including *Oberrealschulen, Realschulen* and curricular equivalents. As an aid to interpretation, enrolments for the year 1885, at about the middle of the process of system constitution, are equated with 100, while earlier and later enrolments are stated as percentages of this standard. Figure 1.3 charts the number of *institutions* in the three main categories from 1832 to 1941 *as percentages* of all institutions. The percentages for the *Gymnasium* type are counted downwards from the top of the graph, those for modern secondary schools without Latin up from

Table 1.2. *Prussian boys' secondary schools and pupils, 1832–1939: full-term and related six-year institutions for selected years*

	All secondary schools			Gymnasien/Progymnasien			Modern sec. with Latin			Modern sec. without Latin		
	No. of inst.	No. of pupils (×1000)	(1885=100)	No. of inst.	No. of pupils (×1000)	(1885=100)	No. of inst.	No. of pupils (×1000)	(1885=100)	No. of inst.	No. of pupils (×1000)	(1885=100)
1832	141			132			9					
1840	171			136			35					
1854	200	48.8	38	149	35.1	43	51	13.7	42			
1860	227	57.6	45	159	39.9	49	68	17.7	54			
1870	399	98.3	76	233	63.0	77	153	32.0	97	13	3.3	23
1875	447	112.2	87	261	68.5	84	169	38.5	117	17	5.2	37
1880	488	123.5	96	283	77.0	94	183	39.7	121	22	6.8	48
1885	552	128.8	100	294	81.8	100	177	32.9	100	51	14.1	100
1890	540	135.3	105	308	81.0	99	172	34.5	105	60	19.9	141
1895	569	140.0	109	318	76.6	97	160	31.4	96	91	29.1	206
1900	608	156.6	122	341	91.6	112	100	22.6	69	167	42.4	301
1905	696	191.5	149	363	102.8	126	125	30.2	92	208	58.5	415
1910	824	226.7	176	374	107.6	132	194	48.9	149	256	70.2	498
1914	894	241.1	187	371	104.7	128	232	59.8	182	291	76.5	543
1926	1102	308.0	239	320	93.4	114	341	99.5	303	441	115.1	817
1931	1101	297.2	231	286	87.0	106	407	122.7	374	408	87.5	621
1936	1021	252.2	196	279	73.5		398	99.8		344	78.5	
1939	831	248.8	193	107	29.9		659	202.9		65	14.5	

Source: Detlef K. Müller, *Datenhandbuch zur deutschen Bildungsgeschichte* (Göttingen, forthcoming).

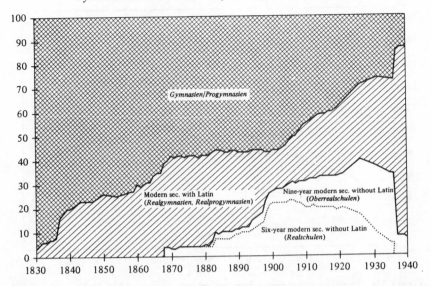

Figure 1.3. Prussian boys' secondary institutions, 1832–1941: the major types as percentages of all institutions (Detlef K. Müller, *Datenhandbuch zur deutschen Bildungsgeschichte* (Göttingen, forthcoming))

the bottom, so that the resulting *areas* represent each type's share of the total. As a further aid, Figure 1.4 graphically represents *absolute enrolments* (in thousands) in the main school types from 1860 to 1940.

While the number of all secondary schools and of all secondary pupils rose continuously from 1832 to 1926, as Table 1.2 indicates, the *Gymnasium* only followed this trend until about 1885, and the *Realgymnasium* only until 1880. *Gymnasium* enrolments actually reached their nineteenth-century maximum of 83,000 pupils in 1887, declined to 79,000 by 1893, and did not recover to the 1887 level until 1897. The *Realgymnasium* reached its nineteenth-century maximum of 40,000 pupils in 1880, then declined to 23,000 by 1900, and did not reattain the enrolment level of 1880 until 1909. During the constitution of the system *Gymnasium* enrolments in fact decreased by 5 per cent (about 4000 pupils) between 1887 and 1893, while *Realgymnasium* enrolments declined by almost 45 per cent (about 17,000 pupils) between 1880 and 1900.

After 1897 *Gymnasium* enrolments recovered to a new high of nearly 108,000 pupils in 1910. Thereafter, however, the *Gymnasium* declined continuously, in both numbers of institutions and of enrolments, until the 1930s. After the equalisation of the three school types in 1900 the proportion of *Gymnasium* graduates actually fell from about 80 per cent to 30 per cent of all secondary graduates by the early 1930s. The National Socialists made

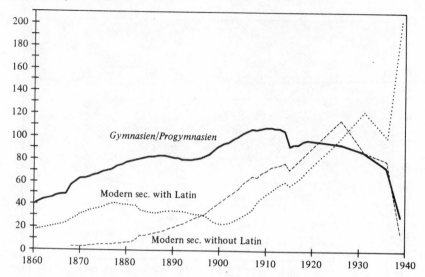

Figure 1.4. Prussian boys' secondary school enrolments, 1860–1940, in thousands (Detlef K. Müller, *Datenhandbuch zur deutschen Bildungsgeschichte* (Göttingen, forthcoming))

this structural change official: *Gymnasien* that had not been able to fulfil the norms of their type because of their locations were transformed into modern secondary schools; of about 280 *Gymnasien* scarcely more than 100 remained, less than had existed before the onset of systematisation in the early nineteenth century.

The *Realgymnasien* after 1906 began a great expansion, from which they emerged as the predominant school type by 1936. The number of institutions and pupils doubled in ten years, between 1905 and 1916; the *Gymnasien* were outstripped by 1926. The school reform of 1936 made the 'reformed' variant of the *Realgymnasium*, which began with Latin in the Fourth, the main type of boys' secondary school, leaving only a residual place for the remaining *Gymnasien*.

The sharp decrease in *Gymnasium* and *Realgymnasium* enrolments during the last third of the nineteenth century was compensated for by an extraordinary increase in six-year and nine-year modern secondary schools without Latin. The number of institutions and of pupils in this segment increased by 85 per cent between 1888 and 1897, and then tripled in the 25 years between 1895 and 1920. In 1926 modern boys' secondary schools without Latin enrolled more pupils than either of the other types, although they then lost ground to the *Realgymnasien* or *Reformrealgymnasien*, surviving only as an exceptional form after 1936.

The changing distribution of enrolments by grade is the subject of Table 1.5 and of Figure 1.6. In Table 1.5 enrolments in the Sixth, Upper Third and

Table 1.5. *Enrolments in selected grades of Prussian boys' secondary schools, 1875–1939, as percentages of relevant age groups*

	All secondary schools			Gymnasien/Progymnasien			Modern sec. with Latin			Modern sec. without Latin		
	Sixth	Upper Third	Upper First	Sixth	Upper Third	Upper First	Sixth	Upper Third	Upper First	Sixth	Upper Third	Upper First
1875	7.4	4.7	1.3	4.3	2.9	1.1	2.7	1.5	0.2	0.4	0.2	0.0
1877	7.7	4.6	1.4	4.4	2.9	1.1	2.9	1.6	0.3	0.4	0.2	0.0
1879	7.3	4.9	1.6	4.3	3.1	1.3	2.6	1.6	0.3	0.4	0.3	0.0
1881	8.3	5.0	1.6	4.9	3.2	1.3	2.9	1.5	0.3	0.5	0.3	0.0
1883	7.0	5.1	1.7	4.1	3.3	1.4	2.0	1.4	0.3	0.9	0.5	0.0
1885	6.7	6.2	1.6	3.8	4.0	1.4	1.9	1.6	0.2	1.0	0.6	0.0
1887	6.9	4.9	1.6	3.8	3.2	1.4	1.9	1.3	0.2	1.1	0.5	0.0
1889	6.8	4.9	1.8	3.6	3.0	1.6	1.8	1.3	0.2	1.3	0.6	0.0
1891	7.1	5.0	1.5	3.7	3.0	1.3	1.8	1.3	0.2	1.5	0.7	0.0
1893	6.6	5.2	1.5	3.4	3.0	1.3	1.6	1.4	0.2	1.6	0.9	0.0
1895	6.2	5.6	1.7	3.1	3.1	1.4	1.4	1.3	0.3	1.6	1.1	0.0
1897	6.5	5.5	1.8	3.3	3.1	1.5	1.4	1.2	0.3	1.8	1.2	0.1
1899	6.9	5.4	1.9	3.6	3.1	1.6	1.0	0.9	0.3	2.3	1.4	0.1
1901	7.2	5.4	1.9	3.7	3.1	1.6	1.0	0.8	0.2	2.5	1.4	0.1
1903	7.4	5.9	1.8	3.6	3.3	1.5	1.0	0.9	0.2	2.7	1.6	0.1
1905	7.8	6.2	1.9	3.6	3.3	1.5	1.2	1.1	0.3	3.0	1.8	0.2
1907	8.2	6.3	2.2	3.6	3.2	1.7	1.4	1.2	0.3	3.2	1.9	0.2
1909	8.6	6.8	2.2	3.6	3.2	1.6	1.9	1.4	0.4	3.1	2.2	0.2
1910	8.2	6.6	2.3	3.5	3.0	1.6	1.9	1.4	0.4	2.8	2.2	0.3
1914	8.4	6.7	2.8	3.3	2.8	1.7	2.2	1.6	0.6	2.9	2.3	0.4
1926	17.8	9.9	3.3	6.0	2.5	1.4	5.8	3.1	1.1	6.0	4.2	0.8
1931	13.0	14.7	6.0	4.1	3.9	1.8	5.9	6.0	2.1	3.0	4.7	2.0
1936	10.0	9.4	7.7	3.1	2.4	2.7	4.1	3.7	2.9	2.8	6.8	2.1
1939	11.7	8.8	0.0	1.1	1.1	0.0	10.6	7.0	0.0	0.0	0.6	0.0

Source: Detlef K. Müller, *Datenhandbuch zur deutschen Bildungsgeschichte* (Göttingen, forthcoming).

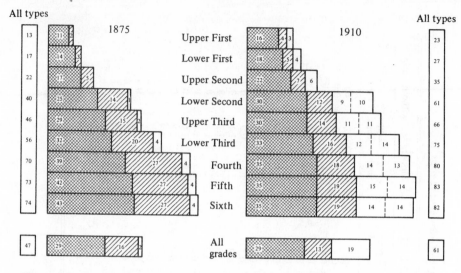

Figure 1.6. Prussian boys' secondary schools, 1875 and 1910: enrolments by grade, per thousands of relevant age groups (Detlef K. Müller, *Datenhandbuch zur deutschen Bildungsgeschichte* (Göttingen, forthcoming)). The blank spaces at the left and right of the figure represent total enrolments in all school types, by grade and in relation to the relevant age–year cohorts. The bars at the bottom of the figure represent *average* enrolments in all grades in relation to the age group 10–18. Differently shaded areas, from left to right, represent *Gymnasien/Progymnasien*, modern secondary schools with Latin (*Realgymnasien/Realprogymnasien*) and modern secondary schools without Latin (*Oberrealschulen/Realschulen*). For 1910 modern secondary schools without Latin are further subdivided into nine-year schools (on the left) and six-year schools (on the right).

Upper First of boys' secondary schools are reported as percentages of the relevant male age cohorts. The 'heuristic force' of Figure 2.2 in Fritz Ringer's chapter, suggested Figure 1.6, which compares total enrolments as well as enrolments by grade for 1875 and 1910, stating enrolments in figures per thousand of the relevant male age groups. In devising Figure 2.2, Ringer did not have data available on enrolments in specific grades. He therefore had to work with total enrolments and rates of graduation to arrive at an estimated 'pyramid of enrolments'. But I can now supplement his Figure 2.2 with precise enrolments per grade and per age group.

In 1875, for every thousand Prussian males aged 10 to 18, some 29 attended a traditional *Gymnasium* or *Progymnasium*, while 18 attended a modern secondary school with or without Latin. In 1910, among every thousand males of the same age group, 29 still attended a *Gymnasium* or *Progymnasium*, while 32 attended a modern secondary school. Thus, whereas the proportion of *Gymnasium* students per age group remained constant, the proportion of modern secondary school pupils increased by almost 60 per cent. To that extent the comparisons seem to confirm Ringer's thesis.

But the numbers being compared for the two years, as I have tried to show, do not refer to the same school forms, or to comparable subgroups *within* the cohort of males aged 10 to 18. Between 1875 and 1910, during the constitution of the system, the *Gymnasium* was altered in its structure, in its educational goals and in the social composition of its student body. In the distribution of its enrolments the *Gymnasium* lost its pyramidal shape and increasingly took on the form of a column. Entry into the Sixth remained open, in principle, only to potential graduates. Enrolment decreases in the lower and intermediate grades were compensated for by increases in the upper grades. In the *Gymnasium* of 1875 the Sixth enrolled 43 pupils per thousand males aged 10, while the Upper First enrolled 11 pupils per thousand males aged 18. In the *Gymnasium* of 1910 the Sixth enrolled 35 pupils per thousand males aged 10, while the Upper First enrolled 16 pupils per thousand males aged 18. Thus the defenders of the *Gymnasium* had not only been able to fend off potential new entrants, but had at the same time virtually insulated their institution from much of their traditional constituency of parents and pupils.

Moreover, Ringer's Figure 2.2 does not distinguish modern secondary schools with Latin (*Realgymnasien* and comparable institutions) from modern secondary schools without Latin (*Oberrealschulen* and comparable institutions), but includes both types under the heading of 'Other'. Such a categorisation may be partly justified if one looks only to the social meaning of curricular distinctions; but it neglects the fact that the *Realgymnasien* did offer Latin. This was important since secondary graduates without Latin had to spend considerable time preparing for a special supplementary examination (*Latinum*) before being able to complete university studies in a variety of subjects. If one groups the *Realgymnasium* with the *Gymnasium* in Figure 1.6., however, one can see the change in the shape of enrolments even more clearly. For as of 1875, the two institutions offering Latin jointly enrolled 70 pupils per thousand of the male age group in the Sixth and 13 in the Upper First, whereas the comparable ratios by 1910 were 54 for the Sixth and 20 for the Upper First. This, too, was a consequence of systematisation.

This essay could not have appeared in this volume if Fritz Ringer had not had the patience to transpose my German version so as to make it translatable, and then to translate it himself. Since the mid-1960s Ringer and I have independently been doing research on structural change in education, with an analytical emphasis upon the relationship between education and society. Dissatisfed with prior publications in the history of education, we were forced to undertake lengthy empirical investigations, in which we reached new and remarkably similar conclusions with respect to Germany, although we long knew nothing of each other's work. Ringer developed a comparative analytical model; my own work was concentrated on the state of Prussia and on selected regions within it. I found Ringer's *Education and Society* fascinating, partly because it offered a complex analytical model for comparative historical research, but also because of the results it contained for England, France and Germany.

My interest in the field had been stimulated by a reading of Brian Simon's *Education and the Labour Movement* in the mid-1960s. Since 1979 Ringer, Simon and I have been working in close co-operation. Ringer held visiting appointments at the Ruhr-University, Bochum in the summers of 1980 and 1985. This greatly aided our work, as did several major conferences sponsored by the Research Project on Knowledge and Society in the Nineteenth Century. The present volume is therefore also a fruit of the Sonderforschungsbereich 119, which I directed from 1979 until 1986.

Since 1979, within the Sonderforschungsbereich, I have been carrying out a project on German girls' schooling in the nineteenth and twentieth centuries. The results of that work require separate presentation, which is in preparation.

2. On segmentation in modern European educational systems: the case of French secondary education, 1865–1920

FRITZ RINGER

In *Education and Society in Modern Europe*,[1] I defined three statistical properties of educational systems: *inclusiveness*, measured in enrolments per age group, *progressiveness*, the degree to which students are recruited from the lower middle and lower classes, and *segmentation*, the subdivision of educational systems into parallel schools or programmes that differ both in their curriculum and in the social origins of their students. The distinction between college preparatory and vocational 'streams' in many American high schools is an instance of segmentation, and so is the subdivision of nineteenth-century European secondary education into classical and non-classical branches or 'tracks'. Segmentation was an outstanding feature of European secondary and higher education between about 1870 and 1920, and some of the most heated public controversies of that time concerned the issue of segmentation. My purpose in the present essay is further to articulate the concept of segmentation and briefly to discuss the causes, social implications and ideological significance of segmentation in European education during our period.

Defining and measuring segmentation

Imagine a society in which there are 1000 fourteen-year-olds from all social classes, of whom 100 reach secondary education in a classical secondary school, 150 reach a non-classical ('modern') secondary school, and the other 750 leave school to seek employment. The society is made up of five socio-occupational groups: (1) a 'non-economic' upper middle class of lawyers, doctors, clergymen, higher civil servants and university professors, (2) an 'economic' upper middle class of big businessmen, industrial technicians and executive-level white-collar employees, (3) a 'non-economic' lower middle class of middle-level government officials and teachers, (4) an 'economic' lower middle class of shopkeepers, independent artisans and middle-level employees, and (5) a working class of petty clerks, workers and domestics. In column (A) of Table 2.1 the 1000 fourteen-year-olds are listed according to the socio-occupational groups of their fathers. In column (S) the same breakdown is provided for the 250 youths who reach either form of secondary education, while columns (C) and (M) report on those reaching classical and modern schools, respectively.

There are two ways to assess the *progressiveness* of this imaginary system. Noting that among the 600 fourteen-year-olds with working-class backgrounds 60 reach secondary education, we may begin by saying that the *access percentage* or *access chance* for working-class youths in secondary education is 10 per cent. But this figure alone tells us little; for if only 10 per cent of the whole age group reached secondary schooling, then 10 per cent for the working class would be very progressive indeed. Thus access percentages are meaningful only relatively, in relation to a norm; and the most appropriate norm is the access percentage for all social groups combined, or for the age group as a whole, which is also the measure of *inclusiveness* for that age group. Thus using the column and row designations in Table 2.1, we arrive at the following:

$$\frac{S5}{A5} = 10\% \quad = \quad \text{\textit{access percentage} or chance for working-class youths in secondary education}$$

$$\frac{\dfrac{S5}{A5} = 10\%}{\dfrac{St}{At} = 25\%} = 0.4 = \text{\textit{relative} access percentage or chance, or \textit{access ratio} for working-class youths in secondary education}$$

And incidentally:

$$\frac{\dfrac{C1}{A1} = 100\%}{\dfrac{Ct}{At} = 10\%} = 10.0 = \text{relative access percentage or chance, or access ratio for the non-economic upper middle class in \textit{classical} secondary education}$$

Table 2.1. *Distribution of students in an imaginary educational system*

Fathers' socio-occupational groups	(A) All youths	(S) Secondary schools	(C) Classical secondary	(M) Modern secondary
(1) Non-ec. up. mid.	20	20	20	—
(2) Econ. up. mid.	60	40	20	20
(3) Non-ec. low. mid.	120	60	40	20
(4) Econ. low. mid.	200	70	20	50
(5) Working	600	60	—	60
(t) All groups	1000	250	100	150

Distributions of (t)

Access to (S)

Access to (C) and (M)

While important British data on education and social class in the twentieth century take the form of access percentages, the nature of the evidence for France and Germany forces us to work with *distribution percentages*. Column (S) of Table 2.1 gives us the distribution of the 250 students in secondary education over the five socio-occupational groups, and we see that the distribution percentage for working-class youths in secondary schools is 24 per cent. Like access percentages, distribution percentages are meaningful only in relation to a norm, which in this case is the distribution percentage for the whole age group. Thus:

$$\frac{S5}{St} = 24\% \qquad = \qquad \textit{distribution percentage} \text{ for, or representation of, working-class youths in secondary education}$$

$$\frac{\dfrac{S5}{St} = 24\%}{\dfrac{A5}{At} = 60\%} = 0.4 = \textit{relative} \text{ representation of, or } \textit{distribution ratio} \text{ for, working-class youths in secondary education}$$

And incidentally:

$$\frac{\dfrac{C1}{Ct} = 20\%}{\dfrac{A1}{At} = 2\%} = 10.0 = \text{relative representation of, or distribution ratio for, the non-economic upper middle class in } \textit{classical} \text{ secondary education}$$

Obviously, the distribution ratio is mathematically identical with the access ratio. Indeed, without that fortunate circumstance, there could be no comparison at all between English and French or German data on the social origins of students.[2]

Even more fortunate is the very close analogy between the measurement of progressiveness and the assessment of segmentation. To find out how much the classical schools in Table 2.1 differed from the modern ones *in the origins of their students*, we proceed exactly as we did a moment ago, except that our questions now pertain to all secondary students, rather than to all members of the age group:

$$\frac{\dfrac{C1}{S1} = 100\%}{\dfrac{Ct}{St} = 40\%} = 2.5 =$$ relative access rate or access ratio for *secondary students* from the non-economic upper middle class in advanced *classical* secondary education

$$\frac{\dfrac{C1}{Ct} = 20\%}{\dfrac{S1}{Ct} = 8\%} = 2.5 =$$ relative representation of, or distribution ratio for, *secondary students* from the non-economic upper middle class in advanced *classical* secondary education

Again the two ratios are mathematically identical. Thus the measure of segmentation within a given sector of an educational system is the degree to which *distribution or access* percentages for particular schools or programmes within that sector *deviate from the norm* provided by the comparable percentages for the sector as a whole.[3] The striking analogy between progressiveness and segmentation is anything but accidental for, as I suggested in *Education and Society*, the divide between those members of an age group who obtain advanced schooling and those who do not is in fact the limiting case of segmentation within any educational system.

The typical form of educational segmentation is socially *vertical*, that is one of the 'tracks' caters to a socially more 'elevated' clientele than the other. There have been circumstances, however, in which segmentation has been *socially horizontal* to some degree. Table 2.1 describes an imagined example. While the upper middle-class groups predominate in the classical schools, working-class youths who reach secondary education at all are markedly overrepresented in the modern stream. This is the typical form of socially vertical segmentation. At the same time, the relative access and distribution percentages for the 'non-economic' upper and lower middle classes are slightly higher, respectively, than those for the 'economic' upper and lower middle classes, with respect to both secondary education in general and classical secondary schooling as a segment *within* the secondary sector. This is socially horizontal segmentation. When it occurs in reality, it indicates a partial divergence or incongruity between the distribution of advanced education and that of other determinants of social rank. One way to interpret such a divergence is to distinguish between 'cultural capital' and 'economic capital', following Pierre Bourdieu; another is to adopt Max Weber's differentiation between 'class' and 'status', where 'class' is identified with wealth and economic power, 'status' with social honour and prestige, including the prestige derived from advanced education. Incongruities between the hierarchies of cultural and economic capital, or of status and class, rarely occur at the very top or in the lowest third of the social scale; they may therefore appear unimportant in comparison with the brute facts of cumulative inequality. For the student of the European middle classes, of middle-class self-images and ideologies, however, these incongruities are quite significant.

Several other empirical aspects of segmentation can be specified. Thus, quite apart from how strongly the several segments of an educational system or sector differ in the social origins of their students, particular segments may be more or less *inclusive*, depending upon how many students they encompass.[4] Segmentation may be more or less *systematic*, in the sense of rigorously defined or codified, and more or less *impenetrable*, depending upon how difficult it is for individual students to cross the boundaries between neighbouring 'tracks'. Further, since segmentation involves a *coupling* of social with curricular differences, one may certainly inquire into the extent of the curricular divergence between classical and modern schools, for example. The significance of such divergences, on the other hand, should not be overestimated, for a classical stream within a secondary system will retain its special position even if the class hours devoted to Latin are reduced.[5] Finally, it may be appropriate to extend the concept of segmentation to cases in which curricular variations between school types are supplemented or even replaced by such non-curricular differences as that between public and private or residential and non-residential institutions, particularly if the associated prestige differences can be signalled by such outward marks of distinctive socialisation as special school 'languages' or modes of speech.

A chronological framework

An early industrial phase in the history of modern European educational systems, I would argue, extended from the early nineteenth century to about 1860 or 1870. The dominant form of secondary education in the major European nations at that time was centred upon the classical languages and literatures. Much of the prestige of this traditional curriculum stemmed from its association with the clerical and governing elites of an earlier era. A few scattered non-classical schools or programmes existed in several European societies, typically at a lower secondary level; but the classical institutions held the centre of the stage. Indeed, as the classical curriculum was more and more rigorously codified by educational bureaucracies, especially in France and in the German states, and as the graduate certificates of the classical schools became prerequisites for entry into the civil service and into the university faculties, the remaining non-classical institutions or programmes were defined in a largely negative way: they did not meet the standards or offer the qualifications of the officially sanctioned classical establishments.

The classical secondary schools and universities of the early industrial period prepared students almost exclusively for the liberal professions, the civil service, the Church, and secondary and university teaching. Together, the members of the 'learned' professions made up a 'mandarin' or 'gentlemanly' elite, an intellectual aristocracy or 'educated stratum' that was largely separated from the commercial and industrial middle class. Secondary and higher education had virtually no positive relationship with the early industrial economy. Advanced schooling channelled young people away from directly 'productive' employment, and reduced opportunities in the economy apparently *increased* university enrolments. An excess of candidates for the learned professions was widely reported in the 1830s and 1840s; it stimulated fears that have ever since been aroused by disequilibria of this kind. Both in Prussia and in France during this period only about one out of three or four entrants to secondary schools eventually obtained a *baccalauréat* or *Abitur*. The secondary 'pyramid' was thus a good deal wider at the base than at the apex. It is certainly possible that many of those who left secondary schools before graduation took jobs in commerce and industry; at the lower secondary level, education may in fact have made a positive contribution to the early industrial economy. Yet, for all we know, a substantial share of early leavers from French secondary schools ended up as marginal Parisian literati, rather than as budding capitalists.

One way to describe the early industrial pattern is to say that education above the primary level functioned as a largely autonomous subsystem within the larger society. While classical secondary schools and university-level institutions prepared candidates for the learned professions, they played almost no role in what upward social mobility there was in the world of economic enterprise. The reproduction of 'cultural' and of 'economic capital', in Bourdieu's language, proceeded in relative isolation from each other. Levels of inclusiveness at all levels above the primary were low and relatively stable. Nevertheless, the degree of progressiveness, at least in the Prussian *Gymnasium*, was surprisingly high. Among graduates of 29 representative Prussian *Gymnasien* from the late 1780s to around 1805, according to Jeismann, about 40 per cent were the sons of officers, university professors, university-educated officials, judges, doctors and apothecaries, and another 33 per cent were the offspring of pastors and secondary teachers; just over 6 per cent came from the families of merchants and 'manufacturers'; some 14 per cent of students' fathers were artisans and workers, non-commissioned officers and primary teachers, and 5 per cent were farmers or farm workers. Less than 2 per cent of the fathers were landowners, and only about 4 per cent of fathers *in all occupational groups* were noblemen.[6] The Prussian *Bildungsschicht* of the decades around 1800, in other words, was certainly self-perpetuating to a substantial degree; but it was also clearly a middle-class 'merit' elite, an aristocracy of intelligence, rather than of birth. The one social group from which it drew very few of its members was the 'economic' middle class.

All this changed during the high industrial phase in the history of European secondary and higher education, which extended from about 1860 or 1870 to 1920 or 1930. Levels of inclusiveness rose steadily during this period, and much of the growth was concentrated in institutions and programmes that were younger and less prestigious than the classical secondary schools and traditional universities. Whether located at the higher primary, secondary or tertiary level, these less prestigious program-mes and institutions specialised in 'modern', 'technical' or 'applied' studies, whose inferior status was typically linked to their supposed practicality. There is no clear evidence that these younger studies actually contributed significantly to the economic development of the period, or that they arose in response to objective and specifiable 'needs' of the high industrial economy. Yet many contemporaries certainly *believed* that commerce and industry would benefit from an increased supply of skilled workers, techni-cians and industrial scientists, and it may be nearly as difficult to show that they were entirely wrong as to prove that they were right.

In any case, the high industrial period, not the early nineteenth century, saw the segmentation of European secondary and higher education reach its most systematic form. Amid anxieties provoked by an 'excess' of graduates and by the spectre of an 'academic proletariat', the future of secondary schooling became the subject of virulent public debates. In this conflictual context, the social and curricular boundaries between traditional and modern secondary schools were defined and redefined, along with the academic and professional options to be opened to their graduates. Analogous issues at the university level were equally contested. Since some of the younger institutions and programmes in fact enrolled increasing percentages of students from the 'economic' middle classes, who might previously have done without much formal schooling, the overall result was the kind of – partly horizontal – segmentation that has been discussed above.

The late industrial phase in the evolution of modern European educational systems began around 1920 or 1930. Since that time there have been extraordinarily rapid enrolment increases in secondary and higher education. There has probably been a relationship between this steep rise in inclusiveness and the expansion of the white-collar hierarchy within the occupational structure. But we do not really know whether the important causal connections ran from occupational change to educational change or vice versa. We do know that an oversupply of candidates for the traditionally learned professions once again raised the spectre of an 'academic proletariat' in the major European nations during the inter-war period, and especially during the 1930s. Violent fluctuations in birth rates during and after the First World War may have helped to destabilise established conventions about the educational qualifications associated with various occupations. In any case, whole new clusters of educated professions have emerged since the 1930s, so that the expansion of the white-collar hierarchy has been virtually identical with the growth of secondary and higher education. At the same time, there has been an increasing degree of *convergence* between the hierarchies of education and of wealth or economic power in contemporary social systems.

Within the educational systems of late industrial societies the increases in progressiveness expected by reformers have not been achieved. Segmentation, too, continues to play a role; but its character has changed in significant ways. In place of a sharp contrast between classical and modern secondary schools, for example, what we find in the major European countries today is a fairly complex pattern of more or less penetrable secondary 'tracks', which now include former higher primary and vocational schools along with 'academic' secondary ones. In this and other respects European secondary systems have begun to approach, if not actually to resemble, the intentionally unsystematic or even disguised 'streaming' characteristic of the better American high schools. One way to describe the change is to say that segmentation in contemporary educational systems is almost exclusively vertical; another is to suggest that the segments of contemporary systems no longer mark out subtle differences between small subgroups or elites *within* the middle and upper middle classes; instead, they legitimate and thus perpetuate the social differences between the upper middle, the lower middle and the lower classes.

Conflicting pressures

In France and elsewhere from the 1860s on, reformers who sponsored non-traditional forms of education often cited the 'requirements' of the modern economy to make their case. Pointing to international economic competition, in which they supposed other countries to have threatening initial advantages, they urged greater attention to the need for trained manpower. Occasionally, they implied that the nation would benefit from a new kind of business leadership, perhaps one with greater scientific or technical expertise. Much more often, what they principally had in mind was a need for new skills at the intermediate and lower levels of the commercial and industrial hierarchy. They therefore recommended or supported a more 'modern', 'scientific' or 'technical' emphasis in secondary or post-primary schools; or they championed 'applied' studies at institutions of a more advanced type that later came to be ranked at the university level. Rarely were educational modernists determined enough to recommend that the established secondary schools and universities be totally transformed or replaced. Sometimes they wanted timely adjustments in the traditional curricula; more commonly they intended merely to introduce or to strengthen programmes that could *supplement* the work of the traditionally most prestigious educational institutions.

In keeping with this outlook the reformers typically saw themselves, and were seen by their opponents, as social and political liberals or even democrats because they proposed to offer educational opportunities and chances for upward mobility to groups that had not previously enjoyed such advantages to any substantial degree. Indeed, the reformers were as often civil servants and politicians as entrepreneurs and scientists; they therefore had their eyes almost as much on the social and political as on the economic consequences of reform. Many of them were interested in a more harmonious and integrated society or polity. In France some of them believed in 'solidarism'; others saw a greater availability of education and of social opportunity as an alternative to class conflict. I see no reason to doubt that many of them held such views in good conscience.

At the same time, most reformers clearly did *not* expect graduates of the schools and programmes they recommended to reach the highest positions in society. The son of an artisan might prepare to be a foreman in a substantial machine shop, while the son of a small merchant might expand his father's business, using skills his father had not needed. Yet as these examples suggest, an increase in 'applied' schooling could be expected to lead to no more than sectorally limited forms of social mobility, particularly in an occupational structure in which artisans and shopkeepers were being replaced by skilled workers and white-collar employees in any case. Thus, until late in the nineteenth century, even determined reformers could share the almost universal assumption of status persistence, and do so 'innocently', without any conscious intent to *limit* mobility. It was apparently possible to believe *both* that the vast majority of sons would continue in their fathers' social stations *and* that outstanding scholarly merit would be recognised and rewarded no matter how humble its origins. As it happened, examples of advancement for unusually talented individuals *through schooling* were probably a good deal rarer in the world of commerce and industry than in the Church, the civil service and, above all, the educational hierarchy itself. Indeed, this may help to account for another assumption prevalent even among educational 'modernists'. This was the more or less explicit expectation that the ablest students would *and should* continue to enrol, where possible, in the 'ancient' institutions and programmes.

One has to remember that the educational reformers themselves usually came from the traditionally prestigious schools and universities. They therefore shared some of the biases of their opponents, even when their conscious convictions were on the side of change. This is a difficult subject; but I honestly wonder how many members of the commercial and industrial 'bourgeoisie' in nineteenth-century Europe were ever wholeheartedly committed to a purely 'middle-class' culture. I do know that many leading entrepreneurs in France and elsewhere sided with the traditionalists in the education debates of the later nineteenth century. Even when they claimed to see a need for more 'practical' training, some of them were apparently thinking more of their employees than of their sons. In short, there was much ambivalence in the camp of the reformers.

The mix of motives in the field of action became even more complex once the newer schools and programmes had their own teachers, students, parents and former students. Their impact is best described under the heading of the 'generalist shift'. This is the propensity of vocational or 'practical' courses of instruction to take on a more 'general' or even 'academic' character with the passage of time. In France the transformation of Duruy's *enseignement spécial* into the *enseignement moderne* during the 1880s provided an example. In England some of the mechanics' institutes apparently went through an analogous process. In Prussia the *Provinzial-Gewerbeschulen*, once converted into *Oberrealschulen*, also moved towards a more general form of schooling. In fact both the teachers and the 'clients' of 'applied' programmes typically tended to imitate their older and more established rivals. The teachers in 'practical' schools were disposed to reduce the grounds for status and salary differences between themselves and their colleagues in the traditional schools. The parents and graduates of the younger programmes had even clearer reasons to seek equality of standing with the more prestigious institutions. At the same time, the supposed demand for specific vocational skills in the job market probably failed to materialise. In any case, the generalist shift had an interesting set of consequences. On the one hand, it demonstrated that even the most carefully restricted educational objectives had a tendency to raise troublesome expectations. On the other hand, it also transformed potentially distinctive courses of instruction, at least initially, into second-rate versions of their more highly accredited rivals. In the process, of course, it steadily aggravated the boundary disputes between the institutions and curricular options that came to coexist in the same sectors of the educational systems.

In France and Germany at least, these disputes became particularly sharp during the 1880s and 1890s in connection with a wave of public anxiety over a supposed excess of educated candidates for positions in the learned professions. The slogan about an 'academic proletariat', coined in Germany during this period, was quickly taken up in France.[7] Interestingly enough, the idea of an 'overproduction' of academic qualifications had weaker empirical foundations in the 1880s than it did during comparable crises in the early and late industrial periods. In Germany at least, the crises around 1840 and 1930 were associated with unusually abrupt enrolment 'booms', which inevitably threatened established conventions about what jobs were appropriate for the highly educated. The enrolment increases that took place in all the major European nations during the late nineteenth century, by contrast, were relatively gradual. On the other hand, they were almost certainly provoked in part by the deep recessionary cycle that threatened the European economies from the mid-1870s. Frightened by uncertain prospects in the economy, the educated upper middle class fought all the harder to protect its 'cultural capital' from devaluation and to pass it on intact to its heirs. It had to fear competition not only from the lower middle classes, but from segments of the economic upper middle class as well. The spectre of an 'academic proletariat' not only accompanied the conflict that ensued; it was also something of a weapon in that conflict. Again and again the traditionalists in the education debate insisted that the modern curricular options prepared adequately for practical work in commerce and industry, but not for leadership in the traditionally academic professions.

When studying the public controversies over secondary education in France and Germany during the late nineteenth century, one is at first inclined to suppose that all the advantages were on the side of the traditionalists, the defenders of the old elite institutions. On looking more closely, however, one finds that even the most powerful participants in the conflict had to adjust to pressures that limited their freedom of action. In fact one can view their tactics as exercises in trial and error. Thus one possible response to the challenge of the natural sciences was simply to add them to the programmes of the classical schools. But this 'encyclopaedic' approach ultimately drew criticism from parents, pedagogues and even medical experts, who worried about the health of 'overburdened' pupils.

An alternative option was to continue with a fully classical curriculum at the elite schools, while denying secondary status to all deviations from the classical norm. But this position eventually became untenable in several ways. For one thing the natural sciences simply could not be ignored in the long run. At the same time, if the non-classical schools were given no weight at all in the job market, the competition for certificates from the traditional schools would inevitably increase. It was all very well to suggest that the steadily rising demand for the classical *baccalauréat* or *Abitur* was due largely to mediocre students from lower middle-class backgrounds, who would be better off in an honest trade. A strictly meritocratic 'weeding-out' of these supposed mediocrities, however, would have threatened upper middle-class students as well. The 'mediocrities' therefore had to be attracted away from the classical and into the non-classical streams. Besides, the clients of the younger secondary schools or programmes gradually acquired a certain political weight of their own. This was true especially in France under the Radical Republic, where competition from the Catholic schools provided an additional incentive to respond sympathetically to all social 'demands' for advanced schooling. In short, the late nineteenth-century contests over the future of secondary education almost *had* to end in compromises that partly reflected and partly disguised the conflicting pressures that shaped them.

Outcomes

The most appropriate way to describe the outcomes of the conflicts that have been discussed would be to report in detail on changes in the structures of secondary and higher education in England, France and Germany during the high industrial period. Differences as well as similarities between the national patterns would have to be considered. Since this cannot be done in a brief essay – and since I mean to look more closely at similarities than at differences between the major national systems – I want to focus here on the case of Prussian secondary education between 1870 and 1911.

There were three types of boys' secondary schools in Prussia by the end of the nineteenth century; each extended over nine grades, and in each case a group of lower schools encompassing only the first six or seven grades was associated with the full-length version. The most prestigious of these schools, of course, was the classical *Gymnasium* (with the *Progymnasium*), which taught substantial amounts of Greek and Latin. Students who earned a graduate certificate (*Abitur*) from a *Gymnasium* were automatically admitted to the German university faculty of their choice. The *Realgymnasium* (with the *Realprogymnasium*) taught almost as much Latin as the *Gymnasium* but replaced Greek with a modern foreign language and made a little more room than the *Gymnasium* for the natural sciences. The

Oberrealschule (with the six-year *Realschule*) concentrated on the sciences and modern languages to the exclusion of Latin and Greek.

The *Realgymnasium* and *Oberrealschule* were sometimes collectively called *Realschulen*, which can be loosely translated as 'realistic' or 'modern' schools. The history of these 'realistic' schools is difficult to summarise. They were not even precisely defined by the Prussian school authorities until 1859, and the full-length *Oberrealschule* did not emerge until 1878. The holders of a modern *Abitur* certificate were largely excluded from the universities until the end of the century. Questions of accreditation in secondary education were publicly debated with particular vehemence in the 1880s and 1890s. Finally, a Prussian decree of 1900 ended the battle of the schools. In theory, graduates of all three secondary streams were henceforth admitted to all institutions of higher education on equal terms. In practice modern school students long continued to face a variety of specific obstacles: they were still excluded from the faculties of theology, and special examinations in Latin and even in Greek survived as preconditions for admission to various courses of university study, state examinations and professions.

Figure 2.2 summarily describes enrolments in Prussian boys' *Gymnasien* (shaded areas) and modern secondary schools (unshaded areas) in 1870 and 1911. The numbers of students at the nine grade levels are related to the relevant age groups. More specifically, the highest of the nine levels is defined by the number of *Abitur* awards per age group. The sizes of the remaining levels are then calculated from the *average* enrolments per age group in the nine-year course as a whole, and this on the assumption that the total loss of students from entry to graduation was distributed evenly over the eight intervals between grades. Further, no distinction is made between the *Realgymnasium/Realprogymnasium* combination, which awarded a few *Abiturs* even before 1870, and the *Oberrealschule/Realschule* segment, which was made up entirely of six-year *Realschulen* until 1878 and which still functioned largely as a non-graduate secondary school at the end of the century. In reality the Prussian enrolment pyramids of the nineteenth century were highly irregular in shape, with a particularly sharp reduction in enrolments after six years of schooling. If one adds that the estimate of 8 *Abiturs* per age group in 1870 may be a little high, one begins to appreciate the degree of abstraction involved in the diagram.

Even so, the table does have a certain heuristic force. What it shows, though in very general terms, is that the net change in enrolments between 1870 and 1911 was a kind of *addition*. The *Gymnasium* did not change very much, although a somewhat greater share of its students stayed on until graduation in 1911 than had done so in 1870. Apparently, the *Gymnasium* enrolment pyramid had been even narrower at the top, in relation to the base, during the early nineteenth century. Yet, for the period 1870–1911 and

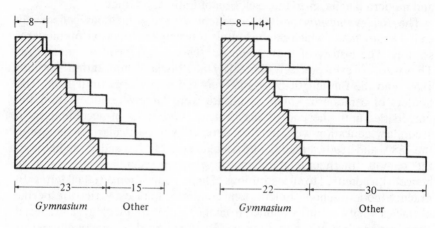

Figure 2.2. Growth and segmentation in Prussian secondary education, 1870–1911: averaged distributions of *Gymnasium* and other students over nine grades (Ringer, *Education and Society*, pp. 54, 272–9). The two shapes stand for distributions of students over the nine ascending grades of Prussian boys' *Gymnasien/Progymnasien* (shaded areas) and other secondary schools (unshaded areas). In 1870 *average* enrolments in *Gymnasien/Progymnasien* and in all boys' secondary schools, respectively, were 15 and 23 students per thousand members of the age group 11–19, while *Gymnasium* and all boys' secondary *Abitur* certificates, respectively, were 7 and 8 per thousand of those aged 19. The corresponding figures for 1911 were 15 and 32 (average enrolments), and 8 and 12 (certificates). All other enrolments represented in the diagram are calculated on the assumption that the loss of students per age group between the beginning of secondary schooling and its completion in the *Abitur* were distributed equally over the eight intervals between grades. The reader may wish to compare Figure 2.2 with Müller's Figure 1.6, which was conceived after Figure 2.2 and along similar lines. But apart from its more abstract character, Figure 2.2 is based on data and calculations in *Education and Society*, not on Müller's latest data and calculations. Note especially that the top lines in Figure 2.2 represent graduations (*Abiturs*), not enrolments in the highest grade, and that age groups in Figure 2.2 are for males and females, whereas those in Figure 1.6 are for males only.

for Prussia as a whole, the net change in the shape of the *Gymnasium* was rather slight. What really happened in Prussia during the high industrial period, therefore, was a significant addition to the modern segments of the secondary system, most notably at the lower secondary level.

Altogether, then, the defenders of the *Gymnasium* won a qualified victory in the battle of the schools. On the one hand, they had to give some ground to the modern curricular options. At least as of 1911, on the other hand, they had managed to keep the enrolment increases of the time entirely outside

Table 2.3. *Social origins and career plans of Prussian secondary graduates, 1875–99, in percentages by column*

Socio-occupational groups	All secondary		Gymnasium		Realgymnasium		Oberrealschule	
	In	Out	In	Out	In	Out	In	Out
Learned professions	19	68	21	75	7	26	5	12
Lower officials	13	7	12	5	15	19	13	13
Primary teachers	6	—	7	—	4	—	2	—
Technical professions	5	11	4	7	7	30	9	56
'Industrialists'	6 }	4	5 }	4	9 }	10	13 }	11
Commerce	21 }		20 }		26 }		27 }	
Artisans	8	—	7	—	13	—	17	—
Agriculture and others	22	10	24	9	19	15	14	8
Absolute totals (thousands)	85.0		71.2		12.6		1.2	

Note: The table reports on the roughly 85,000 students who received the *Abitur* from all Prussian secondary schools between 1875 and 1899. The figures shown are distribution percentages for the occupations of students' fathers (In) and for the intended professions of the graduates (Out). The 'learned professions' include law, the high civil service, secondary and university teaching, theology and medicine. 'Lower officials' also includes the middle ranks of the civil service, along with a few middle-level white-collar employees. 'Agriculture and others' includes the military.
Source: Ringer, *Education and Society*, pp. 71, 280–4.

their own territory. They had thus prevented an inflationary 'devaluation' of the *Gymnasium Abitur*, which none the less remained the royal road to university study and to the learned professions.

In Table 2.3 we turn to the social dimensions of segmentation in late nineteenth-century Prussian secondary education. We are given fathers' occupations and intended careers for all Prussian secondary graduates (*Abiturienten*) between 1875 and 1899. We are in a position to relate the distribution percentages for the graduates of *Gymnasien, Realgymnasien* and *Oberrealschulen* to the corresponding percentages for the secondary system as a whole. The table must be approached with caution because at this level the *Gymnasium* was by far the most inclusive of the secondary 'tracks', whereas the *Oberrealschule* accounted for less than 2 per cent of the graduates. In fact, if the information were regrouped in the form of access percentages, the highest figures for *all* social groups would appear in the column for the *Gymnasium*. Thus among the sons of artisans who obtained the *Abitur* at all, 73 per cent received it from a *Gymnasium*. Even among graduates planning to enter the technical professions, just over half came from a *Gymnasium*. These proportions were low *only relatively*, in relation, that is, to the *Gymnasium*'s huge share of all certificates awarded.

Once that is clear, however, the main conclusions warranted by Table 2.3 are quickly stated. First, the late nineteenth-century Prussian secondary schools in general, and the *Gymnasium* in particular, still prepared most of their students for the traditionally learned professions in law and medicine, the Church, the high civil service, and secondary and university teaching. The only clear exception to this rule was the *Oberrealschule*, which apparently sent many of its graduates into business and, more particularly, into the technical professions, presumably after further study at the technical institutes. In 1900 the most 'modern' of the German secondary schools was still a predominantly non-graduate institution; the evidence about it in Table 2.3 is therefore interesting primarily for what it suggests about students who left it before the *Abitur*.

Second, recruitment into Prussian secondary education towards the end of the nineteenth century was fairly progressive in its way. The vast majority of the graduates came from the early industrial middle and lower middle classes. Only 2 per cent of all fathers were landowners, whereas 11 per cent were farmers. The most prominent group among the parents were the members of the learned professions. Teachers and civil servants below the highest ranks also accounted for a remarkably large proportion of the graduates. Just over a third of the students came from the families of artisans, shopkeepers, merchants and 'industrialists'. Yet many of these 'industrialists' may well have been small independent producers not far above the artisanal level. Thus the commercial and industrial occupations, in so far as they were represented among students' parents at all, suggest the 'burgher' estate of an early industrial economy, rather than the entrepreneurial upper middle class of the high industrial context.

Finally, Table 2.3 represents a classic case of segmentation in a high industrial system of secondary schooling. The socially vertical aspect of segmentation, of course, is immediately apparent. One can hardly miss the stepwise differences of social 'altitude' between the *Gymnasium*, the *Realgymnasium* and the *Oberrealschule*, which are reflected in the decreasing shares of parents in the learned professions, as well as in the increasing proportions of artisans among the fathers. The socially horizontal dimension of segmentation may not be quite as obvious. Yet no unilinear scheme of 'class' rankings could account for the contrasting patterns formed by the percentages for commerce and those for the primary teachers or, even more plainly, by those for the 'industrialists' and those for the learned professions.[8] These contrasts, as I have tried to suggest, testify to a continuing divergence between the economic and the educational hierarchies during the high industrial period.

Segmentation and meaning

Educational segmentation crucially affects what Hans-Ulrich Wehler calls the 'cultural patterns of interpretation' (*kulturelle Deutungsmuster*) that shape the way a society is experienced by its members.[9] Conceptions of education help to define social roles, and social distances are measured by educational differences. This aspect of segmentation strikes me as more important than its tendency to impede social mobility through education. The notion of legitimation comes closer to what I have in mind, but I would want to stress that educational segmentation legitimates social stratification by literally 'giving it meaning'.

Imagine a social world in which all differences of birth, wealth and power were purely accidental and thus totally divorced from men's personal qualities. The contrast between that world and the real one, it seems to me, is due largely to education, which can transform apparently *accidental* into apparently *essential* differences between members of society. The quality of being educated cannot, like wealth, be conceptually separated from the remaining characteristics of those who have it. The educated individual seems to differ from the uneducated one in his whole being, essentially and not accidentally. There have been various ways of describing the personal effects of education, or of distinguishing 'true' education from such inadequate surrogates as 'merely practical training'; but all of these exercises in definition have rotated around the central idea of enriching the student's whole person or shaping his character, rather than simply adding to his skills. This surely helps to account for the strenuous repudiation of useful, instrumental learning that runs all through modern educational thought. Sometimes education has been conceived of as a fulfilment of human potential, and the educated man as the fully 'cultivated', auto-nomous personality. In other contexts the emphasis has been particularly upon the moral or aesthetic attributes of the educated individual. Invari-ably, however, advanced 'general' education has been defined as non-utilitarian in character.

Another way to understand the patterns of meaning associated with education is to focus once more upon the capacity of education to confer social honour or prestige, and thus to sustain a hierarchy of status at variance with the existing distribution of wealth and economic power. Education owes this decisive capacity to its special relationship with tradition, for European educational systems have typically functioned as transmitters of traditional cultural values. That, indeed, is how the contrast between education and property acquired its full significance. For the highly edu-cated were the traditional notables of early capitalist societies. What advanced education conferred upon them can be conceived of as an 'aristocratic' quality derived from immersion in the inherited culture. If it is characteristic of the aristocrat to be defined by what he *is, essentially*, not by what he *does, accidentally*, then nineteenth-century educational ideals were middle-class aspirations to aristocracy.

This is not to deny that the ideal of the gratuitously 'cultivated' personality also contained a utopian potential. The rejection of the merely useful or usable self can attain a critical thrust, in so far as it implies an alternative to the interpersonal relations of the 'cash nexus', of using others and being used in turn. In the English context, as Raymond Williams has shown, the concept of 'culture' drew much of its meaning from the critical contrast with capitalist individualism.[10]

Nevertheless, the ideal of the educated man usually took more commonplace and socially adjusted forms. Thus significant portions of the nineteenth-century middle class in England and elsewhere strove to rise above the world of commerce, whether into that of the civil servant useful only to the nation, or into that of the liberal professions, in which relationships to clients could be pictured as personal, rather than commercial. Sometimes, especially in Germany, the cultivated individual came to inhabit an asocial sphere in which fellow-citizens and fellow-men seemed not to exist. More typically, the condition of being fully and generally educated was taken to confer the right to dominate those trained more narrowly for social usefulness.

As a matter of fact, middle-class ideals of education varied in their social and moral implications, not only from country to country, but over time as well. It will not be possible here to consider the complex and subtle differences between German *Bildung*, French *culture générale* and the English ideal of the gentleman and amateur generalist. On the other hand, I do want to risk a few general remarks, in conclusion, about major historical changes in the educational ideology of the European middle classes over the course of the nineteenth century.

At one level one can conceive of these changes as an actual loss of meaning. Thus the religious overtone, the echo of Pietism, that can still be detected in the German idea of *Bildung* during the early nineteenth century faded with time. Even more important was the impoverishment that overcame the neo-humanist aspirations of the decades around 1800, again particularly in Germany. The early neo-humanists believed, as Matthew Arnold did, that the great classical sources would bestow 'sweetness and light' upon those who approached them. The great Greek and Roman authors were to be moral and spiritual mentors. In the German neo-idealist tradition the experience of the classics was to awaken an inner 'grace' that would otherwise remain a mute potentiality. It was a long road that led from these conceptions to the idea of Latin as mental gymnastics. Somewhere along this road the interest in the spiritual contents was replaced by a fascination with the formal perfections of a literature or even a grammar. To avoid encyclopaedism as a response to the advent of the modern subjects, educational theorists almost had to move from substantive to formalist conceptions. In any case, the violent debates between traditionalists and modernists in secondary education after 1880 caused the *social* significance of educational segmentation, its role in the reproduction of a hierarchic system of social relations, to reach an unprecedented degree of consciousness and public visibility. A largely unreflected assumption of status persistence was replaced by a deliberate intention to *limit* mobility. In the process, the neo-humanist tradition lost its 'good conscience', its initially universalist and potentially utopian significance. It fell into an increasingly defensive ideological posture that both revealed and deepened its moral exhaustion.

At a more practical level these changes of meaning were brought about by the routinisation of classical learning – and of curricular differences more generally – in an ever more comprehensive and consistently articulated system of certifiable qualifications. During the late nineteenth century, even as this 'rationalisation' reached a certain completeness, the early industrial status society was decisively threatened by the high industrial class society, and the forces of change were plainly visible within the educational systems themselves. This was the context in which a formalist variant of the old antithesis between classical cultivation and merely practical knowledge was pushed to an intellectually questionable and socially exclusionary extreme.

Structural change in French secondary education, 1865–1920

In the highly centralised and standardised system of public secondary schooling created in France by Napoleon Bonaparte, the key institutions throughout the nineteenth century were the state *lycées*.[11] Until 1865 the curriculum of the *lycées* was almost exclusively classical, although mathematics held a secure place in the programme of the higher grades. The *lycées*, generally established in the larger cities, were financed directly by the central government. The more numerous public *collèges*, often located in the smaller towns, were partly supported by the municipalities. Their curriculum was that of the *lycées*, but many of them lacked the higher grades. Among the various private secondary institutions that competed successfully with the state schools, the Jesuit *collèges* undoubtedly figured as the most important. Like the public *lycées* and *collèges*, they prepared many of their students for the *baccalauréat*, a state leaving examination and certificate that strongly resembled the German *Abitur*.

The costs of secondary schooling were probably somewhat higher in France than in Germany during the nineteenth century. In addition to tuition, roughly half of French secondary pupils paid fees in order to board at public or private secondary institutions. More generally, secondary education was as rigorously separated from primary schooling in France as it was in Germany. Many of the youngsters who reached the secondary classes of public secondary schools at around eleven years of age came from elementary classes attached to public or private *lycées* or *collèges*. It was certainly possible to transfer to the secondary system after a few years in a primary school, but such transfers were apparently not very common during the nineteenth century. Until 1860, in any case, the teaching of Latin in French *lycées* began at the age of nine.

Having earned the *baccalauréat* at around the age of 18, a French student could proceed to any university-level 'school' or faculty of law, medicine, pharmacy, letters or sciences, where he might prepare for a further state examination and eventual entry into one of the learned professions. He could also seek to pass the competitive entrance examination for a small cluster of elite *grandes écoles*, typically after attending special preparatory classes offered at distinguished Parisian *lycées*.

From *enseignement spécial* to *enseignement moderne*

Between 1863 and 1865 Victor Duruy, Minister of Education under Napoleon III, introduced the so-called *enseignement spécial*. Though not without precedent, this was the first systematic alteration of the French secondary curriculum since the early nineteenth century. Influenced by the example of the German *Realschulen*, Duruy's *enseignement spécial* was designed to provide a clear alternative, at the secondary level and within the existing secondary schools, to the abstract and literary bent of the traditional curriculum. A four-year course beginning at the age of 11 was to emphasise the applied sciences, laboratory work and even manual training. While courses in French literature were to be offered as well, Duruy's scheme had a frankly vocational dimension. In fact, specific programmes within the *enseignement spécial* were to be adjusted to the requirements of local industries.

Both Duruy and his immediate predecessor in the Ministry of Education became interested in technical and vocational schooling partly in response to the International Exhibitions of 1855 and 1862. In justifying his curricular innovation, Duruy repeatedly pointed to the need for economic productivity, and thus for trained manpower in industry, commerce and agriculture. The *enseignement spécial*, while offered at the existing secondary schools and considered 'secondary' in status, was to be sharply distinguished from the 'general', theoretical and classical form of secondary schooling. As initially projected, the four-year 'special' stream was to be subdivided into four internally coherent one-year courses, so that early leavers would not take away a fragmentary education. Those who completed the four-year programme were not to earn the *baccalauréat*; nor were they expected to continue their studies at a post-secondary level. Apparently, Duruy considered the new curriculum particularly suitable for less 'gifted' pupils, who might be discouraged by the level of abstraction involved in the study of the ancient languages.

At the same time, Duruy clearly thought of his reform as a socially progressive measure, one that would create new opportunities for social mobility and help bridge the social 'chasm' between the primary and the secondary schools:

From the foundation provided by an enlarged and unified primary system, two parallel secondary programmes will rise: one classical, for the so-called liberal professions; the other vocational, for careers in commerce, industry and agriculture. [These two] completely different [programmes] will be placed in the same building, under the control of the same administration . . . [Children] of different [social] origins and destinations will thus live together . . . and this contact will profit both groups.[12]

One cannot miss the socially reformist intent in this formulation, but neither should one overlook the tacit – and empirically justified – assumption that most children's social 'origins' would be their 'destinations' as well. In the minds of many nineteenth-century educators this assumption did not conflict with the expectation that a few *exceptional* youngsters from modest backgrounds would reach the 'best' secondary schools, along with *virtually all normal* offspring of the more privileged social groups. In the same way, Duruy could genuinely believe *both* that his reform would encourage social mobility *and* that it would rarely take students far from the social world from which they came.

Yet, whatever Duruy may have intended, the *enseignement spécial* eventually became a serious contender for equality of standing with the classical secondary curriculum. The way in which this happened can best be described as an instance of the 'generalist shift'.

The outward signs of change came mostly in the 1880s. In 1882 the 'special' programme was reorganised into two cycles of three and two years, and the overall course was thus extended from four to five years. In 1886 a sixth year was added. At the same time, a 'special' *baccalauréat* examination and certificate was introduced for students who completed the full six-year sequence, which was no longer subdivided into internally coherent smaller units. The champions of the new curriculum within the Ministry of Education also recommended that the *enseignement spécial* be renamed *enseignement classique français*. While this proposal was rejected by defenders of the traditional classical curriculum, the designation *enseignement moderne* was officially introduced by the Ministry of Education in 1891. By that time the modern curriculum had become quite as 'general' as its classical rival. The 'applied' approach, the shop or laboratory exercises that had characterised the *enseignement spécial* of 1865, had been virtually eliminated by 1886. The new programme henceforth differed from the classical curriculum only in its neglect of Latin and Greek and in its greater emphasis on the natural sciences, modern languages and French literature.

The most important supporters of the *enseignement spécial* in its stepwise 'elevation' were to be found within the Ministry of Education. We have little direct evidence about the attitudes of parents and students, although we know that the new curriculum quickly attracted substantial enrolments. The teachers in the 'special' stream presumably functioned as a pressure group; we know that they had achieved equality of standing and remuneration with their colleagues in the classical branch by 1886. Yet the most forceful agents of change were the reforming politicians and officials who led the Ministry of Education and its section on secondary education from the late 1870s to the early 1890s, among them Octave Gréard, Charles Zévort, René Goblet and Léon Bourgeois. Together with Louis Liard, the famous director of higher education, these men articulated and implemented the activist policies of the Radical Republic in secondary and higher education. Ultimately, of course, these policies and the 'lay' and 'solidarist' ideologies in which they were framed depended upon the electoral support of the broad middle and lower middle classes, who might well have resented the exclusive position of the classical *lycées*.

In any case, it is fascinating to observe how the Ministry of Education gradually transformed the public image of the *enseignement spécial* after 1880. Thus an official report of 1882 referred 'on the one hand' to the need to preserve the 'special' stream in 'its own proper character and its normal direction, not forgetting what category of pupils it addresses, what needs it must serve, and what aptitudes it is designed to enhance'. 'On the other hand', the writer continued, the *enseignement spécial* should fill in, as far as possible, 'the distance that separates it from the classical curriculum, and not only equip pupils with practical and immediately useful notions, but also give them a little of that disinterested and superior culture which is the purpose and honour of secondary education'.[13] The idea of conveying 'a little . . . disinterested . . . culture' implied, of course, that the 'special' stream was a diluted version of the classical curriculum, rather than an alternative to it. The student as recipient of 'a little . . . culture' must learn to see himself as inferior and incomplete.

By 1886 Zévort and Goblet took a more 'advanced' position in trying to impose the label *enseignement classique français*. They saw the younger of the two secondary curricula as both 'general' and 'classical', the latter in the sense of a formal 'culture' or development of the mind and spirit. Zévort considered the new curriculum 'scientific', a term quite different from the French *technique*, and he claimed that it was 'literary' as well. He objected 'in the light of experience' to an overly 'practical' conception of the 'special' programme, stressing the need for the type of practice that is informed by 'theoretical' knowledge of 'scientific principles'.[14]

Apparently, all parties concerned were well aware of the status problems linked to these questions of meaning. The ultimately successful opponents of the term *classique français* recalled that Duruy had initially used such words as 'practical', 'vocational' (*professionnel*) and 'intermediate' to characterise the *enseignement spécial*. In objecting to the designation *classique français*, they said, they meant formally to reject 'the idea of an assimilation of the programme in question to the classical curriculum'.[15]

Nevertheless, the substantive innovations proposed by Zévort and Goblet were implemented, and by 1891 Léon Bourgeois could treat the transformation of the *enseignement spécial* in a generalist direction as a *fait accompli*. Borrowing a tactic from the sharpest opponents of the modern curriculum, he described Duruy's programme of 1865 as self-contradictory: it could not at one and the same time be 'specialised' or practical, and 'general' or theoretical and thus truly 'secondary'. Justice could not be done simultaneously to two sets of parents: those who 'wanted to make their sons workers, foremen, men working directly with their hands', and those who wished their heirs to become 'business owners, manufacturers, merchants, or substantial farmers (*agriculteurs*)'. Since 1880, Bourgeois recalled, great strides had been made in the provision of free and public higher primary and vocational schooling. In the meantime, 'all the reforms instituted in the *enseignement secondaire spécial* since 1870' had tended to turn it into a 'general modern curriculum (*enseignement classique moderne* [*sic*])'.[16]

Bourgeois was arguing in effect that three types of post-elementary schooling corresponded to a presumably natural subdivision of the French middle class into three main strata. Once formed, the old *enseignement spécial* had more or less inevitably gravitated towards one of the two possible positions left open to it, while the new public higher primary schools had taken up the other. As a matter of fact there was probably a grain of truth in Bourgeois' scheme. After the passage of the Ferry laws of 1881–2 two types of free public higher primary schooling were created in France, and a few of the new institutions eventually entered the field of full-time vocational education as well. Just as the *enseignement spécial* was undergoing the generalist shift of the 1880s, in other words, a group of new schools took up the position thus left vacant. Not surprisingly, this process occasioned competitive exercises in social demarcation. The roles assigned to the several segments of the educational system were defined in a systematic, interrelated and even interactive way. Indeed, the *enseignement spécial* may have come to look especially threatening to traditionalists during the 1880s in particular, when it could no longer be 'placed' in the securely subordinate station now occupied by the higher primary schools.

In any case, Bourgeois was not the only one who saw a relationship between the roles allotted to the *enseignement spécial* and to the new public primary stream. As early as 1881 Jules Ferry himself cautioned the higher primary schools against trying to rise above their station. If they did, he said, they would 'sooner or later become an unfortunate imitation of the *enseignement secondaire spécial*'.[17] By 1887 Ferdinand Buisson, the reforming director of primary education, could see the higher primary schools as balancing, 'though unequally, the exercise of the mind and the training of the hand'. He also called for the kind of 'moral education' that would put young workers 'on the right path', and he explicitly repeated the warning against 'aspiring to compete with secondary education, even with the *enseignement spécial*'.[18] Apparently, even the most narrowly 'useful' training could be suspected – with good reason, one is pleased to think – of encouraging troublesome 'generalist' pretensions.

Adjustment and defence in the classical stream

From the 1870s to the end of the century the running debate over the special or modern programme in France was accompanied by an almost equally intensive discussion of the classical secondary curriculum. The basic question was to what extent the classical stream itself could or should be altered to accommodate such subjects as English and German, French literature, history and geography and, above all, the natural sciences. In 1872 this issue was raised by Jules Simon, another reform-minded Minister of Education, who proposed to have the study of Greek begin later than had been the case, to abandon Latin versification and composition, and to devote most of the time thus gained to the natural sciences. Simon's intent was to do justice to the 'needs of the epoch' without overburdening pupils seriously enough to 'tire their bodies, dull their minds, and weaken their wills'.[19]

As it happened, Simon was forced to resign before he could carry out his project. His successors were unwilling to sacrifice any portions of the traditional curriculum or to undermine its socially exclusive position. Yet even the most determined classicists of the 1870s succumbed to the universal sense that education had to be adjusted to the 'exigencies of modern life', or however else the case was put. As a result the discussions of the 1870s ultimately led to a curious kind of compromise. In the curricular reform of 1880 the hours devoted to non-classical subjects within the classical stream were substantially increased, much as Jules Simon had proposed. On the other hand, there was no proportional reduction in the time and effort traditionally devoted to the ancient languages. The 'modernisation' of the curriculum was achieved, in effect, by simple addition.

This helps to account for the wave of public concern that swept France during the 1880s about the 'overloading' of course timetables (*surcharge des programmes*) and the 'overburdening' (*surmenage*) of pupils through over-long school days and excessive homework.[20] In a circular of 1882 the Ministry of Education acknowledged widespread complaints from the parents of overworked students. In 1886 an official described the 'weight' of course work as 'definitely too heavy'. In the same year the French Academy of Medicine warned of the danger to the health of adolescents given too little time for exercise and recreation. Indeed, physical fitness became something of a national passion in France at about this time. Several national sports associations were founded in the years 1887–9, at least partly in response to public anxiety over the health of secondary pupils.

Of course we cannot now assess the objective realities behind these anxieties. We are free to speculate that only the slower learners were truly overburdened. We may also suspect that slow learners who nevertheless continued in school normally had the support of upper middle-class parents; but we cannot directly verify this hunch. It *is* clear, on the other hand, that a certain type of contemporary observer typically made the opposite assumption, tracing the difficulties of classical secondary education to the 'dead weight' of mediocre students.[21] The usual suggestion was that these pupils came from modest circumstances and should therefore have been directed towards the *enseignement spécial* in the first place.

The two major reorganisations of the classical curriculum that followed upon that of 1880 were clearly designed to alleviate the problem of 'overburdening'. In 1884–5, and again in 1890, the number of weekly class hours was substantially reduced. The overall programmes that resulted for the seven years of the classical stream are described in Table 2.4. Obviously the reforms of 1884–5 and 1890 were essentially cuts, in which the classical languages alone retained the full complement of hours assigned to them in 1880.

Yet one cannot interpret the reorganisations of 1884–5 and 1890 simply as traditionalist reactions. Léon Bourgeois, the Minister of Education who presided over the revision of the classical curriculum in 1890, was also responsible for the transformation of the *enseignement spécial* into the *enseignement moderne* in 1891. The instructions he issued in conjunction with the course plan of 1890 provide a first clue to his outlook. Like other educators of the late nineteenth century, Bourgeois placed an unusual degree of emphasis upon pedagogy and the educative effect of a particular curriculum, as against the extent of the subject matter covered. There had always been classicists who recommended Latin primarily as good training for the mind and only secondarily as a means of access to an admirable body of literature. Apparently, this 'formalist' position became more and more common towards the end of the nineteenth century. While Bourgeois himself explicitly repudiated the formalist viewpoint, he did share the formalists' stress on the pedagogic value, rather than the 'content' of a given

Table 2.4. *Distribution of weekly class hours in French seven-year classical secondary education, 1880–90*

Subjects	1880	1885	1890
French	21	17	18
Latin	39	39 ⎫	
Greek	20	20 ⎬	59
Modern languages	18	13	10
History and geography	24	20	17¼
Natural sciences	28	23	16½
Drawing	14	14	10
Philosophy	8	8	6¾
Total	172	154	137½

Source: Clement Falcucci, *L'humanisme dans l'enseignement secondaire en France au XIXᵉ siècle* (Toulouse and Paris, 1939), p. 41.

programme of courses. The ideal subjects, he said, were those 'most useful for their educative value and as intellectual discipline'.[22] Thus one way to explain Bourgeois' willingness to strip modern accretions from the classical curriculum is to say that he replaced encyclopaedism with pedagogy as a response to the 'needs of the epoch'.

Another way to understand Bourgeois' position is to consider curricular diversity as an alternative to the encyclopaedic temptation. Octave Gréard, a leading reformer among French educational administrators, made a persuasive case for diversification as early as 1884: given the steady increase in the quantity of knowledge that one generation must pass on to the next, 'how can youth be prepared to sustain the weight of that heritage?'[23] Gréard's question almost answers itself. There is no way of transmitting everything to everyone. Selection and concentration of subject matter is necessary and helpful, of course, but some degree of diversity – and of choice – is surely unavoidable in the long run. In making this point, Gréard meant to support the claim of the *enseignement spécial* to secondary status. He therefore rejected the idea of a polarity between 'classical' and 'utilitarian' education, noting that the classical curriculum had a 'practical' side, while the 'special' programme was not without broadly 'educative' value.

Even more interesting than Gréard's and Bourgeois' commitment to diversity is a subtle change in the position of the traditionalists towards the end of the century. Thus by the late 1890s the so-called Society for the Study of Questions of Secondary Education was apparently ready to grant secondary status to a non-classical programme, as long as it remained clearly 'practical' in orientation. In a circular of 1898, the Society belatedly announced that Duruy's *enseignement spécial* had been essentially sound and that it should not have been changed or abandoned:

> The Society [recommends] . . . the organisation of a secondary curriculum that parallels the classical curriculum but that, far from seeking to imitate it, is clearly distinguished from it, and is plainly conceived to train farmers, merchants, manufacturers and colonists, not actually to give them the technical knowledge they will only acquire in specialised schools (*écoles spéciales*) or in the very practice of their professions, but rather, through general intellectual training (*une culture générale de l'intelligence*) and a well-directed education of the character and spirit, to develop in them the qualities useful in their occupational life, along with a taste for the exercise of their professions.[24]

The reference to colonists in this passage was not unusual, for colonisation was regularly included among the 'practical' endeavours in which France had to compete successfully with other nations. Equally typical was the idea that a taste for the useful occupations required special nurture and that many of those misled into attempting the classical curriculum ultimately became unsuccessful candidates for public office, or failures and alienated misfits (*ratés, déclassés*). The authors of the circular clearly meant to reduce the competition for the classical *baccalauréat* by channelling a certain class of students into the non-classical stream. To achieve this objective, they were prepared to grant full secondary status to a 'general' but non-classical curriculum and to flatter it with that magical formula about the *culture générale de l'intelligence*. These were unprecedented concessions. By the 1890s, apparently, virtually all participants in the French education debate acknowledged the need for a certain degree of diversity within the secondary system. The attempt to superimpose non-classical subjects upon the classical curriculum had been abandoned. Even the opponents of the modern curriculum recognised that it could no longer be wished out of existence, and the public higher primary schools were firmly established as well. The question left open, of course, was how much hierarchy would remain associated with curricular diversity.

Against this background a parliamentary commission chaired by Alexandre Ribot was convened, in 1899, to undertake a full-scale investigation of secondary education. The Ribot Commission was established in part because the Catholic *collèges* seemed to be drawing students away from the public *lycées* and *collèges*. Once the Commission actually began its work, however, the conflict between the classical and the modern curriculum quickly moved to centre stage. The Commission gathered and subsequently published extensive testimony from a great variety of witnesses.[25] Yet the opinions expressed before the Commission clearly had less impact upon subsequent legislation than the determination of reform-minded officials in the Ministry of Education, who could count on parliamentary support from the left centre in the Chamber of Deputies.

The real outcome of the Ribot Commission's work was a decree of 1902, which essentially ended the French education debate of the late nineteenth century. The decree also established a framework for French secondary schooling that remained in place, largely unchanged, until after the Second World War. The full seven-year course of secondary studies that began with the so-called Sixth at the age of eleven was divided into two cycles, four and three years in length. In the first cycle students chose either a modern or a classical stream, with Greek available as an option on the classical side. In the second cycle those coming from the first-cycle modern programme continued in a course labelled (Modern) Languages–Sciences, while those coming from the classical side could opt for Latin–Greek, Latin–Sciences or Latin–(Modern) Languages. Before entering the last year of the second cycle, students had to pass the first part of the *baccalauréat* examination. If successful, they then enrolled in either the 'mathematics' or the 'philosophy' section of the terminal year, depending on whether or not their second-cycle curriculum had included the natural sciences. After a further examination those who passed earned the *baccalauréat* either in 'mathematics' or in 'philosophy'. The decree recognised no difference of academic standing between the two *baccalauréats*, or indeed between the four paths that led up to them. This, obviously, was the most important educational and political decision embodied in the settlement.

Unfortunately, we are left with a question about the opportunities actually made available to students in Languages–Sciences, the only exclusively modern option covered by the decree of 1902. They could earn the *baccalauréat* in mathematics, which theoretically gave them access to all forms of higher education. In practice they continued for some time to face minor disadvantages in the entrance examinations for the Ecole Polytechnique and for the letters section of the Ecole Normale. As late as 1907 they were required to take a supplementary examination in Latin to obtain the state *licence* for secondary teachers from the university faculties of letters. To be certain how real their legal parity was in practice, we would have to know more about the subsequent careers of French secondary graduates between 1900 and 1930. In the meantime it is probably safest to suppose that the modern curriculum was not much better accredited in France than in Germany after the turn of the century, despite the efforts of the politicians and administrators who managed to impose the settlement of 1902.

The development of secondary enrolments

After remaining essentially stable during the early nineteenth century, total enrolments per age group in French secondary schools increased substantially during the 1850s and 1860s. While the expansion of the 1850s took place primarily in the private secondary schools, which almost certainly benefited from the liberties granted them by the Falloux Law of 1850, the enrolment growth of the early 1860s was directly linked to the introduction of Duruy's *enseignement spécial*. By 1865 more than 13,000 pupils were enrolled in the lowest three grades of the new programme.

The classical stream at public *lycées* and *collèges*, however, was scarcely affected by these developments. Indeed, as Table 2.5 makes clear, enrolments in this key segment of the French system continued largely unchanged from 1865 to 1911. Since the private secondary schools declined steadily during this period, levels of inclusiveness in the traditional sector as a whole were probably not much higher on the eve of the First World War than they had been a full century earlier.

In the 'special' stream enrolments remained concentrated in the lowest three grades until the 1890s; the figures for 1898 in Table 2.5 are the first to suggest the emergence of a new configuration. Thus 'special' secondary

Table 2.5. *French secondary enrolments, 1865–1911, in thousands and in percentages of the age group*

	1865	1876	1887	1898	1911
Lycées and *collèges*					
Elementary classes	17.9	23.7	24.5	(22.0)	
Lower classical	14.8	14.3	18.7	13.6	
Upper classical	12.2	12.4	14.7	16.5	
Lower modern	13.4	19.5	19.3	18.3	
Upper modern	3.5	3.2	3.6	9.7	
Mathematics classes	3.9	6.1	9.0	5.8	
Total					
Public secondary	65.7	79.2	89.9	63.9	67.0
Private secondary	74.6	75.4	68.3	48.8	52.7
All secondary	140.3	154.7	158.2	112.7	119.7
% of age group	2.2	2.4	2.4	2.5	2.6
Baccalauréats	5.9	5.4	6.6	7.8	7.2
% of age group	0.9	0.8	1.0	1.2	1.1
(*Abiturs* per age group)		(0.7)	(0.8)	(0.9)	(1.2)

Note: Students in the elementary classes (below the Sixth, i.e. below the age of 11) are not included in the sums for public secondary education in 1898 and 1911. The 'lower classical' grades encompass the Sixth through to the Fourth; the 'upper classical' grades encompass the remaining four years. The 'lower modern' grades are the first three years in the *enseignement spécial* that was renamed 'modern' in 1871. The mathematics classes were a curricular option in the concluding years of the secondary programme; they are listed separately because they could be reached via the 'special' or 'modern' programme from the 1880s on. The figure for private secondary education in 1898 is an estimate. All secondary enrolments are related to the ten-year age group (8–17) until 1887 and to the seven-year age group (11–17) in 1898 and 1911. The data on Prussian *Abiturs* per age group actually pertain to 1875, 1885, 1901 and 1911; they were included in the table for comparative purposes.
Source: Ringer, *Education and Society*, pp. 135, 140, 316–29 (French data), and pp. 54, 272–9 (Prussian *Abiturs*).

education affected the French system much as the six-year *Realschulen* affected its German (Prussian) counterpart. From its origins in the 1860s to the end of the century, it functioned essentially as a non-graduate (non-*baccalauréat*) form of lower secondary schooling. Simply added on to the existing classical programme which itself changed very little, it modified the pyramid of secondary enrolments primarily by widening its base. By 1921 about one-quarter of French students who passed the first part of the *baccalauréat* examination came from the (Modern) Languages–Sciences option, the heir of the modern stream in the new scheme of 1902.[26] More detailed data might register the arrival of a few non-classical graduates at the level of the *baccalauréat* by 1911; but their share of all certificates earned could not have been great before the First World War. The entries for *baccalauréats* per age group in Table 2.5 reveal no clear trend. They are of the same order of magnitude, interestingly enough, as the comparable indicators for the Prussian *Abitur*. The apparently steady increase in *Abitur* awards per age group during our period, however, had no clear counterpart in France.

Obviously Table 2.5 has its weaknesses. The data it provides – and most of those on which it is based – are highly general and widely spaced in time. Moreover, it includes no evidence at all on the rapid growth of full-time public higher primary and vocational schools and courses during the 1880s and after. Yet as has already been suggested, these institutions in some ways took up the position initially occupied by the *enseignement spécial* of the 1860s and 1870s. It is high time they were given serious scholarly attention.

Secondary students' social origins and destinations

In 1887 Octave Gréard published a statistical study of the 'special' stream at public secondary schools in the Academy of Paris between 1865 and 1886. Like other educational planners of his time, Gréard was apparently anxious to know whether pupils in the 'special' programme were lured away from the 'practical' realm for which they were trained and from which most of them came. His survey of students' social origins and early occupational choices is reproduced in Table 2.6.

In fact the figures for 1865–80 not only demonstrate the importance of industry and commerce for the 'special' secondary stream; they also reveal an extraordinary similarity between the 'inflow' and the 'outflow' of students. At least in its early stages, it seems, the programme was quite as 'functional' as its sponsors meant it to be. It recruited most of its pupils from the families of well-to-do artisans, clerks, shopkeepers and small business-men, and it gave them the status of secondary students. It then returned them to their parents' station in life a little better equipped to take the next step in a slowly changing business environment. Perhaps they enlarged their

Table 2.6. *Social origins and career choices of 'special secondary' pupils in the Academy of Paris, 1865–86, in percentages by column*

	1865–80		1881–6	
Father's occupation	In	Out	In	Out
Liberal professions	2	1	4	2
Other professions	3	7	12	16
Administration	11	8	13	12
Agriculture	23	27	17	16
Without profession	13	—	14	—
Further study	—	11	—	18
Industry	14	14	12	5
Commerce	33	32	28	32
Absolute total known (100%)	4657	3542	4183	3744
Absolute number unknown	1168	2283	58	497
Absolute totals	5825	5825	4241	4241

Note: Social origins are listed under In, career choices under Out. Gréard did not precisely define his occupational categories.
Source: Octave Gréard, *Education et instruction: Enseignement secondaire* (Paris, 1887), vol. 2, pp. 262–5.

fathers' stores and workshops; perhaps they became middle-level employees in one of the larger firms that were growing up. We do not know the details, but we do have grounds to suspect that few of them really left the social world from which they came.

Apparently, this began to change during the 1880s, as the 'special' stream gradually took on the character of the modern secondary branch that officially succeeded it in 1891. After 1880 a sharply increased proportion of students in the 'special' curriculum had fathers in 'administration' (largely, but probably not wholly, government employment) or in 'professional' specialities that were neither liberal nor explicitly identified with industry or commerce. Many of these fathers were probably employees, but they claimed the status of professionals. Among the graduates of 'special' secondary education about a third continued even after 1880 to enter commerce, but there was a marked reduction in those who opted for industry or for agriculture. Almost a fifth sought additional education, and close to another third chose 'administration' or one of the 'professions'.

The transformation of the 'special' curriculum after 1880 was thus a perfect instance of the 'generalist shift'. The movement from vocational to general education was accompanied by a drift towards the white-collar graduate and away from the skilled artisan or industrial foreman. A mere 5 per cent of those leaving 'special' secondary courses in the Academy of Paris during the 1880s went directly into industry. Against the intentions of its founders, the 'special' stream became a less prestigious form of academic

Table 2.7. *Social origins and educational/occupational choices of French public secondary pupils about 1863, in percentages by column*

University-level institutions and occupational groups	All secondary		Special secondary only	
	In	Out	In	Out
Ecole Normale	—	1.5	—	0.5
Ecole Polytechnique	—	3.7	—	0.3
Mining (civil engineering)	—	1.7	—	0.1
Ecole Centrale	—	2.5	—	0.2
Arts et Métiers	—	1.9	—	6.4
Ecole Forestière	—	0.7	—	(—)
Officers/military schools	2.4	6.2	1.0	2.3
Law	6.4	12.3	0.6	1.6
Medicine	4.5	9.2	1.0	2.3
Other university level education	—	1.7	—	1.6
Religion	0.3	2.0 ⎫	0.8	0.7
Arts, writers	1.0	0.8 ⎭		
Subtotal	14.6	44.2	3.4	16.0
'Education'	2.3	1.7	0.4	0.2
Primary teachers	1.7	2.7	3.0	6.2
High(er) officials	1.6	0.1 ⎫	2.0	0.7
Middle officials	2.0	0.3 ⎭		
Lower military	1.3	4.6	1.2	5.7
Subtotal	8.9	9.4	6.6	12.8
'Propertied'	17.0	2.8	13.5	3.4
Industrialists	2.9	0.7 ⎫	3.6	1.0
Engineers	0.5	0.3 ⎭		
Large merchants	9.7	2.8	7.4	2.4
Subtotal	30.1	6.6	24.5	6.8
'Industry'	1.3	3.3 ⎫	1.2	4.2
Railroads	0.1	0.3 ⎭		
'Commerce'	7.3	13.4	8.8	17.0
Shopkeepers	7.0	2.3	10.7	5.1
White collar	7.8	6.8	5.8	10.8
Subtotal	23.5	26.1	26.5	37.1
Clerks	2.7	4.4	2.8	8.5
Farmers	12.3	7.3	21.4	11.4
Artisans	6.1	2.0	12.5	6.9
Workers	1.9	0.4	2.4	0.8
Subtotal	23.0	14.1	39.1	27.6
Absolute total known (100%)	12,603	26,066	1548	1849

Note: The In columns report the occupations of students' fathers; the Out columns cover the educational or occupational plans of students in 1864, as well as the educational institutions or occupations actually reached by students who left the secondary schools (most of them with the secondary schooling. What social mobility it may have provided remained sectorally limited, as intended; but the programme ultimately catered more to the white-collar elements within the middle and lower middle classes than to artisans and small manufacturers. What set if off from the traditional secondary path was no longer an alternative model of education, but a mere difference in social elevation within the middle-class spectrum. The conflict over the divide between French classical and modern secondary education around the turn of the century was thus essentially a contest between the upper and the lower middle classes.

Unfortunately, good data on the social origins of secondary students did not begin to be systematically published in France until the late 1930s. The major exception, apart from Gréard's study, is a survey conducted by Victor Duruy in 1864 that has recently been extracted from the archives by Patrick Harrigan and that is briefly summarised in Table 2.7. Within the limits of occasionally awkward categories this valuable new evidence does give us a glimpse of the French public secondary system as a whole, and of the early *enseignement spécial* as well. At the time of the survey pupils leaving the small 'special' programme after a maximum of four years' study typically went into 'commerce' (17 per cent) or agriculture (11 per cent), or into various intermediate (11 per cent) or lower-level (9 per cent) white-collar positions. The vast majority of students in the secondary system as a whole, of course, were enrolled in the classical stream. Among them about 44 per cent proposed to continue their studies, or actually continued them, beyond the *baccalauréat* at the university-level faculties and *grandes écoles*, while 23 per cent became large merchants or entered 'commerce' or other white-collar occupations.

Among fathers of all students the traditionally educated professions were less prominently represented, at around 17 per cent (including 'education'), than the economic upper middle class of the 'propertied' (*propriétaires*, 17 per cent), large merchants (10 per cent) and industrialists (3 per cent). The intermediate layers of the economic middle class accounted for a further 24 per cent of the sample, while 12 per cent of the fathers were farmers, 6 per cent were artisans, 3 per cent were clerks and 2 per cent were workers.

---

baccalauréat) from the late 1850s to 1863. Harrigan used a code of 96 basic educational/occupational categories to record both fathers' occupations and students' goals, along with a summary code of 20 educational/occupational groupings. I have partly rearranged Harrigan's groupings to specify important distinctions, in so far as Harrigan's basic categories themselves made this possible. The grouping 'white collar' as used in this table covers a cluster of predominantly private white-collar employees of a middling or unspecified level, while the grouping 'clerks' represents the French *employés*.
Source: Patrick Harrigan with Victor Negila, *Lycéens et collégiens sous le Second Empire: Etude statistique sur les fonctions sociales de l'enseignement secondaire public d'après l'enquête de Victor Duruy (1864–1865)* (Paris, 1979), pp. 18–21, 27–30 and Tables 1, 8, 9.

The differences of social origin between the *enseignement spécial* and the public secondary system as a whole provide a perfect example of socially vertical segmentation. Among the parents of pupils in 'special' secondary education, the liberal and educated professions were most markedly under-represented, at distribution ratios of 0.1 for law, and 0.2 for medicine, for 'education' and for the highly educated as a group. A less pronounced degree of underrepresentation, with distribution ratios around 0.8–0.9, characterised the middle and higher officials, as well as the economic middle and upper middle class of *propriétaires*, large merchants, intermediate-level white-collar employees, and men grouped vaguely under 'industry' and railroads. Slight to moderate overrepresentations can be calculated from the data for industrialists and engineers (1.06), 'commerce' other than large merchants (1.2), shopkeepers (1.5), farmers (1.7), primary teachers (1.8) and artisans (2.0). Clerks and workers, oddly enough, were only mildly overrepresented in the 'special' programme, at distribution ratios of 1.04 and 1.3, respectively; but these surprises may be due to imprecise categories and low absolute numbers.

None of these figures suggest the socially horizontal dimension of segmen-tation that characterised Prussian secondary education during the later nineteenth century. In closing this essay, therefore, I can only repeat some of the comparative conclusions I initially proposed in *Education and Society*. Despite a whole series of striking similarities, the French and German secondary systems of our period apparently played subtly different social roles. The Prussian *Gymnasium* of the nineteenth century was almost certainly more progressive in its recruitment than the French *lycées* and *collèges*. Among the fathers of *Gymnasium* students and graduates the dominant presence of the traditionally educated upper middle class was strongly supplemented by a non-economic middle and lower middle class of Protestant pastors, lower civil servants and primary teachers. The economic middle classes, having held a comparatively weak position in the *Gymnasium*, became particularly prominent clients of the modern second-ary schools toward the end of the century.

In the French *lycées* and *collèges*, by contrast, the economic upper middle class typified by the *propriétaires* was overwhelmingly dominant well before the arrival of the *enseignement spécial*. As a result the social divide between classical and modern secondary schooling came essentially to separate the established upper middle class as a whole, the *bourgeoisie*, from the middle and lower middle class (*classes moyennes*) of small producers, of shop-keepers and, increasingly, of white-collar employees. In France, throughout the nineteenth century, classical learning served almost exclusively to enhance and to legitimate social positions that were based primarily on wealth. In Germany, *for a time*, the traditional forms of secondary schooling helped to sustain a 'status' order that was partly incongruent with the emerging capitalist class structure. That is why the development of segmentation in German (and in French and English) secondary education during our period can also be conceived of as the creation or systematisation of a stratified school system capable of reproducing and legitimating the modern class society.

3. Systematisation and segmentation in education: the case of England*

BRIAN SIMON

In considering educational change in England in the mid to late nineteenth century it may be as well, first, to define what features appear as specific to England at this period, compared with France and Germany. There are two aspects which should be stressed: the first concerns chronology, or the sequence of events; the second, the means by which the transformation was brought about.

The state and educational change, 1850–70

First, as I have argued in detail elsewhere, the crucial 'moment of change' in England was the period 1850 to 1870.[1] It was during these 20 years that a series of Royal Commissions were appointed, with the brief of examining and making recommendations for the reform of all levels of education from the elementary schools to the ancient universities, and including, as a crucial aspect, the provision of schooling for the various strata of the middle and professional classes, gentry and aristocracy. Each of these Commission reports was succeeded by the passage of an Act of Parliament which laid down the statutory basis for reform. The patterning and restructuring that resulted (which, of course, was inevitably based to some extent on contemporary developments within the institutions concerned) began to be

* I have to thank my co-editors, Detlef Müller and Fritz Ringer, for many discussions on the issues covered in this chapter, as also David Reeder, whose advice and support has been consistently stimulating and helpful. I also owe a debt to David Allsobrook, whose unpublished PhD thesis (noted below) casts much new light on the social factors affecting educational restructuring in England in the period covered by this essay (see his *Schools for the Shires* (Manchester, 1986)).

implemented from the 1860s on, but it was in the last decades of the century that this restructuring became firmly grounded in institutional change. The full consequences, and implications, of the measures determined between 1850 and 1870 were by no means immediately realised, but took several years fully to work themselves out.

Second, as also argued elsewhere, this restructuring was brought about by the direct intervention of the state.[2] The technique used – that of the appointment of a Royal Commission, normally with powers to require submission of 'evidence', subsequent publication of the Commission's report and evidence (often in many volumes), followed by public discussion and Parliamentary debate leading to the passage of a Parliamentary Act – was one which was widely used by reforming Parliaments in the nineteenth century (for instance, in relation to the Poor Laws, Municipal Reform and so on). This clear involvement by the state has not, traditionally, been accorded its full significance by historians of education, who have tended to interpret state intervention in England only in terms of the development of elementary education – from the point when the state was directly involved in making financial grants to such schools (from 1833) and the subsequent foundation of an Education Department to administer such grants. The central role played by the state in the restructuring of secondary and higher education in mid-century has tended to be ignored while attention was focused, in the latter half of the century, on the Elementary Education Act of 1870 and subsequent developments in this field.[3]

While no direct financial support was provided by the state either for secondary or for university education in the mid-nineteenth century, the transformation brought about through state intervention (and subsequent legislation) was directly concerned with the redistribution (and the use) of actually existing financial resources, which were then seen, in a sense, as a public trust. These were the endowments, sometimes substantial, which assisted in the financing of most grammar and 'public' schools, as well as the universities of Oxford and Cambridge. It is this point that is overlooked. The restructuring that took place involved not only the transformation of existing institutions and the emergence (to some extent) of new institutions (for instance, girls' grammar schools),[4] but also the relations between the different levels or 'subsystems' that were developed with each other and with the state. In all this the role of the state, as exemplified by the new statutory requirements and the actions of Commissioners with executive powers appointed to carry these through, was of primary significance.[5]

These issues will be considered in more detail later. In the meantime two points may be made in a comparative study of this kind. First, in England,[6] conflicts between different social groupings leading to a basic restructuring of education, which were fought out with considerable energy during the first half of the century, led to decisive action some twenty to thirty years earlier than was the case in France and Germany, as the preceding chapters by Ringer and Müller make clear. This, it seems probable, was the outcome of the earlier impact of industrialisation and urbanisation in England compared to the Continental countries. In particular, the continuous critique, by representatives of the new industrial and commercial middle class (represented in the early years of the century by the utilitarians, or philosophic radicals, led by Bentham and Mill) as well as by other sections of the population (for instance, advanced groupings of the emerging working class, now becoming conscious of itself as a class), reached a point of what might be called crisis by the early 1850s. At this point the industrial middle class, which had been gaining economic power and wealth with great rapidity, now also gained a measure of political power through increased representation in Parliament, partly as a result of the Reform Act of 1832 – an increased power epitomised in their victory over the repeal of the Corn Laws in 1846. At the same time, the traditional educational institutions – Oxford and Cambridge and the leading 'public' and grammar schools – were being perceived as increasingly dysfunctional and were themselves undergoing a crisis of survival (particularly the 'great' schools such as Winchester, Westminster and Charterhouse). It was this concatenation of circumstances, embodying different (and even opposite) perspectives on the part of widely differing social groups or classes, that created a climate where change, reform and even transformation now came on the agenda, the need for it being widely recognised.

It is along these lines, it may be suggested, that an explanation can be found as to why it was that decisive, even ruthless measures were determined on in the period 1850 to 1870. To put the matter simply (and, no doubt, crudely), there was, on the one hand, a growing pressure for reform from those sections of society (middle and working classes) that wanted change and modernisation and who were demanding access to a set of transformed educational institutions, and, on the other, a growing realisation on the part of the dominant sections of the social hierarchy (gentry and aristocracy) of the urgent need for reform if the traditional institutions of the country were to preserve their hegemony and not be supplanted by new institutions representing the interests and aspirations of new social classes – now perceived as representing a serious threat to the established order.

The second point, which has already been referred to, concerns the means by which this restructuring was brought about. In France, for historical reasons, the state certainly played a major role in the control and shaping of the educational structure, at least since Napoleonic times. In Germany, as Müller makes clear, the Prussian state had also been involved at all levels, at least from the early years of the century, and, as Prussia expanded after 1866 through the assimilation of new principalities such as Hanover, a degree of centralised planning was directed towards ensuring development on uniform lines (in both the *Gymnasien* and universities) in the new, expanded Prussia (and, after 1870, in the new unified Germany). England is generally regarded as exceptional in that it has been held that the state was not directly involved in controlling or shaping the system. While it is certainly the case that direct control over individual institutions was never exercised, nevertheless in the restructuring of the system as a whole, as has been argued, a crucial role was in fact played by the state. Indeed, without intervention on the scale experienced, such a finely defined restructuring as was achieved could hardly have taken place. The interesting point is that this process involved features of systematisation and segmentation very similar to that brought about in France and Germany a generation later.

There is one further, and perhaps modifying, feature that might be stressed at the start. This is the important role that market forces were able to play in England before, during and after the overall restructuring that took place. Before 1850–60 some grammar schools, for instance, were already tapping what might be called the national market, so that a process of differentiation was, in a sense, endemic in the situation. Again, in the latter decades of the century, as Hilary Steedman makes clear in Chapter 4, a clear tension developed between market forces and government-inspired blueprints so far as the endowed schools were concerned; such tensions clearly affected outcomes.

Here also, then, was an important difference between the situation in England and that in France and Germany, where market forces seem less influential. There was, in England, nothing equivalent to the system of state certification that Müller describes for Germany. Qualification for different levels of employment depended more directly on the status conferred by schooling – a situation which again gave scope to market forces in determining the process of school differentiation and therefore the nature of the hierarchical system that resulted.

Social class and educational change

Any attempt to 'make sense' of the overall transformation of education in England at this time – from a relatively inchoate structure at the beginning of the century to a system comprising a finely differentiated or segmented set of interrelated 'subsystems' at the close – must involve definition of the main social forces bringing it about. As a preliminary generalisation, study of the period and of succeeding events seems to indicate that the factors involved (specifically in the differentiation process) were primarily of a social and political character rather than directly economic.

Changes in the economy based on scientific and technological advance certainly underlay social developments in the nineteenth century. The growth of industry, commerce and banking led not only to the formation of new social classes – in particular of an industrial and commercial middle class and, with the growth of factory production, of the working class or proletariat – but also to an increasing complexity of occupational structure, in particular among what may be called the middle strata – professional and other white-collar occupations. Indeed, Geoffrey Holmes has recently analysed, in a fascinating study, the extraordinary rise of the professions in the early eighteenth century, a process which continued with considerable force through the eighteenth and early nineteenth centuries.[7]

In addition, the first half of the century, following the traumatic experience of the French Revolution, which had its repercussions in England as well as elsewhere, was a period of sharp social conflict and instability, when even the new power of capital itself was under attack. In this sense, powerful economic and political factors certainly underlay the educational changes of the mid-century. These, however, it appears, were mediated through changes in the occupational structure which directly led to new demands on, or requirements of, an educational system that reflected the needs of an earlier dispensation. The fact that institutional change was already taking place under the influence of market forces early in the century has already been mentioned. This, however, partly as a result of legal conditions as then interpreted, was inadequate to meet the force of criticism and pressure, which had mounted considerably by mid-century.[8]

As restructuring (of individual institutions as well as sets of institutions) became a political necessity, conflict about its nature necessarily surfaced. It seems that the dominant social forces of the time were now able to use the situation so created to determine the direction and character of this restructuring. Without these forces necessarily having clear overall intentions, the fact is that the *outcome* of this overall restructuring was the establishment of a system which reflected – and provided for – different levels in the hierarchy of social strata then existing. As the Schools Inquiry Commission was to put it, 'education has become more varied and complex . . . the different classes of society, the different occupations of life, require different teaching'.[9] It could be said that the function of education emerging from the measures adopted in mid-century was not so much that of ensuring the *reproduction* of society with a divided social structure as the actual reinforcement and more precise refinement of an hierarchical society in which each stratum knew, was educated for, and accepted, its place.

Discussing mid-Victorian education, the historian Geoffrey Best, for instance, characterises the changes made as not only creating a system which reflected class differences, but as being deliberately patterned to perpetuate them. 'Educational systems', he writes, 'can hardly help mirroring the ideas about social relationships of the societies that produce them.' Education became a 'trump card' in the great class competition. The result was that the schools of Britain 'not only mirrored the hierarchical social structure . . . but were made more and more to magnify its structuring in detail'.[10] So, in Best's view, education reinforced and exacerbated class differences. This view is generally held among historians. Thus Harold Perkin characterises developments in the 1860s as intended 'to put education in a straitjacket of social class'.[11]

Such analyses, in terms of social class, clearly owe much to Marx's approach. However, the Marxist theory concerning the relation between changes in the economic base (or 'forces of production') and the 'superstructure' (law, ideology, institutions, for instance), while having a clear significance in terms of overall revolutionary change as, for instance, from one economic–social formation to another (e.g. feudalism to capitalism), cannot be taken to imply a direct, linear (or mechanistic) relationship between 'base' and 'superstructure' within a given economic–social formation, as is argued by some Marxists and even neo-Marxists (for instance, Bowles and Gintis, whose 'correspondence theory' reflects such an approach).[12] Such a 'model' runs the danger of vulgarising Marxism.

The issue, it seems, is a great deal more complex than is recognised within such formulations. Education as a system comprising what are often powerful and interrelated institutions has, it is now generally accepted, a certain 'autonomy' (or a 'relative autonomy'). In the Marxist sense this implies that educational institutions and ideologies are not *directly* affected by changes in the economic structure (in Bourdieu's sense it seems to mean that education has a certain *apparent* independence from the state and dominant social forces, so that it ensures more effectively its function of securing social reproduction).[13] Specific developments in education, as in mid-nineteenth-century England, appear above all, as mentioned earlier, to be subject both to market forces and to political pressures, influences and measures. These latter, which appear dominant in any organised action by the 'state', primarily reflect the interests of dominant social classes (or class alliances). It is in the interpretation of the formation of such classes (and strata), and of the changing relationship between social classes, their conflicts and alliances insofar as these affect, or are embodied in, their educational actions, that the Marxist approach can be helpful – if only in giving an overall orientation to such interpretations.

In England, for instance, modernisation of the educational system dates from the Reformation.[14] It was at this period – from the early mid-sixteenth to the mid-seventeenth century – that 'grammar schools' were established in most market towns, with separate school buildings being erected and teaching being developed as a profession, and that a systematic approach to the structuring of the content of education (the curriculum) took root. Two or three hundred years later, in the mid-nineteenth century, as a result of industrialisation and the social changes that resulted, that system stood in urgent need of reform if it was to meet both the new pressures and demands arising from occupational change and the perceived requirements of social strategy in terms of maintaining, or reinforcing, social stability. It is something of a paradox that, by the end of the century, what actually transpired was not so much a system reflecting the needs of the economy (for instance, giving primacy to science and technology and being open-ended and supportive of individualised endeavour, as perhaps in the United States), as the creation of a set of more or less closed subsystems of institutionalised education at different levels, which were only articulated together to a limited extent and, as Best and Perkin describe it, had the primary function of reinforcing class divisions. It is these developments that require explanation.

Education and the industrial bourgeoisie

It is a striking fact that, in spite of the rapidity and force of industrialisation in England, and so of scientific and technological change, no serious attempt was made in the middle of the century to create new forms of education specifically related to this energetic upthrust; or, if such attempts were made, their success was marginal.

It is worth remembering that in the closing decades of the eighteenth century Literary and Philosophical Societies, which united industrialists, scientists and professional men (particularly medical men), did in fact give priority to, and were successful in creating, just such institutions – the Manchester College of Arts and Sciences, for instance, as well as the Manchester Academy in the dissenting, but now Unitarian tradition.[15] These provincial Societies, the most famous of which was, of course, the Lunar Society grouped around Boulton and Watt at Soho in Birmingham, were directly concerned with scientific investigation and advance, and with its practical application in the new technologies of the day (particularly the chemical industry related to cotton manufacture). Members of these groupings were profoundly interested in education, if for their own children and groupings in particular, and advanced new theories which embodied a philosophically materialist outlook and an all-round humanist–scientific perspective.[16]

These institutions, however, did not survive in their original form far into the nineteenth century. The new spokesmen of the industrial middle class – the utilitarians – narrowed the perspectives of their predecessors, although again emphasising the need for modern knowledge and a total reformation of the curriculum. Such a programme is best epitomised in Bentham's *Chrestomathia*, his plan for a new school on new lines which it was hoped could be erected in Leicester Square (in London).[17] This deliberately rejected the procedures and ethos of the traditional institutions of the country by embodying a specifically utilitarian approach to education, with the curriculum determined by the two principles of utility and facility (the promotion of ease of understanding through the logical arrangement of the sequence of studies).

It was at this period – in the 1820s and early 1830s – that what might be called a specifically *bourgeois* (or middle-class) thrust in education began to express itself forcibly. The establishment first of University College (1828) and later of the University of London (1836) again reflected the aspirations and objectives of social groupings excluded, for religious, financial or other reasons, from the ancient universities. University College certainly embodied new conceptions as to the role, character and function of a university and was seen as a clear challenge by Oxford and Cambridge, who fought its establishment extremely bitterly.

There was, then, a definite thrust from the new social forces at this time. This period also saw the founding of a whole set of interconnected institutions in the provincial cities, particularly those of the Midlands and the North, which were developed throughout the middle years of the century. These cities were the home of a scientific culture (epitomised by the important part played by the Literary and Philosophical Societies), of an independent liberal press (for instance, the *Manchester Guardian* and the Leeds *Mercury*) and of a series of cultural institutions (Athenaeums, for example), while the whole culture was linked together through the espousal, often by the leading industrialists, merchants and professional men, of Nonconformism, and especially of Unitarianism. These institutions played a dominant and crucial role in many provincial cities in mid-century, and of course earlier (especially after 1835, with the passage of the Municipal Reform Act).[18]

There was, then, a clear challenge to the hegemony of the culture of the gentry and aristocracy as embodied in traditional educational institutions. However, it was not this trend and these interests which carried all before them in the process of restructuring between 1850 and 1870, and later. In fact, developments took an opposite direction. Study of the classics – the traditional subject matter of the curriculum – was revitalised in the latter half of the century as the curriculum considered appropriate to the Victorian upper middle class. The ethos, mores and indeed the institutions of traditional education became the models increasingly accepted by the middle class and the new social forces now bidding for hegemony. The culture of the gentry and aristocracy was ·in fact accepted by leading sections of the bourgeoisie – perhaps predominantly by that section defined recently by Rubinstein as comprising those involved in commerce and finance (based in London), rather than industry (based in the North).[19] It seems that this new class, now achieving positions of power, took over the existing symbols of dominance and excellence, which still retained their significance. However this may be, there is no doubt that the challenge from the new social forces was now muted. The educational objectives of the new middle class now became ambivalent.

Even if it seems strange and contradictory, it is worth recalling that Gladstone himself, leader of the great reforming Liberal party from the 1860s on, was himself the son of a Liverpool merchant of Scottish (and trade) descent, had himself been schooled at Eton, was himself a distinguished classical scholar and, in a well-known letter to the Royal Commission on the Public Schools (the Clarendon Commission), stated his firm conviction that only a classical education was, or could be, appropriate to that small section of the population destined to attend the leading 'public' schools and then to assume responsibility for governing the country. Indeed, he went so far as to suggest that Greek civilisation had been providentially brought into being precisely to provide a suitable subject matter for the education of the English gentleman![20]

Engels' comments on the bourgeoisie at this time are very relevant to this analysis. 'In England', he wrote (in 1892),

the bourgeoisie never held undivided sway. Even the victory of 1832 left the landed aristocracy in almost exclusive possession of all the leading government offices. The meekness with which the wealthy middle class submitted to this remained inconceivable to me until the great Liberal manufacturer, Mr W. E. Forster, in a public speech implored the young men of Bradford to learn French, as a means to get on in the world, and quoted from his own experience how sheepish he looked when, as a Cabinet Minister, he had to move in a society where French was at least as necessary as English.

The fact was, Engels goes on,

The English middle class of that time were, as a rule, quite uneducated upstarts, and could not help leaving to the aristocracy those superior government places where other qualifications were required than mere insular narrowness and insular conceit, seasoned by business sharpness . . . Thus, even after the repeal of the Corn Laws, it appeared as a matter of course that the men who carried the day, the Cobdens, Brights, Forsters, etc., should remain excluded from a share in the official government of the country, until 20 years afterwards a new Reform Act opened to them the door of the Cabinet.[21]

Even then, their representation remained small. In 1869 John Bright entered the Cabinet. In 1880, Joseph Chamberlain. But by now a new phase had opened.

In the period of restructuring, the traditional classical education was legitimated anew in the reformed institutions for the middle and upper classes, as we shall see. Science, although strongly pressed (by scientists), for instance in evidence to the Clarendon Commission, was regarded as of inferior value and relegated to subsidiary streams or institutions – an example of segmentation as interpreted by Ringer. Technology was not, at this time, even considered as a possible appropriate subject matter for these classes.

Nor did science and its application in technology gain more than a slippery foothold at other levels until the 1880s and 1890s, when there were a number of developments of some significance, particularly concerning the development of the new universities and colleges in the great provincial cities (Manchester, Birmingham, Leeds, Sheffield, Newcastle, Bristol) as well as London. At this point there were also significant developments at lower levels, including the beginning of the upthrust of the higher grade (elementary) schools and the system of 'organised science schools', financed through the Department of Science and Art, which now came into being, again largely in the great provincial cities of the Midlands and the North. Nevertheless it remains true that in England industrial development in mid to late century still owed little to institutionalised education.[22] Towards the close of the century another factor began to influence the situation – the development of imperialism. The massive export of capital that this entailed – the seeking of a higher rate of profit by investment abroad than could be obtained in England – militated against the modernisation of the technical and industrial base, for this was held not to be necessary.[23] This factor clearly operated against ensuring high levels of scientific and technological education, even if, as in the mid-1880s, a powerful pressure group like the National Association for the Promotion of Technical Education now began to press for change and to compare English developments in the area adversely to what they perceived to be happening in Germany, Switzerland and other European countries by this time – a point of view also strongly pressed by the Royal Commission on Technical Education, which reported in 1884.

What, then, was the basis of the restructuring and systematisation of education in nineteenth-century England? As indicated earlier, although the industrial bourgeoisie in the great provincial cities did develop their own scientific culture and specific religious outlook (Non-conformism), this hardly found expression in a coherent educational policy or ideology in the crucial mid-century years;[24] nor did they then articulate any overall proposals for action for educational change for the middle and upper strata, either locally or nationally. Those grouped around the Anti-Corn Law League of the 1840s focused their thrust in the Lancashire-led campaign for the provision of popular education for the working classes, founding the Lancashire (later, the National) Public Schools Association and campaigning energetically in the 1850s for rate-supported, locally and democratically controlled, secular (or non-sectarian) systems of elementary education.[25]

As far as other classes were concerned, the initial thrust both of the

Unitarians in the late eighteenth century and of the utilitarians in the 1820s and 1830s was forgotten, or at least not developed further into a specific programme of change – though the influence of Bentham's mid-century followers such as Chadwick, Nassau Senior and even Henry Brougham, who was still active, should not be under-estimated. Nevertheless, as David Allsobrook has shown in a recent detailed study,[26] the main force or thrust for change locally, regionally and ultimately nationally now came from the traditionally dominant classes – the landed gentry and aristocracy, assisted by the specific expertise of representatives of the professional groupings linked traditionally with these classes. Among these, Frederick Temple, headmaster of Rugby and later Archbishop of Canterbury, played a leading part, drafting two of the crucial chapters of the Schools Inquiry Commission Report, while James Bryce and T. H. Green, both Assistant Commissioners, particularly the latter, influenced the final recommendations concerning grading and restructuring.[27]

These groupings were concerned to restructure, and to some extent to modernise, local and, later, national systems of schools – not so much for themselves, but more particularly for the various levels of the middle class (farmers, the professions and the minor gentry, including artisans). They now formed 'County Committees', made experiments in agricultural education and sought to link the reform of local 'systems' with Oxford University by establishing examinations appropriate to this initiative.[28] Among them the liberal academics were also becoming closely concerned about the possible alienation of professional and business elements in the middle class from the largely Anglican-dominated universities and endowed grammar schools, and were themselves considering the need to restructure education in the cities as well as in the rural areas. The main issue in both town and country was the revitalisation of the ancient system of grammar schools, now often decayed and increasingly useless to the 'middle classes' – or at least perceived as being so. The fact that, according to their original statutes, still in force, these schools often now gave a free education to the poorer classes was seen as an undesirable wastage of valuable endowments, which might now be put to a 'better' purpose. It was through reorganisation of the resources available in these endowments (whose misuse – often scandalous – had already been revealed by a Parliamentary inquiry early in the century),[29] that these groupings saw the means of constructing a rational structure of schooling to meet the requirements of different strata in the social hierarchy.

In the 1840s and 1850s, when these movements were already under way, England was only beginning to emerge from the turbulence of Chartism. The increasing prosperity of the 1850s, which affected both the agricultural world and industry, was now leading to a period of social stability which was to last, in general, to the mid-1880s. This, then, was a suitable time to encourage the development of new educational structures that could both go some way to meeting the new pressures arising from occupational and political change, and at the same time stabilise, or even reinforce, the emergent hierarchic social structure.

It was at this period (the 1850s to 1860s), then, that these elements began to pressurise succeeding governments, and Parliament generally, to set up a Royal Commission of Inquiry into the endowed (grammar) schools and the private and 'proprietary' schools which had come into being in large numbers to meet the new demands. This initiative had already been preceded by Commissions investigating other areas – the ancient universities, the 'public' schools and the elementary schools.[30] With the appointment and report of the Schools Inquiry Commission and the Act which followed it (1869), the basis had been laid for the reform of education for the middle and upper classes. The seal would be set on the total system with the passage of the Elementary Education Act one year later, in 1870. The blueprint for mid-century restructuring was now complete.

The Schools Inquiry Commission

Although the Schools Inquiry Commission (SIC) was the last of the Commissions that reported between 1850 and 1870 to be appointed, it may be convenient to deal with it first since it was directly concerned with the secondary education of the middle classes or middle strata. This Commission, as is well known, had the brief of examining all schools lying between the 'great' (or 'public') schools (which had already been investigated by the Clarendon Commission) and the elementary schools on which the Newcastle Commission had reported in 1861. Its proposals provide a classic example of what Ringer defines as 'vertical segmentation'.

The proposals, which cannot be considered here in any detail, were concerned to establish three grades of school, each designed for a specific level among the middle classes. In order to free resources for this restructuring, the Commission proposed to put an end once and for all to free education (an age-old right in many schools) and so to exclude the poor or working class. The proposals also involved putting an end to class-mixing (or heterogeneity) in the schools' intake (several had traditionally recruited students from different social strata) in order to develop a differentiated system of schools, each with a different leaving age and different curricula. With the object partly of sugaring the pill, provision was to be made from the endowments for a limited number of scholarships (or exhibitions) in the higher-grade schools which might be won by working-class or artisans' children in the lower (third) grade, thus building into the system a procedure allowing a strictly limited degree of social mobility.

The Commission was very clear that their primary objective was to bring some order into the work of the schools they examined. The schools 'need to have their work defined and then to be kept to that work', they reported. 'Each type of school should have its own proper aim set before it, and should be put under such rules as will compel it to keep to that aim.'[31] Their view was that sets of schools at different levels, or grades, needed to be created to serve different sections of the so-called 'middle-classes'. These are defined as the 'upper middle class', the 'middle middle class' and the 'lower middle class' (with which the Commission was particularly concerned).

In terms of the differentiated curricula proposed, first-grade schools were to focus on classical studies, both Latin and Greek. While second- and third-grade schools were both to teach Latin, only in first-grade schools could Greek be taught. As Greek was an essential requirement for entry to both Oxford and Cambridge at that time, this effectively restricted entry to these universities to pupils who attended first-grade schools. This recommendation appears as a piece of overt political (or social) engineering: it was during the last half of the century that the 'public' (and first-grade) schools almost entirely monopolised entry to Oxford and Cambridge.[32]

First-grade schools were to serve the upper middle and professional classes which the Commission defines as, first, those with large unearned incomes, along with successful professional men and business men, 'whose profits put them on the same level', and second, clergy, doctors, lawyers and the poorer gentry, who 'have nothing to look to but education to keep their sons on a high social level' (an interesting premonition of the concept of cultural capital).[33] In fact, several local endowed schools investigated by the SIC were already developing as 'public' schools in the 1860s – for instance, Oundle, Uppingham and Repton – and some of the schools in the SIC's first grade became part of the revitalised 'public' school system in the period under review. First-grade schools were for children who would stay until the age of 18.

The second grade of school proposed was for children who left school at 16; these were day schools (not boarding) which, it was proposed, would prepare pupils for the army, the medical and legal professions, civil engineering, business and commercial life. It was envisaged that these should be patronised largely by the mercantile and trading classes – defined as larger shopkeepers, rising men of business and substantial tenant farmers. Latin would be included in the curriculum, as already indicated, but not Greek. Otherwise the curriculum would be modernised to include English literature, political economy, mathematics and science.[34] Here, then, was a deliberate attempt to meet the needs of the lesser bourgeoisie.

The third grade of school was designed for those leaving at 14, for 'a class distinctly lower in the scale', that is for smaller tenant farmers, small tradesmen and superior artisans. The establishment of efficient schools on this level was, the SIC held, of first importance. Their curriculum should (significantly) also include 'the elements of Latin' or a foreign language, English, history, elementary mathematics, geography and science. No one should be permitted to stay beyond 14.[35] It is worth noting the special attention given to the creation of third-grade schools in the light of the clear objective of attaching, by this means, the petty bourgeoisie and the upper working class firmly to their social superiors in the renovated grammar school system, and so isolating them from the working class with whom in the past (for example, the Chartist period and earlier, and in the 1860s franchise agitation) they had formed a sometimes powerful and threatening alliance.

The proposal to abolish free education, which was certainly implemented, involved charging sometimes quite substantial fees. It was proposed that these should also be graded, the highest, of course, being those for the first-grade schools, the lowest for third-grade ones.

Such was the neat, highly differentiated scheme proposed by the SIC. One thing that is certain, however, is that this scheme was not brought in in the pure form here proposed. No central or regional authority was set up to mastermind this reconstruction, as proposed in the Report. Instead, three Endowed Schools Commissioners were appointed, under the Act which followed the Report, with executive powers to implement reorganisation school by school, using the SIC Report as a guide to classifying individual schools. After five years, as a result of a Tory–Church backlash to their reforming activities, these powers were made over to the Charity Commission (a government office established in 1853). But statutory authority continued to be exercised, if now in a muted form, and on this basis change took place along the lines proposed in the Report. A new statutory basis for most of the endowed grammar schools was established during the thirty years following the 1869 Act, and to some extent these accorded with the Commission's proposals. Precisely how far this was the case we do not know, as this period has not, as yet, been effectively researched.[36] There is a great deal that needs doing to sort out how things actually developed during these years. Hilary Steedman's later chapter in this volume, however, lays the basis for a modern interpretation of the nature and significance of these changes.

We have dealt so far with the middle strata and the proposals for educational reconstruction for this central grouping in the mid to late nineteenth century; but this period also saw what may be regarded as a classic case of systematisation with a clear class significance: the evolution of the independent or so-called 'public' schools as a cohesive, organic and self-contained grouping having the closest links with the ancient universities, and through this route with government (both Parliamentary and the civil

service). The system that evolved, again partly as a result of state intervention, is unique to England and still obtains, though it may be said that in the
last forty years or so it has lost something of its pre-eminence.

The 'public' schools developed as a 'system', as John Honey shows in
Chapter 6, in the period from 1860 to 1900. The Clarendon Commission,
which reported on the leading 'great' schools in 1864, laid the basis for this
development – for the reinvigoration and 'reform' of the traditional schools,
which formed the core of the system. These were now, however, joined by
the aspiring first-grade schools that the SIC had reported on, as well as by
schools newly founded on their model.

The system of 'public' schools, as it developed in the closing years of the
century, was of course entirely independent of the state, at least in a formal
sense. These schools received no financial support directly from the state,
were generally governed by a variety of (now reformed) semi-public, semi-
private bodies, and were profoundly concerned to preserve this
independence. When we speak of a 'system' of 'public' schools, it must be
understood that this had no formal existence, except that the heads met
together and organised the Headmasters' Conference, which had been
brought into being in 1869 to defend the 'public' schools, 'in their hour of
danger' as one headmaster put it,[37] that is the danger of being taken over by
the state, which was now becoming increasingly subject to popular pressure
as a result of the extension of the franchise in 1867. These schools did,
however, form close links with each other, as Honey has shown, thus
reinforcing a hierarchy, with the most prestigious, such as Eton and Harrow,
at the top, and the least prestigious, for instance Dover College, at the
bottom.[38] No doubt each level within the total system could be characterised
in terms of the social origin of their pupils and their occupational level after
leaving school. As mentioned earlier, very close links were maintained with
the individual colleges at Oxford and Cambridge, which were also
independent foundations.

These schools played a key role in the symbiosis, or fusion, of the
industrial and commercial (and financial) bourgeoisie and the aristocracy,
together with leading elements from the liberal professions, into what is
called the Victorian upper middle class. Having a high social status, they
conferred that status on their pupils where these did not come from the
gentry and the aristocracy. To have been educated at a 'public' school
became, by the close of the century, the *sine qua non* for most leading
positions in society, government, the civil service, law, the Church and the
professions generally – and it was to these callings that many sons of
industrialists now aspired. This, then, was a process which evolved as the
industrial middle class began to demand a 'public' school education for their
sons in place of the system of apprenticeship, family connections and the like
which they had still relied on at mid-century.[39]

It is difficult to find any direct relationship between these schools and developing industry. In a sense these schools, even those specifically patronised by industrialists, turned their backs on industry and scarcely recognised it. Situated normally in remote rural areas, the schools pursued the ideal of a kind of country life-style in which games and the worship of athletics increasingly dominated from the 1860s on.[40] The central focus of studies, as recommended by the Clarendon Commission, remained the classics; modern studies, though now included, were given little time or prestige and remained peripheral. The 'hidden' curriculum was concerned not so much with cognitive (intellectual) development (though here there were exceptions) as with the development of character – reliability, conformity, honesty, courage, integrity – the sort of qualities, perhaps, that were now required of the governing caste in a rapidly developing imperialism. Some historians now ascribe England's economic difficulties in the second half of the twentieth century to what now appears as the deliberate rejection of science and technology (and of concern with industry) in the leading schools and universities in the late nineteenth century.[41]

Reverting to the Marxist model discussed earlier, it is difficult to make a case for a direct relationship between economic development and industry, and the nature and content of 'public' school education in the late nineteenth century. Clearly these were important institutions in terms of underpinning the social order, but their relations with industry were tangential, to say the least. Those schools that were popular with the industrial bourgeoisie in the north of England, for instance Uppingham and Radley (the latter established by a group of business men), developed similar life-styles to the ancient schools which they took as their model – a classical education together with games and athletics. The whole inner structure of these schools, largely boarding, with 'houses', pastoral care by the teachers (as a primary and important function), the system of prefects and fags, and so on, had evolved over a long period and was by now both general and adapted to the perceived requirements of the period in terms of educational outcomes. These were now 'total institutions' (in the sociological sense), providing a very carefully controlled and structured environment as the means of induction for the upper middle-class young. Their role was social and political rather than economic.

Is there a stronger case, to move to the other end of the social spectrum, for arguing a direct relationship between the provision of universal elementary education and the economic requirements of mid-century? A Royal Commission had also investigated this area (the Newcastle Commission), reporting in 1861, but in this case the key legislation was postponed until 1870 (and succeeding Acts to 1880), when a compromise but widely supported system, involving a degree of local finance and control, was finally brought into being.

Certainly it is generally acknowledged that economic considerations were one factor leading to this measure – in particular the perennial argument that England was being overtaken, in terms of industrial and technological developments, by Prussia, France, Switzerland and other European countries, most of which had already established systems of universal compulsory elementary education well before England. The relatively poor showing of the British exhibits at the Paris Exhibition of 1867 was adduced as evidence for this. It was also argued, by manufacturers in the mid-1860s, that universal education was required in order to select, from the mass of the workers, those who, responding well to schooling, would make good foremen on the shop floor. But a close study seems to suggest that the centrally accepted motivation for this measure was not so much economic as directly political. This relates to the successful struggle of the Labour movement and the radical bourgeoisie for the extension of the franchise, as shown by their relative success in 1867 – and with the likelihood of a further extension in the not too distant future.

In England measures related to popular education in the nineteenth century were often specifically related to the extension of the franchise. It was the radical bourgeoisie (or rather, its ideological spokesmen) who first deliberately developed this policy in the early years of the century – as the means by which the industrial and commercial middle class might oust the traditional governing classes and achieve political power, in the early nineteenth century monopolised by Whigs and Tories, the two 'factions', as James Mill put it, of the aristocracy.[42]

How could this situation be transformed? Only by the massive extension of the franchise would it be possible for the middle class (bourgeoisie) to gain control of Parliament and overturn the rule of the aristocracy (or landed interest). But, if the working class were given the vote, would they not then have the power to overturn the existing social order in their own interests ('the world turned upside down')?

Hence the solution, strongly argued from the 1820s on by Mill and Bentham, the philosophic radicals: educate the masses; enlighten them; let them understand that their true interests lay in uniting with capital both economically and politically; let them understand the laws of political economy – especially the iron law of wages.

So the advanced industrial bourgeoisie favoured, on the one hand, the extension of the franchise to all males (in Bentham's case females as well), together with a massive extension of popular education. We have seen that, in the 1840s and 1850s, Cobden and other liberal manufacturers threw their weight strongly behind the mass provision of popular education.

Popular demand for the extension of the franchise reached a new peak in the mid-1860s. In 1867 three days of demonstrations in Hyde Park swung the issue. The Tory government of the day now conceded an extension of the franchise, so bringing a million artisans (or skilled workers) on to the voting registers for the first time. Robert Lowe's famous remark, 'I believe it will be absolutely necessary to compel our future masters to learn their letters', encapsulates the view that he and others now held.[43] Now was the time for a serious extension of popular education. The last two or three years of the sixties saw a sudden consensus around the issue of the provision of universal elementary education. This seems to indicate that the 1870 Act was a *political*, rather than an economic necessity.

So there was constructed, at the close of the crucial decision-making period – building, of course, on earlier developments – another level of schooling, again for a specific class (the working class, as written into the Act itself), which was largely self-contained and had no organic relationship at that time with the other levels of schooling now being brought into being.

The emergent 'system'

Whatever the intentions, the outcomes of the mid-century educational reorganisation in England are clear enough: three main levels of schooling came into being in the period 1860 to 1900.

First, a cohesive grouping of 'public' schools for the upper middle class. Second, elementary schooling for the working class. The first of these was 'independent' of, but closely woven into, the state. The second was directly controlled and financed by the state, though in 'partnership' with the new local authorities (School Boards) and the voluntary bodies (the Churches).

At the same time, a third set of schools was brought into being, with the aim of restructuring education for the middle strata (or class) on three levels. The outcome, then, was the establishment of a highly differentiated system in which each level served, in theory at least, a specific social class (or subsection of a class), with each having a specific function.

In this situation the struggle between classes expressed itself in different ways. For instance, the early socialist and Chartist movements' concept of the content and character of popular education (as defined, for instance, in Lovett's *Chartism* in 1841) was very different from that of the system finally imposed. Again, the perspectives embraced historically by the industrial and commercial middle class, partly for reasons discussed earlier, differed radically from the nature and content of middle-class education as actually imposed, even if there was some acceptance of modernising tendencies.

The system that was imposed, in the period of reorganisation, was precise and neat, involving clear forms of differentiation (or segmentation); but there were many loose ends. Indeed by the 1890s it erupted in crisis, but this represents a new phase in developments.

To conclude, the reorganisation of education in England in the mid to late nineteenth century resulted in the construction of a highly differentiated system comprising several levels of schooling, differentiated in terms of curriculum, fees, length of school life and ethos. Each level was intended to cater for a specific section of the social spectrum. The resultant structure both reflected, and fed back into and so perpetuated, the existing social structure.

These developments do not bear out a strict reproduction model of the relations between education and society, as elaborated, for instance, by Bourdieu in relation to contemporary systems, since such a model (admittedly highly theoretical and challenging) cannot explain change. Yet the period from 1860 to 1900 was a period of rapid change, both in society *and* in education. How can a reproduction model account for the fusion, or symbiosis, of aristocracy and bourgeoisie, as cemented through the 'public' schools, which had the clear function of promoting such a fusion? Only, perhaps, if one accepts that the reproduction of social hierarchies may take different forms; and that this development in a sense simply meant that new means were found to ensure the, otherwise insecure, perpetuation of existing class relations.

Nor do developments in England bear out a linear model of the relationship between education and economic development. Indeed, economic developments appear in this period to have little direct relation with educational change. Later in the century, in the later 1880s and 1890s in particular, the new universities established in the provincial cities apparently responded more directly to economic requirements than any institutions in the period of restructuring. Changes in the 'base' (forces of production) certainly affected education indirectly (as argued at the start of this chapter) through urbanisation and population growth, and through the consequent emergence of a complex occupational pattern, particularly affecting the middle strata. But educational restructuring was not spearheaded by those representing economic or industrial interests and developments. Rather, this role was played, at a crucial phase, by those representing the aristocracy and gentry, who were concerned to preserve social stability and reinforce emerging social hierarchies.

The English experience, then, tends to the conclusion that education has a large degree of autonomy from the economic base. The forces primarily involved in restructuring and systematisation are political and social rather than economic. Gramsci's analysis, relating to hegemony and the role of civic society, seems central to an understanding of these developments. Unlike the French Marxist Althusser, Gramsci fully accepts that education can be a site of struggle between classes with different objectives and that the struggle of subordinate classes for hegemony may conflict with the role of 'established' culture. It is along these lines, I suggest, that educational developments in England at this time may best be interpreted.[44]

The closing decades

This chapter has focused on the significance of the educational measures determined on in the period 1850 to 1870. As mentioned at the start, these measures preceded similar developments in France and Germany, which focused more particularly on the final decades of the century. However, the period from roughly 1860–70 to 1900 were also years of important developments in England, when the full implications of the measures that had been decided were realised.

Of key importance was the reconstruction of the endowed grammar schools along the lines proposed by the Schools Inquiry Commission's report of 1868. In Chapter 4 Hilary Steedman contributes a pioneering study of these developments. Here she develops her theory of 'defining institutions' by which these schools, consistently subject to market forces, became polarised into 'successful' schools and 'unsuccessful' ones. Her chapter discusses some of the difficulties and conflicts experienced in the struggle of these schools for status, and on the precise working-out of the graded blueprint of the Commission. As mentioned earlier, this period has been little studied, but Steedman's investigation indicates that these schools did develop into a differentiated hierarchy close to the proposals of the Commission itself.

The late nineteenth century certainly also saw an energetic upthrust within the centres of urban culture in the main provincial cities. This took various forms, but the outcome generally was the beginning of the development of an 'alternative system' which deliberately rejected traditional institutions (endowed grammar schools and ancient universities) in favour of support for higher-grade schools and organised science schools, emerging technical institutions (and colleges) and, above all, the 'modern' universities established mainly in these cities in the period from 1860 to 1900. Such a system was now developing cohesive relations between the various stages, had a quite different ethos and different objectives to traditional institutions, and so in this sense now represented a new and real threat to the hegemony of established (or traditional) institutions.

These developments are the focus of David Reeder's study on 'The Reconstruction of Secondary Education in England'. In this chapter he analyses the basis of and the social forces behind, this movement, as well as considering its outcomes in the new restructuring that took place. This culminated in the Education Act of 1902 and the administrative measures related to it, but Reeder takes the analysis further into the early twentieth century, when new forms of differentiation and systematisation, adapted to the new circumstances, took the place of the old.

It was in the closing decades of the nineteenth century, too, that the 'public' schools developed as an identifiable and cohesive grouping of schools of a special type, independent of the state yet closely linked with it. These schools, still today in the form in which they developed at this time, continue to play a major role in the body politic and are unique to England. In Chapter 6, John Honey, who has made a major study of these schools, analyses this phenomenon and attempts to account for it. As the dominant educational institutions of the country, as far as schooling was concerned, these schools continued greatly to influence the accepted concept of secondary education as new institutions came into being in the early years of the twentieth century.

Finally, in Chapter 7, on 'Structural Change in English Higher Education, 1870–1920', Roy Lowe carries the analysis into the university field, showing that here, too, segmentation became the rule in the clear differences (and similarities) between the ancient universities and the modern. Here, too, the role of classical and humanistic studies is stressed. If mid-century school restructuring resulted in the reinforcement of social hierarchies, the same influences also appear to have been at work within higher education during this period. Indeed the educational system as a whole, as determined by mid-to-late century restructuring, still in essence maintains the main characteristics laid down at this stage. In this sense the crucial changes of mid-century have had a tenacious and lasting effect. It is for this reason that study of the period retains its importance.

Part II
Structural change and social reproduction in England

4. Defining institutions: the endowed grammar schools and the systematisation of English secondary education

HILARY STEEDMAN

Detlef Müller's concept of the systematisation of schools understood as part of the wider social process of social reproduction enables us to perceive a logic in the informal status hierarchy that emerged in English secondary education during the last third of the nineteenth century. Basically schools succeeded or failed to the extent that they linked pupils to the prestigious network of Oxford and Cambridge colleges by means of scholarships and exhibitions. A result of this objective was the standardisation of curricular patterns of 'rising' or 'successful' schools. This process of standardisation, which involved, for some schools, increasing the amount of Latin and Greek in the curriculum and consigning 'modern' subjects such as science to the non-scholarship streams, has been identified and discussed by Fritz Ringer in his studies on France in terms of 'a generalist shift'. Ringer's elaboration and illustration of this concept both in this volume and in *Education and Society in Modern Europe* makes it much easier for us to understand that the strengthening of classical studies in English secondary education at this period was not an example of idiosyncratic English traditionalism but an integral part of a social process which affected France, Prussia and England in similar ways.

The concept of defining institutions

Ringer has himself put the essential question which is raised by the identification of the generalist shift as part of a wider process of systematisation in the following way:

If we are agreed that the ways in which the European middle classes were educated was not simply forced upon them by economic or technological 'necessities', then we have to ask ourselves how more or less 'arbitrary' curricular patterns and modes of socialisation did in fact arise.[1]

Ringer's question makes it clear that the dominance of classical studies in all three countries constitutes an apparently irrational element in an otherwise coherent structure based on participants' decisions and established connections between jobs, status and educational qualifications. Ringer attempts to come to terms with the problems raised by the generalist shift in his chapter in this volume, and to do so in terms of the dependence of educational 'meanings' on the definitions of status perpetuated by vertical segmentation as it existed in France and Germany at this period. Traditional learning, with a built-in legitimation, was established as the curriculum of the segment with the highest through-put in terms in social status, and traditional learning in both countries was humanistic, based on the classics.

What we are talking about is a process of conversion of social hierarchies *into* academic hierarchies in such a way that academic hierarchies became the obligatory mediators for social groups maintaining or improving status between one generation and the succeeding one. Now, while it is possible, especially in the case of France and Prussia, to discuss this process, as Ringer does, in terms of carefully defined and recognised school types, in England for the same period, commonly used labels do not denote a homogeneous group of schools.

I would therefore suggest that Ringer's approach to the questions raised by the generalist shift needs a different emphasis in the case of England. Furthermore, I consider that the case of England may lead us to place less emphasis on the *nature* of the generalist shift, that is from practical–scientific to abstract–literary, and to look more closely at the power of institutions to establish dominance not only by means of types of knowledge but also by means of school ethos and organisation.

The first point to be stressed is that, in contrast to France and Prussia at this time, in England government had no role in the provision of secondary education. The result was not an absence of *system*, but an absence of a set of stable categories of schools, changes in the curriculum of which could be fairly safely dated and documented as they are by Ringer in the case of French and Prussian education. Indeed, John Honey's chapter makes this very point – that the term 'public school' continued to defy definition throughout our period, even *after* the point of official definition and legitimation conferred by the Royal Commission of 1864. When we look at the process of the conversion of social hierarchies into academic hierarchies in England, where the progressive introduction of open examinations for the civil service, the armed forces and for certain professional careers is fairly close to the Prussian system of official qualifications, we can see that this conversion was the product of the existence of the recognised 'public' schools. Without being subject to the authority of the state, this group of schools was *invested with* the authority of the state because their former pupils dominated both government and administration and constructed the open examinations mentioned above in such a way as to ensure that this dominance continued.[2] England, unlike France and Prussia in the period of high industrialisation, had no defining authority in the field of secondary education but a group of defining institutions which defined originally in their own right but then increasingly in terms of the prestige based upon traditional Oxbridge links.

We can only understand systematisation and the concept of the generalist shift for England in terms of the 'public' schools and their role as defining institutions. Because of the long-existing symbiotic relationship between these schools and Oxford and Cambridge, Oxford and Cambridge tested what the 'great' schools taught, that is Latin and Greek, even for students of science and maths; other schools had to approximate to the fierce concentration of the 'great' schools on classics.[3] Since secondary schools other than the 'great' public schools were competing in the same market as these schools, they were necessarily bound to shift their curriculum in the direction of the market leaders.[4] But schools below the 'great' public schools came under pressure to approximate to the defining institutions of their day not merely in terms of the three fundamental criteria – Oxbridge scholarship and other examination successes, the school-leaving age, and the classical curriculum – but also in terms of school organisation, more particularly the strengthening of boundary definition between school and the outside world. We can identify four principal aspects of secondary school organisation not belonging to the strictly academic curriculum which were widely adopted by even the humblest of secondary schools in the 1890s and which directly imitated what were perceived to be the defining features of 'public' school education.[5] These features were (i) uniforms, (ii) organised team games, (iii) chapel (or assembly where chapel was unavailable) and (iv) a house system.

The most interesting aspect of these approximations to the defining institutions, in contrast to the three adaptations more directly related to social reproduction, is their purely symbolic value when applied to the lesser secondary schools. Whereas features (i)–(iv) above performed a *necessary* role in tightly controlled total institutions such as the 'public' schools had become by the 1870s, these features were widely adopted by *day schools* where, for example, a house system was peculiarly inappropriate (houses originally being just that – places where boys lived while at school).

These widespread attempts by the less prestigious secondary schools to approximate not only academically but also in a wider symbolic sense to the leading schools underlines, in my view, the role and power of this group of schools to define all other components of the secondary system in their own image. Given that this process undoubtedly took place in England in the last quarter of the nineteenth century, the area that needs to be researched is how and at what juncture in a school's fortunes these practices were introduced. We can already make some informed guesses about the importance of the movement of former 'public' school masters to become headmasters of less prestigious secondary schools.[6] However, questions of the mechanics of such a process must be asked in the wider context raised by Ringer of the construction of social meanings. By 1890 the idea of a secondary school became less diffuse (the social mix was reduced and the curriculum standardised at a more advanced level) and academic goals *in the context of a certain type of school organisation* marked both successful and unsuccessful secondary schools. How powerful and enduring are the social meanings of institutions? I do not intend to answer this question, but I raise it in order to draw attention to the fact that in England in the 1980s many state-maintained schools both primary and secondary insist on uniform, have flourishing prefect and house systems, compulsory sport as an integral part of the curriculum, and the descendant of chapel (transmuted by necessity into the daily assembly enshrined in the 1944 Education Act). One way of answering the question of the importance of social meanings of institutions would be to investigate the English public's prestige rankings of maintained secondary schools with or without the above characteristics.

The concept of defining institutions could be used within national contexts other than that of England, and not only as a descriptive term but as a starting-point for analysis. This is clear both from Müller's account of systematisation in Prussian secondary education and from Ringer's treatment of French secondary schooling. Thus the modifications undergone by the *enseignement spécial* were very similar to the changes in curriculum and length of school life made by the English grammar schools in an attempt to approximate to 'public' schools. The struggle of the *lycées* for a defining role in the French system raises the question of whether such a struggle also took place in England or Prussia.

With respect to England I have made it sound as if the 'public' schools slipped unchallenged into the role of defining institutions. Closer analysis of the records and histories of individual secondary schools of the period reveals strong resistance from 1830 onwards to the classical curriculum in secondary education from the industrial and agricultural bourgeoisie whose challenge to the ruling and predominantly landowning class was a real threat to the social order at least until 1850. In fact, what is characterised as systematisation in this chapter is, viewed from another perspective, the definitive defeat of the aspirations of this challenging class for a curriculum which would more closely correspond to their own needs.

The concept of defining institutions is thus in itself not a new or original idea, given that it is implicitly present in many of our cross-cultural studies. But the *delineation* of properties and roles entailed by the elaboration of the concept has the value of shifting our attention from idiosyncratic properties of institutions at different levels of educational structures in different national contexts towards similar roles performed by institutions in the formalisation of educational structures and their significance in terms of class competition.

The endowed grammar schools, 1867–97

Levels of education that prepare directly for professional careers or higher education will become crucial elements in the process of social reproduction, once limited meritocratic criteria are introduced to determine entry to elite status. Within the framework of this wider social process of reproduction parents inevitably make decisions about the most advantageous placement of their children within the school system. Parental decisions both condition and are conditioned by the school response to the demand for schooling, and the schools' need to respond to demand also means that they must react to the changing requirements for access to higher-grade occupations. We can expect to see developing in the period 1867–97 a process of interaction the essential elements of which are, on the one hand, the necessity for the schools of satisfying parental demand within the restraints of parental income and, on the other, the range of careers for which pupils could be prepared. From this process of interaction we may expect to be able to identify a process of systematisation for educational institutions in which the schools' attempts to promote the interests of their pupils, and thereby their own institutions, bring about a redistribution of schools on a status continuum determined by their success in providing access to high-level occupations.

The period opens with the publication in 1868 of the Report of the Schools Inquiry Commission (SIC), a minutely detailed investigation and analysis of every endowed educational institution in England and Wales, as well as of some important proprietary and private secondary schools. The only exceptions to this investigation were the schools known as the 'great' schools, referred to hereafter in this study as the 'Nine'.[7] These schools had been the object of a government-appointed Commission of Inquiry published in 1864.[8] While the SIC provides us with excellent, detailed and reliable information on the schools under investigation in this study, the subsequent reorganisation of the endowed secondary schools under the Endowed Schools Act of 1869 has, as yet, scarcely been investigated. Brian Simon has pointed out this important gap in his contribution to this volume. There is a lack of contemporary research of a scope wider than the histories of individual schools. Furthermore, there is equally a lack of statistical information apart from the 1868 survey, as was admitted by the Education Department in 1897:

In England there are no official statistics showing the number of pupils receiving instruction in the schools which fill the gap between the public elementary schools and the universities or university colleges.[9]

The approach adopted in this study is therefore based of necessity upon sampling of the schools concerned. The first of our two samples was randomly selected and was obtained from secondary sources, that is histories of individual schools. This first sample, 30 school histories from a published total of over 500, has been used as a substitute source of basic data on the growth or decline of pupil numbers in secondary education in the period 1867–97. School histories were used for this purpose because the files on individual schools housed in the Public Record Office are so voluminous and do not always contain data on pupil numbers for the period concerned.[10] It should be noted, however, that although the sample was randomly *selected*, it cannot be said to be a random one in the real meaning of the term, since in most cases only those schools which managed to survive the difficult years from 1867 to 1902 have produced school histories. These schools can thus be seen as relatively successful; yet they nevertheless yield striking divergencies in growth and development, as recorded in Figure 4.1. This fact encourages me to regard this sample as indicative of genuine trends in school systematisation.

The second sample – based on the detailed examination of school prospectuses, school timetables and inspectors' reports available in the files housed in the Public Record Office – was used first of all to establish whether a detailed analysis of primary sources confirmed the trends in pupil numbers and associated school characteristics that were derived from the first sample. It also made it possible to go beyond inference in associating school success or decline with certain characteristics of the curriculum, and to observe and record these associations at first hand. A regional sample was chosen because it was felt that the competition of schools for the clientele of a given locality should be observed. Three schools mentioned below were added to the sample because two of them fall into the interesting category designated as Subset Y of Set B schools in Figure 4.1, and it was considered important to attempt to observe how they had improved their academic status between 1867 and 1887. The study of Pocklington Grammar School represents the beginning of an attempt to study Set A schools in more detail.

The second sample is therefore a selected one and comprises firstly all the endowed secondary schools in one geographical–administrative area, namely Westmorland, together with Pocklington Grammar School and Newcastle under Lyme Grammar School, Staffordshire. The development of these schools was studied from primary sources, that is from the files of the Charity Commissioners on individual endowed schools housed in the Public Record Office.[11]

However, before proceeding to a description and analysis of these two samples, I intend to provide a wider framework relating to developments in educational and occupational qualifications within which the two samples can be situated.

It is implicit in the construction of this volume of studies that one point of comparison with other European systems at this time should be the response to the increasing need to ensure the social reproduction of a dominant professional–administrative elite through education rather than through the channels of family and influence which had been predominant in a period before limited meritocratic principles were introduced. Comparison should therefore concentrate on the process of social reproduction, and the institutions to be examined cross-culturally should be those providing access to elite status posts. Whereas in Prussia it is possible to identify this set of institutions as corresponding to the *Gymnasien*, the definition of such a set of institutions in England in the period 1867–97 presents considerable problems. Yet it can also be appreciated, from the initial statement of the aims of this study, that the first step in a study of schools within the context of social reproduction must be a definition of qualifications in their widest sense as the necessary but not sufficient condition of access to high-status occupations. The principal problem for this study if it is to serve as a basis for cross-cultural analysis is the formal nature of qualifications in Germany and France and the lack of similar structures in England at this time.

My solution to this problem of cross-cultural analysis is to identify a widely accepted criterion of academic access likely to give access to elite status, and to define a set of high-status institutions according to their performance measured against this criterion. It should be pointed out that this procedure is not as arbitrary as it sounds, since the *Pall Mall Gazette* was identifying groups of schools in precisely this manner during the decade (see below). The schools in Set B of Figures 4.1 and 4.3 represent the application of this procedure, that is schools are judged successful if they succeed in gaining open and, to a lesser extent, closed awards to Oxford and Cambridge both in 1867 and in the period 1885–92.[12]

In Prussia the most prestigious qualification was that which enabled the holder to enrol at the university, and the schools entitled to confer this qualification were strictly limited in number. In England, however, entrance requirements to Oxford and Cambridge were extremely elementary in character, and no one type of secondary school could be said to have had a monopoly of such preparation. However, examination of sources of this period does reveal that the extent to which schools succeeded in obtaining awards at Oxford and Cambridge was widely accepted as the academic criterion by which educational institutions were judged and graded.

The importance of Oxbridge awards as a criterion for distinguishing a set of successful schools emerges at the beginning of the period in Appendix VII, Table IV of the SIC Report.[13] This table ranks all the schools which came within the scope of the SIC according to the number of former pupils in residence at Oxford and Cambridge, the number holding open and closed exhibitions and scholarships, and the number of undergraduates as a percentage of the total number of scholars in the school. The schools highest in the list were, of course, those endowed schools which were entering the category of 'leading schools' alongside the Nine. These schools were also characterised by a substantial boarding element and were not distributed evenly throughout England and Wales. It seems justifiable, therefore, to assume that this data provided the grounds for the SIC's major recommendation, the establishment of different grades of secondary school. Let us examine the relevant passage of the Report recommending the setting-up of first-grade schools. The SIC states that its concern is for a class which

has nothing to look to but education to keep their sons on a high social level. And they would not wish to have what might more readily be converted into money, if in any degree it tended to let their children sink in the social scale. The main evil of the present system in their eyes is its expense. The classical education of the highest order is every day to a greater degree quitting the smaller grammar schools for the great public school, and others of the same kind. Those who want such education can no longer find it, as they could in the last century, close to their doors, all over the country. They are compelled to seek it in boarding schools, and generally in boarding schools of a very expensive kind.[14]

This paragraph establishes three important points which support the approach adopted in this study. The first relates to the growing importance of education in this period as an essential element in social reproduction and to the desire of parents to see their sons placed in a similar occupational status to their own. The second is the importance of a 'classical education of the highest order' as the prerequisite for high-status positions. The third point to emerge is the SIC's determination to provide a route to elite status in addition to the 'public' schools.

The SIC saw as one of the tasks of reorganisation the definition of a group of schools which in facilities and curriculum could compete with the already existing 'public' schools and merge with them into a single class of institution. These schools would give realistic access to Oxford and Cambridge awards, but at a lower fee, easily affordable by clergymen and other struggling members of the professional classes. The need was for a sound financial basis for these first-grade schools which could be derived neither from fees, which must be reasonable, nor, on ideological grounds, from state resources. The solution to this problem adopted by the Endowed Schools Commissioners, at least up until 1879, was first to establish a list by county of all schools having an endowment of more than £500 per annum,[15] and then to select at least one such school to serve as the first-grade school for the county.[16]

An interesting conclusion emerges from the first ten years of the Commissioners' grading activities which is both relevant to the discussion at the end of this study and to the wider debate taking place among contributors to this volume. This is the fact that while in 1868 a total of 152 endowed schools are listed in the SIC's Table IV as having former pupils in residence at Oxford and Cambridge, by 1879 the Commissioners had designated only 60 endowed grammar schools as first-grade schools. This means that 12 years later, 92 endowed grammar schools which had been sending pupils to Oxford and Cambridge in 1867 were either still awaiting reorganisation or had been relegated to second- or even (e.g. Lucton Grammar School) third-grade status. These facts suggest that the Commissioners intended to restrict the number of endowed grammar schools which would be allowed to compete with the established 'public' schools. Unfortunately, after 1879, the Commissioners ceased to publish lists stating the grades assigned to different schools and this information must be laboriously gleaned from the schemes drawn up for individual schools. In the absence of information as to the grading of schools, we can, however, compare the numbers of endowed grammar schools sending pupils to Oxford and Cambridge in 1867 with those of 1887. This may be done very simply by examination of the schools contained in the intersection of Sets A and B in Figure 4.1.

The information for 1867 is taken from the SIC Table IV quoted above, and that for 1887 from lists of award-winning schools published in the *Pall Mall Gazette* for Saturday 15 October 1887. As the latter source only includes schools obtaining at least one open scholarship, the same criterion has been applied to the 1867 list. The Nine were not included in the 1867 list and have been similarly excluded from 1887. After 20 years of the Commissioners' activity we can see that the *number* of endowed grammar schools sending pupils to Oxford and Cambridge with open awards had been reduced from 88 to 58 – at a time when the number of undergraduates at the two universities was increasing. There is no problem, however, in reconciling the Commissioners' reduction in the *number* of schools and their concern to make Oxbridge access more widely available. The pre-eminent need, as will be clear from our small sample, was for a group of schools which could compete with the vast resources of the Nine and yet charge reasonable fees. This entailed the *concentration* of existing resources on a reduced number of schools.

Up to this point we have merely stressed the importance attached by the Commissioners to Oxbridge awards. However, we can also find a wealth of contemporary sources to confirm their growing importance in the period up to 1900. The issue of the *Pall Mall Gazette* already quoted observes that 'even those who object to our method (of publishing Oxbridge results) the most strongly do not hesitate at speech days and in school calendars to make elaborate parade of their "honours" '.

This assertion can be substantiated by reference to school calendars and

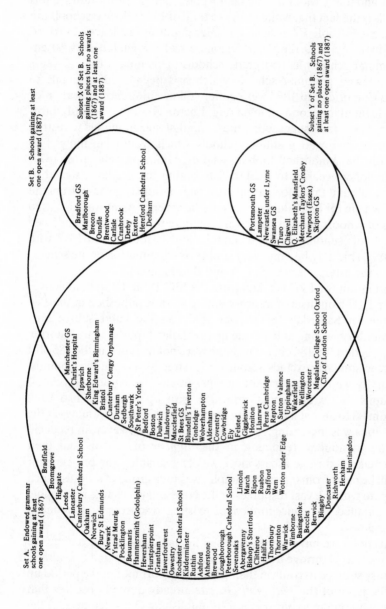

Figure 4.1. Continuity and change in sets of endowed grammar schools sending pupils to Oxford and Cambridge, 1867–87.

prospectuses of the period. Pocklington school calendar for 1895 states that 'Pocklington Grammar School is richly endowed and possesses good scholarships tenable both at the school and university. It also has the right of competing for the Hastings Exhibitions at Queen's College Oxford which are of the value of £90 p.a. for five years.'[17]

Pocklington's calendar concludes by printing a league table of open scholarships to the university gained by other Yorkshire schools which it considered its nearest rivals. The list provides illuminating insight into the extent to which schools identified themselves as belonging to a definite group of similar institutions within a given geographical area.

Portsmouth Grammar School in its Class Lists of 1891 boasts an extremely wide and impressive set of achievements in almost the entire professional career spectrum of the period.[18] The headmaster draws attention not only to the open awards gained at Oxford and Cambridge but also to the school's success in sending pupils *directly* to Sandhurst and Woolwich, an unusual event at the time. Another aspect of the school's success, referred to in the Class Lists of 1892, is success in examinations for a commercial certificate awarded by the Oxford and Cambridge examination syndicates. In fact, there is evidence here of the school's efforts to respond flexibly to changing occupational opportunities: 'the work is of a most varied character as in addition to the ordinary curriculum, special classes are formed to meet the requirements of all who desire to be prepared for a definite profession or business.'[19]

As the stress laid by the schools themselves upon examination success, and in particular open awards, is so important in establishing the growing importance of the school as the agency of access to elite status, I shall quote, finally, from the Heversham school prospectus, which has some interesting features. Firstly, the prospectus, which is not dated but refers to the period 1892–4, opens with the words: 'By the new scheme of the Endowed Schools Commissioners this old foundation is classed as a FIRST GRADE SCHOOL thus securing to it all its University Scholarships.' This, it should be noted, is the only prospectus in the detailed sample of schools to mention its connection with the Commissioners, but more interesting, it is the first indication that status other than first-grade may have entailed the loss of awards to Oxford and Cambridge which were formerly attached to a particular school.

The Heversham prospectus lists the same *wide range* of careers as Portsmouth: 'Boys are fully prepared for the Universities, Civil Services, the various Professional Preliminary Examinations and for Mercantile and Business Pursuits.' The prospectus then lists a variety of successes similar to those of Portsmouth. The final place of honour is given to an item which we can also find in the Pocklington and Portsmouth prospectuses and some others of the sample. It reads as follows: '*Public Schools* Open entrance scholarships at Charterhouse, Rugby etc.'[20]

Portsmouth boasts a scholarship to Epsom College, one in the following

Table 4.2. *Open scholarships to the university: Yorkshire schools*

School	Pupils	Awards
Bradford Grammar School	430	6
Pocklington	130	4
Giggleswick	210	1
Leeds Grammar School	160	1
Ripon	108	1
St Peter's York	115	1

year to Wellington, and in 1899 a scholarship to Winchester. This phenomenon of using the first-grade grammar schools and minor 'public' schools as a springboard for entry to the high-status 'public' schools was also found to be very widespread in the larger sample of schools. Nevertheless, the more established 'public' schools attracted parents by more than scholarship-winning ability alone since Portsmouth, Heversham and Pocklington, for their size, offered equally good chances of Oxbridge awards as the established 'public' schools. Status distinctions undoubtedly existed within the group of schools that we are suggesting can be identified by their capacity to ensure pupils' access to high-status careers, and this fact can be easily accommodated within the hypothesis put forward in the opening section of this study.

What is important for our argument here is that within the context of middle-class parents' career aspirations for their children and the accompanying financial constraints, there is, in 1887 and in succeeding years, an identifiable group of academically successful schools whose common characteristic is their ability to gain entry for their pupils to elite status occupations. This fact is stated bluntly in the *Pall Mall Gazette*:

In the first place the winning of money prizes *is* one of the objects – and the legitimate objects – of a public school education. A very large sum of money is given away every year in scholarships at Oxford and Cambridge. With many parents it is of the utmost importance that these prizes should be won by their sons. They could not afford to send the boys to college without scholarships . . . Of course, there are other lucrative things to aim at besides university scholarships such as admission to Woolwich, the Indian and the Home Civil Service, etc. Some schools make a speciality of these things, just as others make a speciality of cricket.

The way in which small schools in particular survived by this very technique of 'playing the academic market' emerges from our small sample. Heversham, a relatively tiny school of 60 pupils, gained its considerable success at Oxford and Cambridge by concentrating on mathematics to a startling degree. The timetable for the sixth and fifth forms for 1895 shows 26 of the 38 weekly lessons devoted to mathematics, the remainder to Latin and Greek.[21] Pocklington identified another strategy which helped it to revive following its decline in the 1880s. The school calendar of 1895 advertises 'the study of Hebrew, with a view to preparation for the Theological and Semitic Language Honours Schools at Oxford'.[22]

Another example, and one which will be analysed in detail below, is provided by Windermere Bowness Grammar School. Classed as third grade by the Commissioners, the school declined in numbers until 1892. Then, with a new headmaster, came a concentration on science teaching, especially chemistry, the building of a chemistry laboratory, and, finally, the winning of a senior open scholarship in Natural Science at Clare College Cambridge.[23]

It is evident, then, that in accordance with our initial assumptions, parents played the market, choosing to send their sons to schools well provided with awards and with a good academic record. Schools, for their part, sought out new openings by which their pupils could win success at university, hurriedly setting up departments to prepare for whatever new set of examinations was being introduced.

Yet, as has already been stressed, whatever the means employed, the achievements were in the end identical, and it is possible to identify a substantial 'hard core' of schools from which pupils proceeded to high-status positions, or to Oxford or Cambridge. Figure 4.1 refers only to endowed grammar schools. To obtain a complete picture of the 'hard core' we need to examine the full list in 1867 (endowed, private and proprietary schools) and in 1887 as set out in Figure 4.3. The 'hard core' can thus be seen to consist of a group of institutions composed principally of endowed grammar schools but also including a number of private and proprietary institutions. These schools were already sending substantial numbers to Oxford and Cambridge in 1867 and continued to do so until 1890 at least. When we examine this set of schools, we must be struck first by the continuity of the set during what has always been thought of as a period of active intervention and reorganisation of secondary education in England. Only 19 institutions (Subset P and Subset Q) joined the club over this period, and of these only 10 were endowed grammar schools.

Having identified this group of schools and established the wider social significance of membership of the 'core', we should now analyse the first and larger of our two samples of endowed grammar schools in order to ascertain what other common factors are associated with the 'hard core' and with the group of schools excluded from it.

The larger random sample yielded some useful information on two points. Firstly, we can see how the endowed schools outside the 'hard core' prospered during this period, and we can identify their principal common problems.

The total sample of schools is presented in Table 4.4, which shows numbers in the school in 1867 as reported by the SIC and numbers in the period after 1890, where the source is the history of a given school. The first

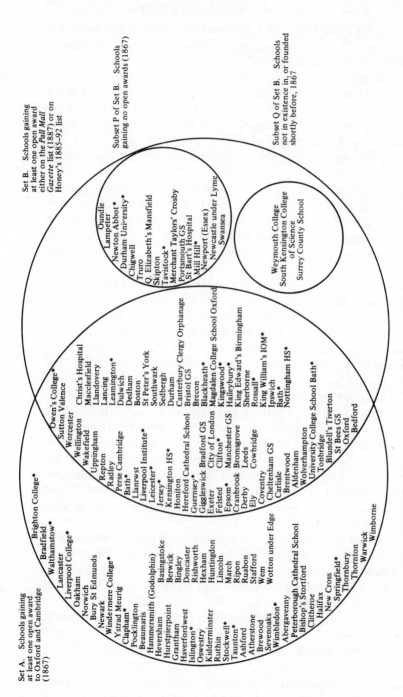

Figure 4.3. Continuity and change in sets of schools sending pupils to Oxford and Cambridge, 1867–87 (excluding the Nine and Marlborough and Cheltenham Colleges).

and most obvious point which emerges from consideration of Table 4.4 is that the 30 schools divide into two groups: 19 schools whose numbers actually fell during this period and 11 schools whose numbers rose.

Two points should be remembered when considering the significance of the fall in numbers. The first of these points is that this sample represents schools which *survived* the period 1867–97 to be revived with state-provided and local funds in 1902, after which most went from strength to strength. A totally random sample could have been expected to provide evidence of an even sharper decline, with 'successful' schools forming a smaller proportion of the total. The second point is that the decline in numbers attending these 19 endowed grammar schools must be seen in the context of an expansion in the total number of boys being educated in the categories of school with which we are concerned. In fact, the number of boys in endowed grammar schools in England increased from 35,738 in 1868 to 59,517 in 1897.[24]

The most striking common feature of the larger group of 'sinking' schools in the sample is the decline in numbers. There are, however, a number of other features which these schools have in common. A point made by almost all the historians of these schools, either implicitly or explicitly, is the low leaving age of pupils – few stayed beyond 15 – and the tendency to stay for only two or three years before leaving, or moving to another school. Of Bolton School we learn that 'under Lipscomb (1903) the great and abiding weakness of the school was the number of early leavers, including the sons of richer parents who went at 13 to boarding school'.[25] At Chesterfield Grammar School most boys left at 14 and only one had gone to a university since 1862. Numbers continued to decline despite reorganisation as a second-grade school by the Commissioners in 1879.[26] Marjorie Cox, writing of Sir John Deane's Grammar School, Northwich, points out that the new headmaster 'faced a problem common to most Cheshire schools – the failure of boys to stay long enough in the upper school'. In 1877 there were four boarders and fifty-one day scholars, of whom seven were over 15 and only one over 17.[27]

Although a comparatively successful school, the case of Ilkley Grammar School spells out the dilemma of the poorer schools which had not succeeded in establishing links with the universities: 'Finance was a problem throughout Mr Swann's regime. The building schemes reduced capital so that the endowment income barely met such overhead expenses . . . fees could not be raised to meet losses. If fees had been raised higher, parents would have sent boys to Bradford Grammar school.' At a later point Salmon observes that not only was Ilkley Grammar School threatened by competition from above – by the highly successful Bradford Grammar School – but, according to the report of the school's first general inspection, 'the fees are high . . . the poorer classes find it cheaper to send their sons to the Higher Grade School at Leeds'.[28]

Even Hull Grammar School, which succeeded in increasing its numbers in

Table 4.4. *Schools in the random sample grouped according to the criterion of increase or decrease in numbers, 1867–90*

	'Rising schools'			'Sinking schools'	
School	Nos. 1867	Nos. c. 1890	School	Nos. 1867	Nos. c. 1890
Chigwell*	20	80	Appleby	49	26 (1901)
Felsted*	95	241	Ashby de la Zouch	196	50 or 60
Hull GS	55	218 (1897)	Ashton in Makerfield	52	24 (1900)
Ilkley GS	48	104 (1896)	Bentham	96	40 (1894)
		64 (1902)	Bolton	67	37
Manchester GS*	250	700	Bosworth	82	5 (1886)
Nottingham HS*	192	381	Chesterfield GS	108	78 (1894)
King Edward Retford	58	100	Dartford GS	reopened	
Sedbergh*	23	147 (1887)		1866	25 (1902)
Truro*	28	41 (1892)	Loughborough	64	53 (1893)
Wallasey GS	95	180	Lymm GS	14	20 (1889)
Queen Mary's GS			Middleton GS	37	5 (1902)
Walsall	73	109	Nantwich and Acton	67	53 (1893)
			Northwich	45	38 (1897)
			Richmond	108	25
			Stamford	80	60
			Stockport GS	179	17 (1887)
					80 (1903)
			Tuxford GS	55	13 (1896)
			Alleyne's		no figures but
			Uttoxeter	75	'diminishing
					numbers'
			Whitney GS	29	14 (1896)

* Indicates school gaining at least one award (1885–92).

the later 1890s – from 98 in 1893 to 218 in 1897 – suffered acutely from the problems outlined above. In 1893 Lawson states that the average duration of attendance at the school was a mere three years two months, a point which makes the numbers in the school appear less impressive. Furthermore, the situation was not very different four years later, in 1897, when of 218 boys, only three were over 16 and only twenty over 15.[29] When we turn to the successful schools – those that steadily increased their numbers during this period – we find that many of the names are already familiar. In fact, among this 'rising' group six schools – Chigwell, Felsted, Manchester Grammar School, Sedbergh, Truro and Nottingham High School – all gained open awards in the period 1885–92.

Before considering the significance of this striking divergence of development in the sample, let us examine a number of other 'rising' schools, like Retford, Wallasey and Hull, to see why they appear among the group of 'rising' schools, although not gaining awards in this period. The answer, as far as Retford is concerned, is that its 'success' in 1890 followed a period of extreme instability when numbers had dropped to 30 (1883). The arrival of a new headmaster (1887) revived Retford temporarily, as it had revived Hull in 1893. Yet despite the increase in numbers, for Retford, the words of Church, a former headmaster of the school, remained true: 'The fact is, that during the last half of the century, the whole situation of secondary education has changed . . . Any competition with the great public schools is a hopeless waste of energy.' Church's pessimism was borne out by his successor's experience, for the school's historian, A. D. Grounds, tells us that in the last decade of the century the school's boarding side was affected by the increasing tendency of the professional classes to send their sons to 'public' schools. 'Most pupils', he writes, 'came in at eleven or twelve and left, on average, at fifteen.'[30]

Although Hull and Retford appear at first sight to have been successful schools in terms of increasing numbers, fluctuations in these numbers, partly as a consequence of pupils leaving early, place them more appropriately in the category of struggling schools.

Wallasey Grammar School is perhaps the most interesting of these three schools. The school itself was, of course, situated in a fast-growing middle-class suburb, but in this it is not unique in the sample. Its first major distinction lies in its having developed into exactly the opposite type of institution from that envisaged by the SIC and later by the Charity Commissioners. Both these bodies were convinced that the inefficiency of the old endowed grammar schools stemmed to a large extent from their trying to combine too many functions – university preparation, commercial education, education of a post-elementary type – and from doing none of these well. They resolved on *separate* institutions for the different functions – first, second and third grade, distributed as far as possible according to (a rather unscientific) projected social demand. Yet an invaluable portrait of the social organisation of Wallasey Grammar School in the last years of the century, written by an old boy of the school, shows all these functions and all the social classes which the Commissioners tried to separate, brought under one roof:

Boys in the Sixth Forms were destined for the universities and seemed to come from the more affluent homes, where the paying of fees for six or more years as well as the employment of a private tutor presented no difficulties. Tall, elegant and already well-advanced by home tutors . . . they were coached for the universities or early directorship. The intermediate forms were where the honest to goodness middle class were found. Sons of lawyers, doctors, parsons, heads of small manufacturing firms, etc. The two lowest forms contained boys whose fathers were small shop-keepers, builders, artisans. These being mostly destined for the trades were in those days apprenticed at the age of 14.[31]

Another interesting tendency can be noted at Wallasey Grammar School which, in my view, qualifies it for inclusion with the Oxbridge scholarship schools, even though its name does not appear among the list of schools winning such success. This is the fact that the school seemed to encourage its boys to enter Oxbridge after a period spent at Victoria University, Manchester. Eggleshaw recounts the history of one such scholar who, after five years at the school, won an open scholarship to Victoria University, proceeding from there to Balliol College, Oxford, where he graduated with a first in Mods. and a first in Greats. The role of the civic 'universities' at this time – both Durham and Manchester figure in the 1887 list of institutions gaining open awards – probably masks the university preparatory role of a number of grammar schools such as Wallasey.

On the basis of this examination of the large sample, two conclusions emerge clearly. Successful schools – defined in terms of steadily increasing numbers, a sizeable sixth form and an average school life of at least five years – were those schools which belonged, or virtually belonged, to the set of Oxbridge scholarship schools. The unsuccessful schools found that the demand envisaged by the Commissioners for schools which did *not* prepare for university or the professions did not exist. Instead of three grades of school, each flourishing separately and catering for a different social class, we find the gap between the successful and unsuccessful schools becoming wider. This process can in fact be conceived of in terms of a polarisation of endowed grammar schools into two groups in which the positive characteristics of the successful group find an exact counterpart in the negative characteristics of the unsuccessful group. These differences are far more pronounced in the 1890s for the schools in the sample than they were in 1867. The position of the two groups can be summarised thus:

'Rising' schools	'Sinking' schools
Numbers increase steadily.	Numbers fluctuate and decline.
Well above 1867 level by 1890.	Usually below 1867 level by 1890.
Curriculum includes Latin and Greek.	Little classical teaching. Wide range of 'modern' subjects, often taught by one or two masters.
Significant group aged 16 and over. Steady flow to universities and professions.	Boys stay for two or three years. Few over 15. Some transfer to 'rising' schools.

The larger random sample provides us with very little detail of this process of polarisation of schools into two types, and of the effects of the successful schools on the unsuccessful. This process is best observed in the smaller regional sample which I shall now discuss. The strictly regional sample comprises six schools, Appleby Grammar School, Kirkby Lonsdale Grammar School, Heversham Grammar School, John Kelsick's School, Ambleside, Windermere Bowness Grammar School and Kendal Grammar School, all in the county of Westmorland.[32]

Before we look at this sample, however, it is important to clarify what was understood by the Charity Commissioners' definitions of first-, second- and third-grade schools. They differed in three crucial areas: (i) in the curriculum, (ii) in the leaving age, and (iii) in the scale of fees. No one of these components was interchangeable, that is the Commissioners would not countenance a hybrid school with a first-grade curriculum and a second-grade scale of fees, or a third-grade curriculum and a second-grade leaving age. The patterns laid down are shown in Table 4.5. The schools in our regional sample were graded as follows:

First Grade	*Second Grade*	*Third Grade*
Heversham	Kendal	Windermere Bowness
Appleby	Kirkby Lonsdale	John Kelsick's Ambleside

This grading corresponded closely to the level of work that the schools had been doing in 1867, with the exception of Kendal, which at that time had been classified as a non-classical school.

As far as the two first-grade schools were concerned, the Commissioners appear to have been happy to grant first-grade status, not on the grounds of endowment (Westmorland being one of the few counties with no rich schools), but probably because of the value of the schools' exhibitions, which included the right to compete for the valuable Hastings exhibitions. In view of the small endowment and the small population of the county, these schools were expected to prosper by expanding their already existing boarding houses. Kendal Grammar School, a second-grade school, was expected to be mainly a day school, although it had a boarding house. Of the two third-grade schools, John Kelsick's School at Ambleside was to be devoted to elementary education, with provision in the scheme (1872) for an upper department providing third-grade education at fees of between £2 and £5 per year. It is significant for the argument to be developed here that by 1880 no parents had been found willing to pay the fee for the upper department.[33] The other third-grade establishment, at Bowness, Windermere, was established in 1883. Its amazing history is best dealt with in the section which follows, which examines the development of the schools and compares this development with the Commissioners' three-tiered conception of education in the area.

Appleby Grammar School, which we have already encountered in the larger sample, did not prosper as a first-grade school, and a new draft scheme was put forward in 1890 for comment by the governors which would have made Appleby into a second-grade school with Greek as an optional extra and a leaving age of 17. The governors complained that 'there is little chance of success for the School if conducted on classical lines – competition from Carlisle, St Bees, Heversham . . . Sedbergh, Durham, etc.' But the governors complained equally bitterly when confronted with a scheme for second-grade status. Supported by letters from Queen's College, Oxford,

Table 4.5. *The three grades of school: Charity Commissioners' definitions*

	Curriculum	Age	Fees (per annum)

First grade	English
	Latin and Greek languages
	  and literature
	Arithmetic and maths
	Geography
	History
	At least one foreign
	  European language
	Natural science
	Drawing and vocal music
		8–19	£8–12

Second grade	Geography
	History
	English grammar and
	  composition
	English literature
	Maths
	Latin
	At least one foreign
	  language
	Greek to be an optional
	  extra for which a fee must
	  be charged
		8–17
		(could be extended to 18 at
		discretion of governors)
			£6–12

Third grade	Geography History English grammar and composition Maths Drill, vocal music Latin Modern foreign languages Natural science Drawing	8–15 (could be extended to 16 at discretion of governors)	£4–8

which had a representative on the school's governing body, they maintained that although they would like a modern curriculum and lower fees, they could not think of losing the chance of competing for the Hastings exhibition. This chance would be lost if boys stayed on only until 17 and if Greek were merely optional. A compromise was reached in the new scheme of 1891 and the school allowed a leaving age of 18. Yet Leach, a Charity Commissioner, reporting in 1894, finds the school – and Queen's College – still dissatisfied:

The Governors want the leaving age raised to 19. Queen's College also favour this as it will allow them to compete better for the Hastings Exhibitions. The College authorities are of the opinion that Northern boys develop later. If there is anything in the idea, Queen's College ought to know if anyone does. At all events it is likely to handicap the school in competition if the limit is not raised.[34]

Appleby was unhappy within the straitjacket of first-grade status, but while wanting more flexibility was not prepared to lose the chance of preparing pupils for Oxbridge scholarships. Meanwhile, Kendal Grammar School was equally dissatisfied with the restrictions of second-grade status. The school possessed a number of valuable exhibitions which could be held at Oxford or Cambridge, and also acquired the right to compete for the Hastings scholarships. Although the school opened in new buildings only in 1890, by 1895 it had 104 pupils. Yet soon after the school had opened, the headmaster petitioned the Commissioners for a change in status. His description of the school sounds very similar to that of Wallasey Grammar School, mentioned above. The school, he wrote, contained three groups: a small number preparing for Oxford and Cambridge, a larger number preparing for professional examinations, and a still larger number who desired to be prepared directly and practically for business.[35]

According to the Commissioners' theory, Kendal should have contained only the second of these three groups, and they decided to ignore the headmaster's request 'as it was made informally'. It is in the case of Kendal Grammar School that we can clearly see the extent to which second-grade status, if strictly adhered to, made it extremely difficult for a school to gain membership of the Oxbridge scholarship school group. The first obstacle encountered by the second-grade school was the restriction that Greek could only be taught as an optional extra and at an extra fee. This may at first sight appear to be of little importance, but from the debate over the regrading of Kendal, Greek emerges as *essential for success* in gaining Oxbridge awards. A letter from the Provost of Queen's College, Oxford, dated 9 March 1898 and supporting Kendal's case, states that no scholar would be allowed to compete for the Hastings exhibitions *unless he offered himself for examination in Greek*.[36] And second-grade status meant not only the handicap of optional Greek but also a maximum leaving age of 18, whereas Queen's had asserted most strongly in the case of Appleby that for university entrance, a leaving age of 19 was desirable. Finally, we learn from the correspondence between Kendal Grammar School and the Commissioners that at that period, at least, membership of the Headmasters' Conference was denied to schools where an extra fee for Greek was imposed, that is second-grade schools. Kendal Grammar School finally won the battle for Greek in 1898, but the Commission stood firm on one point. Greek as part of the curriculum meant first-grade status and first-grade status meant first-grade fees: 'To concede it [Greek] at £5 would be most unfair to Keswick, Appleby and other schools in the district. *We cannot look on these matters as they affect only one school.*'[37]

Kendal was not the only second-grade school to apply for and win first-grade status in the last decade of the century. Portsmouth Grammar School, which had risen even more meteorically from a school with no pupils to a place in the *Pall Mall Gazette* of 1887, also requested and obtained first-grade status in 1892.

If second-grade status proved in the long run to be an undesirable state of limbo, then from our small sample, at least, third-grade status just did not work at all. Mention has already been made of the third-grade upper department at John Kelsick's School in Ambleside, where no parent was interested in paying the fee demanded. Even more remarkable, as I have already suggested, was the story of Windermere Bowness Grammar School, founded as a third-grade school in 1883. Nine years later, in 1892, the school only had 8 pupils, but after the arrival of a new headmaster in 1892 and considerable reorganisation, numbers rose to 51 by 1893. Chemistry and Greek were introduced into the curriculum, a chemistry laboratory was built and a sound commercial department was started. By 1896 the school had started to win scholarships, and in 1897 the school had a sixth form and a pupil had obtained a senior open scholarship in Natural Science at Clare College, Cambridge.[38]

Almost as soon as the new headmaster arrived in 1892, he and the governors had raised with the Commissioners the question of first-grade status for the school, stressing particularly that they would like Greek to be taught. The headmaster also added in a letter that 'he has 2 boys now in the school who, if they are allowed to remain until 19 are certain to obtain Open Scholarships at Oxford'. On this occasion, however, the Commissioners refused to give way, stating that '*it would be unwise to add to the supply of First Grade boarding schools in the district*'.[39] By 1901 a report shows that Windermere Bowness Grammar School had reverted to low-level work and was merely entering pupils for the Oxford Local Examinations.

The Charity Commissioners' main concern, as it emerges from this detailed study, appears to have been the viability, as classical schools preparing for Oxford and Cambridge, of the group of first-grade schools. This viability could only be maintained by protecting this group from aspiring lower-grade schools by means of curricular obstacles, notably Greek, and by structural obstacles such as the upper age limit of boys in the school. This policy might have succeeded if the SIC had made a correct analysis of the way in which demand for secondary education would develop in the following thirty years. Our analysis suggests, however, that all three grades of school, as conceived by the SIC and put into practice by the Endowed Schools Commissioners and by the Charity Commissioners, were unviable in their pure form.

Discussion and conclusion

During the period 1867–97 an identifiable set of schools emerged which was publicly defined by its ability to place pupils in high-status positions. These schools have been generically characterised as 'schools gaining open awards at Oxford and Cambridge'. A process of differentiation thus emerges based on the schools' relationship to the social structure. Yet the Oxbridge scholarship schools are not only identifiable in terms of the careers of their pupils, but also share common features of structure and curriculum. The existence in the schools of a number of pupils aged 18 and over and the teaching of Greek as an integral part of the curriculum have been seen to be crucial for membership of this group. Consequently, when we confront the two poles of the secondary system in 1897 we find surface structural and curricular differences which do not appear to relate instrumentally to the 'deep' social structure (see Table 4.6).

What we must supply and interpose between deep and surface structure are the assumptions of this period about the hierarchy of knowledge which served as a basis for judging a pupil's fitness for occupational status. The fact that we can see the 'surface' structures of the group of successful schools emerging as a result of changes in the type of qualification required for access to elite status does not answer the question of *why* these particular structures? The conventions of meritocratic selection which became institutionalised in the nineteenth century were not the result of an objective appraisal of the capacities required for high-status positions. At the origin of the development of education as a system linked to occupational status lies the definition of the criteria by which suitability for elite status is to be determined. In England the criteria selected were those qualities and styles of thought traditionally fostered in the schools of the upper classes. This 'cultural style' was elevated to the level of a set of objective criteria to be used in the selection of an elite. The notion of 'cultural style' enables us to link the *apparently arbitrary* elements of 'surface' structure and 'deep' structure, instead of merely noting the links in terms of the circular flow of generations of individuals through a set of educational institutions and occupational statuses.

It is thus being asserted that the cultural style of the upper classes in early nineteenth-century England resulting from the interaction of what Gladstone called 'birth and training' was gradually institutionalised after 1830 into the essential element of qualification for high-status positions. Since the 'public' schools in the narrowest sense (the Nine) had traditionally provided the training element or secondary socialisation of the upper classes, they became the *defining institutions* of the emerging system of secondary education. Their curriculum, length of schooling and the like became the norms to which institutions aspiring to elite status had to approximate. This is powerfully demonstrated, in my view, by the fact that the SIC *started* their analysis of a possible structure of secondary education in England from the *existence* of 'public' schools, their strong ties with elite institutions and by implication with elite status. First-grade schools were then *necessarily* defined by the Commission as schools which positively approximated as closely as possible to the existing set of 'public' schools, the defining

Table 4.6. *Two poles of the secondary system*

	Oxbridge scholarship schools	'Struggling' secondary schools
Surface structure	Greek Pupils over 18	No Greek No pupils over 18
Deep structure	Access to high-status positions	No access to high-status positions

institutions. Second- and third-grade schools were also defined in terms of the 'public' schools, but as negative approximations, as sets of schools which could not achieve the cultural style of the 'public' schools because of deficiencies in their surface structure (for example, the limit on the length of schooling and the absence of Greek).

While the positive and negative approximations persisted throughout the period 1867–97, our regional sample has shown that schools were not bound by the Commissioners' grading but aspired successfully or unsuccessfully to a positive approximation. Both the regional and the random samples demonstrate the general unviability of the negative approximation, and our analysis supplies the grounds of this unviability. Second- and third-grade schools were not designed positively to prepare for a particular group of occupational positions, but were designed negatively by the Commission *not* to prepare for high occupational status. The schools that grew and flourished, both first- and second-grade, were those which acquired a positive approximation to the defining institutions. The schools which we described as struggling, both first- and second-grade, were those which failed to break out of the negative approximation and its negative connotations.

This study took as its starting-point general assumptions of the increasing importance of social reproduction through schools in a period when qualifications assumed greater significance for high-status posts. This was followed by an empirical examination of school types in this period. From this empirical examination more precise statements have emerged about the process of interaction between the sets of schools composing the system. What has been noted is that the group of schools identified as successful in terms of Oxbridge scholarships can be seen to share with each other common characteristics of structure, curriculum and development. At the same time, the group of schools characterised as 'struggling' and whose pupils do not win Oxbridge awards also manifest common characteristics of structure, curriculum and growth. It is in this sense that the idea of the *systematisation* of secondary schools in England *can* be put forward, that is the emergence of groups of schools clearly distinguishable from each other in their surface structures and in their relationship to the occupational structure.

5. The reconstruction of secondary education in England, 1869–1920

DAVID REEDER

The contention of this chapter is that educational development in England, as in other European countries, was associated with a movement from a relatively undifferentiated set of institutions to a differentiated system. A key element in this movement was the grading of schools, as we have seen in Chapters 3 and 4. The principle of grading was not only operative in the provision of schools for the higher reaches of society. In the later nineteenth century the evolution of publicly provided, as well as privately sponsored, systems of schooling involved a range of responses to the needs of increasingly differentiated social groups. As society became more complex, so the principle of grading schools was extended further down the social scale, although developments on the ground were not necessarily in accord with official policy. The claim of this chapter, indeed, is that developments in the cities generated a new and critical phase of structural change. The chapter draws on the existing historical literature on the emergence of secondary education as a concept and as an organised provision of state-assisted municipal schools, to provide a case study. What has to be explained is how the adaptation of English education to economic and social change, as represented by the development of local urban systems, came to be regulated eventually by a common acquiescence in a status hierarchy at whose apex were the 'public' schools and Oxbridge.[1]

The evolution of publicly provided schooling involved the establishment of different types of school with different curricula, leaving ages, staffs and clientele. This differentiation can be regarded in one sense as an outcome of the schools' response to market forces operating at a grassroots level. One ingredient in these forces was the growth, and more importantly, the diversity of demand for secondary instruction on the part of the middle classes, as has already been illustrated.[2] A related ingredient was the status aspirations of larger sections of the population, particularly the lower middle class and upper working classes. As W. E. Marsden's socio-geographical investigations have shown, 'the characteristically English influence' of 'a compulsive, individualistic quest for status' not only contributed to the development of forms of post-elementary schooling but had implications for the organisation of elementary schooling as a whole in the larger towns and cities.[3] It seems that a process of ecological adaptation was taking place after 1870, with school catchment areas reflecting the emergence in the towns and cities of territorially bound, socially homogeneous communities. The charging of school fees made possible the grading of schools and enabled a perceived hierarchy of schooling to develop related to the social tone of different neighbourhoods.

This chapter traces out the impact of social pressures on grammar schools and the emergence of a putative modern sector of education based on the post-elementary schools in late Victorian towns and cities. However, an account of structural change presented only in terms of social demand pressures would be too deterministic. The pattern of development was not simply a function of impersonal market forces mediated by headmasters and school managers. It was also a function of the growing involvement of the state in education through the creation of new local and central bodies. This account adopts the view that such governmental agencies not only contributed to a greater complexity of administration, as those who defended the Education Act of 1902 claimed, but also brought political and ideological attitudes and interests to bear on the situation. The implications of developments in post-elementary schooling for the future of secondary education, and for the crucial divide beween the elementary and secondary levels, were such as to embroil city schools in a conflict between local ambitions and centralist anxieties. This chapter will argue that new political and bureaucratic initiatives were taken to overcome what was perceived as a structural crisis in the provision of education at the local level, a crisis fuelled by, and gaining in significance from, the impact of industrialisation and urbanisation on older cultural assumptions and on dispositions of social power.[4] Centralist intervention was the decisive factor in the reconstruction or reshaping of secondary education, as carried through by the early twentieth century.

The conviction that a reconstruction of schooling was needed, first came to the fore in England as a public issue in the early 1860s, and in relation to the education of the middle classes, as Brian Simon has explained. Several elements in the mid-Victorian situation require to be restated briefly as pointers to later developments. It is worth reiterating first that the Schools Inquiry Commission was a product of concern about the relevance of traditional institutions, and of the associated ideas of liberal culture, to a new society. The Commissioners were persuaded of the social dangers implicit in a threatened hiatus between the schooling of the middle class and the liberal training of the universities. They were concerned, therefore, to devise a plan that would provide in middle-class schools an educative core of liberal study, whilst allowing for the modernisation of the curricula, and that would take account of the different levels of income and aspiration among the middle class. Hence the idea of grading. The Endowed Schools Commissioners, set up in 1869, were intended to use the Report of the Schools Inquiry Commission as a guide to classifying schools 'to meet the different demands for education existing in society'.[5] In the event, the reconstruction of middle-class schooling was not to be achieved in this way despite the number of schemes that were made for individual schools.[6] It would have been a herculean task given the number (nearly 3000) of endowments, their maldistribution, and the complicated legal procedures; but any ambitions for systematic reconstruction were to be defeated by intense local hostility towards the schemes, which derived not only from principled opposition to their proposals, but also from the vested interests of individual headmasters and local groups. Nevertheless, the idea of a three-grade system was an enduring one, notably among members of the educational bureaucratic establishment being formed in the later nineteenth century; it was still being invoked, for example, by staff inspectors of the Board of Education in the early twentieth century in relation to the public provision of secondary schools.[7]

The Schools Inquiry Commission had been convinced that grammar schools would not be able to meet new demands unless endowments could be reorganised. They were able to point to the growth of private and proprietary schools as filling the void – the 100 proprietary schools, 72 founded since 1820, and an estimated 10,000 private schools, of which an unknown proportion were private English and commercial schools.[8] The grammar schools had been responsive to some extent, however, to demand for elementary and commercial subjects despite restraints on change in the statutes of foundations. By the 1860s, of 820 endowed grammar schools investigated, a total of 198 schools functioned only as elementary schools. The implication of this 'decline' according to one commentator is that endowed grammar schools were becoming increasingly schools for the children of the working class,[9] but the data on the occupational backgrounds of pupils gathered by the Schools Inquiry Commission does not support such a claim. In south-west Lancashire, to take a district for which this data has been carefully studied, in respect of eight non-classical or semi-classical schools and two classical schools, only 10.5 per cent of pupils (56 out of a sample of 531 pupils) had working-class fathers (artisans and labourers). These schools were serving predominantly a middle-class clientele.[10] Furthermore, there was no correlation between the list of lower-class pupils and 'free' places. On the contrary, in this district, as elsewhere in the country, the chief beneficiaries of foundation places were shopkeepers and tradesmen (and to a lesser extent skilled artisans) – a process of lower middle-class 'takeover' begun in Lancashire after the turn of the eighteenth century when the provision of schools of all kinds had failed to keep pace with population growth.[11]

The pressure of demand from lower middle-class parents also affected the curriculum and social composition of the Church schools subsidised by the government in order to provide an elementary schooling for working-class children. In some parts of the country, for example, Church schools were developing classes beyond the standards in 'higher tops'. As an Assistant Commissioner to the Schools Inquiry Commission pointed out with regard to a manufacturing 'frontier' district in Lancashire, Privy Council (grant-aided) schools were being used to a very large extent 'by those of what would be counted a socially superior class'.[12]

This use of elementary schools by children of the lower middle class anticipated later developments. But it had already become an anxiety for government education officials in the 1860s, who made efforts to define more strictly the clientele of grant-aided elementary schools.[13] The Schools Inquiry Commission, too, concerned to ensure that the lower middle class would not patronise the elementary schools, established effective third-grade grammar schools offering a curriculum not very different from that available in the higher classes of elementary schools. This was necessary because a common accusation against the endowed grammar schools as they existed was that they frequently turned out very bad clerks for the sake of a few good scholars.[14] The Commission also sought to introduce scholarships for elementary school pupils to replace the 'free' places that had been available in the endowed schools. This served to underline further the class divide as between elementary and secondary 'third-grade' schooling. In addition the meritocratic principle which the idea of such scholarships implied provided a rationale for diverting charitable funds to the extension of middle-class fee-paying education.

All of which points to social pressure for higher-level elementary provision building up before the Education Act of 1870. Whilst the Anglican education society (The National Society) subsidised Church middle or commercial schools, Non-conformist school managers also seem to have responded by forming what was in effect a new order of school for the upper working-class and lower middle-class fringe population. These Non-conformist schools were largely self-supporting 'and regulated in fees beyond the means of the poor'; the fees charged, however, were pitched sufficently low to bring criticisms of subsidising the middle classes.[15] The argument that middle-class parents should pay a proper level of fee for the schooling of their children was to be repeated in later debates.

It is also important to notice how new developments were affecting the middle-class patronage of the town grammar schools in the mid-Victorian period. Among these developments were the revival in the demand for classics, the charging of capitation fees and the growth of boarding, developments which enabled a school to expand beyond the confines of a town and to tap a national market. In consequence some endowments began to move in the direction of the wealthier sections of the middle class, as Hilary Steedman has shown in Chapter 4. In the Schools Inquiry Commission's Return of 820 endowed grammar schools, 100 were already classifiable as first-grade schools, providing mainly a classical education to the age of 18, and the majority of these were boarding schools or mixed day and boarding, with an average size of 94 pupils. In contrast, 472 second- and third-grade schools had an average size of only 58 pupils.[16]

The growth of boarding and improvements in railway communications meant that schools could operate independently of the size of local settlements; indeed, many prestigious boarding schools were located in rural districts, small country towns or historic centres. Amongst these, the so-called 'great' schools had consolidated their position as upper-class schools by the middle of the century. Further pressure on boarding-school facilities continued to be exerted, it seems, by upper-class parents and this was the dominant factor in the unprecedented rise in the number of minor 'public' schools between the 1840s and the 1870s.[17] At the same time, the establishment and growth of new private and proprietary schools as 'public' schools evidently owed much to demand from the 'economic' middle class for this kind of education, although it seems probable that parents with children at such schools were more likely to have a commercial or financial background, as opposed to a manufacturing one, until the later nineteenth century. The best of these schools may have drawn from metropolitan-based wealth rather more than from provincial-based wealth, partly because the upper reaches of the London middle class were in any case closer to the old society anyway.[18] In the 1860s an Assistant Commissioner was able to claim that the real distinction in middle-class education lay between parents of great wealth and those of moderate affluence. For the former, boarding schools offered an opportunity of associating with members of the higher professions and were attractive to those restlessly eager to seek after alliances 'with the landed gentry, with Parliament, with the magistracy'. For other parents local schools were more appropriate.[19] Thus it was possible for some of the city grammar schools to retain the patronage of a local professional and business class as classical schools and on the basis of a judicious mixture of day and boarding, as in the case of Birmingham's Grammar School.[20] The success of Liverpool Collegiate Institution, a well-known proprietary school, on the basis mainly of day scholars, but organised into three types of school, may have been exceptional.[21] However, some of the London schools successfully moved to first-grade status with a considerable day clientele because of the diversity of railway communications.[22] Nevertheless, the implication of John Honey's account (in Chapter 6) of the formation of a 'public' school system is that the social spectrum of higher-status schooling was eventually enlarged to incorporate the children of a provincial business and professional class based on the cities – and this was even more the case with high-status girls' schools.[23] Here was a development with implications for local urban elites whose family dynastic ambitions drew them into patronising 'public' schools even when their civic loyalties and the locus of their wealth were centred on the industrial and commercial cities. Whilst it was possible in an old commercial city such as Bristol for the local elite to support the founding of a prestigious boarding school with some day scholars (Clifton College), the tendency in the northern and Midland cities was for the top elite to educate their own children out of the city. Given this latter tendency, it may have been easier for local elites to adopt expansionist and meritocratic policies with regard to local schooling, as they did in Birmingham, for example, in the last two decades of the century.[24]

Hilary Steedman's argument in Chapter 4, on the basis of a systematic regional analysis, for a polarisation between the most successful of the endowed grammar schools and the rest after 1869 is very relevant to the situation of the town schools, many of which failed to make the top grade and remained dependent on a local clientele. There was considerable variation in experience, but the grammar schools, in the market towns especially, found the task of reappraising their role particularly difficult and fraught with conflict.[25] In these market towns the grammar school was frequently regarded as *the* town school, and attempts to change its status were fiercely resisted. Conflicts arose over the nature of foundation places, the charging of capitation fees, boarders, and the relevance of the classics to local needs. The group most involved in resisting change was a petty bourgeoisie of tradesmen and shopkeepers excluded from the costlier and more select of the private schools, who preferred the cheapness and the aura of gentility of the grammar school to the private commercial school.[26] In towns with large endowments, as at Bedford, it was possible to preserve the status of the classical grammar school whilst funding new developments to accommodate local pressures, whether by the introduction of modern sides into the grammar school or by the founding of an entirely separate modern school, variously called a 'middle', or an English or commercial school.[27] The latter schools contributed yet another strand to the genesis of a modern sector, except that the tendency to horizontal segregation implicit in the differentiation of curriculum and schools was limited by financial resources and overtaken by events. In any case many schools survived only by developing a kind of *à la carte* curriculum of different subjects or groups of subjects in a catch-all manner.[28] It was not impossible for a well-placed school, such as the United Westminster Schools in London, to establish a credibility which enabled it to retain a considerable social mix; yet there were many schools which failed to establish a social identity and suffered in consequence from fluctuating rolls. In the larger cities an added complication was the cost of erecting new buildings in an effort to pursue the middle class into the suburbs, thus creating financial burdens of the kind that dogged Bristol Grammar School, for example.[29]

After 1870 the urban endowed grammar schools were caught up in an increasingly fluid situation, especially in the larger cities, having to relate to new institutions of technical and higher education and coming up against competition from new types of municipally controlled higher elementary schools. The paradox of the 1880s in urban education is that whilst this decade witnessed a peak in the grading of schooling at all levels, new developments seemed to threaten an 'alternative' system involving the higher elementary schools, evening classes and technical day classes in colleges, a system rendered cohesive by the provision of scholarships. In fact the situation was not quite so straightforward; but when the Royal Commission on Secondary Education reported in 1895 they recognised that higher elementary day and evening classes were to an extent making good the failure of the Endowed Schools Act to reform the grammar schools and make third-grade provision more readily available.[30]

Developments at the municipal level were in themselves a stimulus to a growth in demand for secondary instruction, but the extent and nature of demand reflected major changes in the economy in the later nineteenth century. The most important of these was a structural shift from manufacturing to commerce and services and, consequent on this, the expansion and transformation of the lower middle class by a new group of salaried clerical and commercial employees and members of the minor professions, including the elementary school teachers. A striking feature of the late Victorian economy was the overall growth of specialised non-manual occupations, which increased by 72 per cent between 1881 and 1911, compared with an increase of 48 per cent in all occupations and 41 per cent in manual occupations.[31] Meritocratic career opportunities were no longer expanding as they had done, for the rate of increase from 1881 to 1901 in the growth of professions was not much more than that of the population as a whole. However, new career opportunities were becoming available because of the growth of specialised non-manual occupations where large-scale organisations of labour were occurring. The increasing scale of organisation involved changes in methods of recruitment, as in clerking for example, with positions opened up to competitive examinations, or at the very least the public notification of job vacancies.[32] A consequence was that schooling came to be valued more than hitherto, both as a means of social ascent for the children of working-class parents and as a way by which lower middle-class parents might consolidate their social position. In this last respect it has been noted that the expansion of a 'white-collar' work force was associated with a heightening of the anxiety and frustration characteristic of the ambiguities in the status position of the lower middle class. This may have been the most important factor accounting for the pressure on educational facilities in the last decade of the nineteenth century.[33]

The impact of changes affecting manufacturing industry on the school situation in the later nineteenth century is more problematic. In so far as industrialists had any interest in school qualifications, the tendency was for them to have a low estimate of their value as far as their employees were concerned. A tradition of recruiting to supervisory posts from the industrial–practical man rather than from the technically qualified man was strongly persistent in British industry.[34] Yet in a period of growing anxiety about economic forces abroad and declining competitiveness at home, the argument for an expansion of scientific and technical education in the 'national interest' had more credence. Moreover, the introduction of new technology in some industries, and the consequent growth of larger concentrations of capital, meant that employers and workers were having to adapt to new conditions. An increase in the tendency to recruit at a variety of levels and an acceptance of the need for educational certification for many trades were two developments facilitating technical education as represented by the growth of day science classes and schools and the proliferation of evening classes with specific vocational courses. The little evidence we have about the kind of post-elementary education preferred by different class groups suggests that skilled manual workers in particular might be more inclined to favour a technical education for their sons (and a literary or commercial education for their daughters).[35] Nevertheless, a greater proportion of clerks and elementary school teachers – male as well as female – were being recruited from the working class in the later nineteenth century.

The overall expansion of post-elementary education and the growth of scholarships fostered a limited degree of social mobility through education. The number of scholarships provided by local authorities increased tenfold between 1895 and 1906, with the extent of provision varying between localities.[36] These scholarships were competed for, in the main, by children from parents of a lower middle-class or skilled artisan background. Since there was a much greater number of minor scholarships than major scholarships available, access to office and commercial employment was opened up more readily than that to higher-level occupations. This situation created a dilemma for the publicists of scientific and technical education: in seeking to enlarge the pool of talent available for industrial occupations by encouraging meritocratic policies, they were in effect encouraging the diversion of children from artisan backgrounds into clerical and commercial occupations.[37]

New developments were centred on the cities and industrial districts, whose elective municipal school authorities, the School Boards, pressed ahead to improve the quality and duration of elementary schooling as the Education Act of 1870 had intended. If progress was slow in rural areas, it was quite otherwise in many urban districts, where School Boards began to provide instruction beyond the elementary grades (or standards), promoting in effect secondary instruction of a practical and quasi-vocational nature, either in the higher grades of the existing schools or in separately established higher-grade and day science schools. The formation of pupil-teacher centres to recruit and train elementary school teachers, and the development of evening continuation classes, also constituted additions to post-elementary provision in the cities.

The higher-grade schools, as embodiments of a new order of secondary school, were the most important of these developments. They were frequently purpose-built showpiece schools, larger than the average grammar school, often with a thousand or more pupils, and provided with good laboratory and workshop facilities. They represented a considerable investment on the part of the School Boards. Although the number of schools actually built by 1902 was relatively small – probably about 85 – the ones that had been built were thriving, well-supported schools, and from the point of view of the School Boards and the National Union of Teachers a portent for the future.[38] They were most numerous in the towns and cities of the West Riding of Yorkshire and parts of Lancashire, where endowed school provision was particularly weak. Bradford provided one model, with six schools by the 1890s situated peripherally in socially respectable areas, graded in fees, but with a good level (25 per cent) of scholarship entry. In contrast, Sheffield went for a large, centrally situated school intended for clever and deserving children across the city.[39] Others followed the example set by Bradford and Sheffield, but not until the 1890s. Thus Bristol, an old commercial centre with a range of endowed schools, began to support higher-grade provision only after the annexation of new suburbs, whilst Southport, a northern residential town with much private schooling, set up two centrally located schools, only to see the Education Act of 1902 lead to their loss of higher-grade status.[40] Overall, higher-grade schools drew on the same clientele as the smaller grammar schools, that is on the lower-middle and upper working-class groups, but they were probably more progressive in drawing a greater proportion of pupils from the lower class groups (see Table 5.1). Many of them had low fees relative to grammar schools or no fees at all.

It seems likely that post-elementary provision contributed more than traditional schooling to the growth and inclusiveness of English education in the last two decades of the century. Between 1870 and 1901 the proportion of 14-year-olds enrolled in some form of schooling rose from 2 per cent to about 9 per cent. The official statistics show a pronounced increase in the

Table 5.1. *Socio-economic classification of parents of scholars at selected public secondary and higher-grade board schools, 1897, in percentages*

	Secondary boys	H-g boys	H-g girls
Upper middle class	38.9	11.0	10.6
Lower middle class	46.6	42.0	45.2
Skilled artisans	8.1	32.7	29.6
Unskilled	1.0	7.3	7.8
Others	4.2	6.2	6.0

Source: Board of Education, *Return Concerning Certain Higher Grade Board Schools and Public Secondary Schools, 1898*, LXX, pp. 10–11.

proportion of the age group 12–15 on the registers of the public elementary schools. On the other hand, the endowed schools cannot be altogether discounted as contributors to growth despite the uneven provision.

The situation was complicated by the availability of finance intended for the support of science and technical education, which could be drawn on by grammar schools as well as by higher-grade schools. From 1870 the Department of Science and Art, a central examining and financing body, considerably extended its activity. By 1898–9 a total of 53,628 students were attending day science classes linked to the Directory of the Science and Art Department. Of these, 27,399 students were enrolled in the municipal higher elementary schools, but there were 8,092 students enrolled in science classes in 162 endowed grammar schools – a testimony to the success of the Department in overcoming the prejudices of the headmasters of the smaller grammar schools about the 'intrusion' of science.[41] These latter schools had a greater proportion of ex-elementary pupils than the first-grade schools, which had relatively few or none at all.[42] Nor were science grants and scholarships the only financial incentives to specialisation on the part of lesser grammar schools. The passage of the Technical Instruction Acts of 1889–91 empowered County and County Borough Councils, first brought into existence in 1888, to levy rates and draw on a government subsidy to finance technical education, defined very broadly to include a variety of modern subjects. Some of the money voted for this purpose found its way by various channels to irrigate the wider field of secondary education in the form of junior and senior scholarships and in building and other grants.[43]

The impact of such developments on the evolving pattern of secondary education at the local level is difficult to assess because of different local policies and circumstances. A number of County Councils set out to foster the grammar schools as 'intermediate' schools linked by scholarships to new provincial institutions of higher education. In such circumstances lesser town grammar schools were revived or reconstituted (often as mixed schools) with the aid of technical instruction funds.[44] And in some of the cities the elective School Boards also developed a perspective of having a cohesive system in which grammar schools might be accorded a secure place within a local status hierarchy. In Birmingham, for example, the higher elementary schools of the School Board were relegated to a lower division linking up mainly with the municipal technical college and its evening classes. The Birmingham grammar schools forged links with the local university college, whilst the high school had links with Oxbridge.[45] But in other parts of the country, in other cities as well as in rural districts, the situation was more confused, with grammar school headmasters feeling threatened by higher-grade provision and the potential loss of scholarship winners. Even *The Times* recognised that opposition to the higher-grade schools 'comes now from small endowed schools, which are beginning to feel their competition, and from those persons who wish to see Secondary Education placed under County Councils and find that in the large towns School Boards are already in the field'.[46] There were reasons for such anxieties as some grammar schools were suffering from falling rolls. The problems of grammar schools were such that until about 1911 most university colleges found themselves undertaking secondary instruction in order to remedy the low attainments of former grammar school students. In a sense the higher-grade schools might have been perceived as less of a threat if they had remained schools of science or concentrated only on practical and quasi-vocational subjects; but they were combining that kind of bias with a variety of subject offerings and with aspirations to develop a school ethos and become fully fledged secondary schools providing students for the university colleges. In so far as higher-grade provision represented a continuity of schooling with the elementary sector, as it did, these schools can be represented as an 'organic' growth which threatened to overcome the vertical segmentation of the system.[47]

In this light the Education Act of 1902 had structural as well as administrative implications. After 1902 secondary (grammar) school education was to come under the aegis of County and County Borough Councils in new local education authorities, with the finances of the grammar schools being drawn from local rates and central exchequer grants. Within a few years 494 endowed (foundation) schools were taken over and brought onto the grant list (for some of which the grants offered a financial lifeline). The Act of 1902 made possible the reinstatement of the grammar school as the only recognised type of public secondary education.

The 'consensus' view of the Act of 1902 is that legislation was necessary to rationalise a confusion of administrative authorities and to lay the basis for an expansion of secondary provision within a co-ordinated national system. The need for rationalisation was put forward in the Report of the Royal Commission on Secondary Education (1895), whose recommendations were mainly intended to overcome what the Commission saw as the administrative and conceptual problems inhibiting the development of an 'organic' system. As for the structure of secondary education, the Commission was content to recommend an updated version of tripartite grading, but incorporating technical education as a 'species of the genus'.[48] The general outlook of the Commissioners was symptomatic of a developing 'establishment' view about the need for social and cultural unity in the context of anxieties about national efficiency and the urge to reassert the values of 'Englishness'. But in the case of secondary education the consensus formula was overtaken by political and social conflicts (not to mention religious conflicts) about who should have control over schooling in the interests of new policy objectives. Political and ideological differences emerged to shape perceptions of an educational crisis and the way it was to be resolved.

The impetus for change in the later nineteenth century had come mainly, as earlier, from Liberal reformers – politicians and educationists – active in forming a climate of opinion favourable to expansionist and meritocratic educational policies, and prominent also in emphasising the need for modernising the curriculum of secondary instruction. The Liberal campaign influenced developments in several ways. It was a factor, for example, in the work of the more vigorous of the Technical Instruction Committees and, to that extent – in giving County and County Borough Councils a stake in the administration of secondary schools – paved the way for the Education Act of 1902. However, the Liberal campaign also reinforced the political and civic ambitions of members of elective urban School Boards (many of whom were Liberal Non-conformists). By the 1890s the extension and defence of the work of some of the largest of the School Boards had come to be based on an alliance between anti-Church radical Liberals and new Labour organisations in a form of popular politics. This last development was crucial in generating a vigorous political reaction to School Boards and their policies on the part of a powerful Conservative–Anglican alliance. As Brian Simon has documented, the Education Act of 1902 was conceived in a climate hostile to the political as well as to the educational ambitions of the cities.[49]

This overtly political reaction can be regarded as an aspect of a wider regrouping of social and educational forces led by representatives of established elites recruited from the 'public' schools and Oxbridge. Endowed school headmasters formed one such group, campaigning against higher-grade schools even after the agreement to recognise the claims of these schools in a joint memorandum of 1897 with the Association of Higher-Grade Headmasters.[50] In the debate about the formation of the Board of Education in 1899, endowed school headmasters enlisted the aid of the ancient universities to defeat the threat of an administrative takeover by upstart officials of the former Department of Science and Art.[51] In consequence the administrative control of secondary education was separated from technical education and a new group of Oxbridge civil servants was put into a position to influence subsequent developments.

One of the first moves against the higher-grade school was to define, by a minute of 1900, the 'inferior' character of all higher elementary schools, which were not to keep children beyond the age of 14 and were to be regarded as preparatory to manual and industrial occupations – a conception which was to influence the character of subsequent developments in higher elementary schooling throughout the inter-war years. As the Consultative Committee to the Board of Education made clear in 1906: 'The higher elementary school completes the regular course of organised schooling; the secondary school not necessarily. The two types of school prepare for different walks of life – the one for the lower ranks of industry and commerce, the other for the higher ranks and for the liberal professions.'[52] After 1902 local authorities were left in no doubt about the critical attitude of the Board of Education to the erstwhile higher-grade schools in view of the difficulties experienced in having these schools recognised as Division A (science bias) secondary schools, in contrast to the more favourable treatment of the endowed schools. The recognition of higher-grade schools could only be obtained at the cost of separation from elementary teaching and the raising of fees.

There were two key elements in these attitudes. One was the suspicion and hostility of Board officials and some of the staff inspectors towards elementary school teachers, especially the new breed of higher elementary teachers, trained and certified, some with part-time degrees, and with experience, possibly, of teaching in the pupil-teacher centres. It is worth noting that in the centres and some of the colleges, intending teachers were making use of a range of texts with pedagogical theories which relayed a generally optimistic view of the potentiality of the population at large for educational improvement.[53] The teachers bore the brunt of a diffuse attack on the educational ambitions of the School Boards, an attack which reflected contemporary anxiety about the cultural isolation of the entire white-collar stratum. The Secretary to the Board of Education, Robert Morant, a civil servant of strong hierarchical views, made much, for example, of the need for prospective teachers to pass through the grammar schools and come under the influence of liberal culture.[54]

A second key element in the attitudes of the Board of Education was that of the relationship between the centre and the localities. The Regulations of 1904 on the curriculum of public secondary schools should be assessed in this light. These Regulations attempted to impose a balanced curriculum of general education on all grant-aided secondary schools, a conception which reflected contemporary educational unease about premature specialisation and curricular distortion from an undue concentration on scientific and technical subjects.[55] But there was more involved. The Regulations were influenced in part by Treasury opinion about how best to control expenditure on secondary education.[56] Above all, they were a way of establishing Board control over the curriculum and hence the social composition of the secondary schools, as Morant had intended. In that context the inclusion of science in the balanced curriculum had considerable ideological significance.[57] The Regulations were subsequently relaxed, making possible both a renewed debate about the nature of secondary education and a degree of differentiation – the latter through the introduction of practical subjects, especially in the curriculum of the early leavers.[58] Yet the conception of a balanced curriculum remained and was reinforced by the subject groupings and philosophy of the School Certificate examinations, introduced by the Board of Education in 1918 to be operated in conjunction with university matriculation boards. These examinations enabled the local grammar schools to extend their links with provincial universities; they also provided a means of prescribing a defined amount of liberal culture for all grammar school children, including the majority of children for whom the 16-plus examination was a leaving certificate. The future of the grammar school in a local status hierarchy was assured when employers began to insist on university matriculation standards as necessary for employment in commercial and professional occupations.[59]

Fritz Ringer has observed that in England an academic type of education was extended to a wider range of social groups than in France or Germany.[60] This was a concomitant of the rigid separation of secondary grammar from post-elementary forms of schooling. On the one hand, the restrictive role of higher elementary schools meant that they were not able to thrive and could not successfully divert working-class children away from secondary education. On the other hand, the new pupil-teacher Regulations of 1903, bursaries for those pledged to teaching, and the free place system introduced in 1907 to satisfy the meritocratic principles of Liberals (and pressure from Labour sources), all contributed to a change in the social composition of the grammar schools as the number of children entering from elementary schools and the number of girls increased. Hence by 1911 there were under 8000 higher elementary pupils, but over 82,000 ex-elementary pupils on scholarships in secondary schools.[61] If the assumption is made that free places – amounting to about a third of all places in 1908–9 – were taken up by children from the working class, this must have contributed to improving the progressiveness of traditional secondary education. Thus in 1913 just over 20 per cent of the boys in grammar schools had working-class fathers, albeit mainly in skilled manual occupations (see Table 5.2).

It is by no means clear, however, how far access ratios were increased after 1902. On the face of it the 1902 Act made possible an expansion of secondary education, although it was some time before new schools were built in any numbers. Much of the expansion came initially from increases in

Table 5.2. *Occupations of fathers in secondary schools, 1913, in percentages*

	Boys	Girls
Professions	18.8	19.2
Farmers	5.5	5.0
Traders and contractors	32.5	31.6
Minor officials	7.1	7.0
Clerks, travellers, agents	13.9	13.2
Skilled manual and domestics	18.2	19.0
Unskilled	2.4	2.6
Not given	1.3	2.4

Source: Board of Education, *Returns* of Secondary Grammar Schools on the grant list.

the size of schools brought onto the grant list. The total number of schools amounted to 736 by 1910, of which 554 were taking part in the education of bursars or pupil-teachers. However, the founding of new schools undoubtedly contributed to the expansion of the following decade, when the proportion of pupils (per thousand population) enrolled in secondary education more than doubled to reach 10.4 in 1929–30.[62]

What cannot be assessed is whether opportunities for secondary education available before 1902 in higher elementary schools were fully replaced by the expansion of the grammar schools. We need to know more about the nature of the brief experiment in higher-grade schooling to judge the educational and social potential of these schools better. It is worth noting, for example, that girls did not necessarily benefit more from post-1902 schools, since the coeducational higher grades may have opened up a much wider range of employments and careers for girls than the somewhat genteel grammar schools were able to do for many years.[63] These are hypothetical speculations. What does not seem in dispute is that the grammar school was able to win the battle for the lower middle class, with the municipal grammar school functioning most frequently as the third-grade school in the inter-war years.

The reconstitution of the grammar school after 1902 was associated then with a trend away from specialisation back to general education. This was accompanied by moves to arrest earlier tendencies towards horizontal segmentation. A perceived educational and social crisis had been overcome by incorporating elements of the curricula and institutions of a late Victorian modern sector into the redefined cultural ethos of the grammar school, an ethos which elementary school teachers were now implicated in maintaining. The grammar schools were enabled to grow in strength and confidence during the inter-war years by adopting more and more the institutional values of the socially exclusive but culturally inclusive upper-class 'public' schools. The grammar school, a President of the Board of Education remarked, was the inheritor of a 'public' school tradition 'which is really the traditional spirit of the nation planted and acclimatised by the culture of centuries in the society of the school'.[64]

The structural characteristics of English education in the early twentieth century have to be understood, therefore, in terms of a historical logic whose outstanding feature was the resilience and extension of older cultural models suitably modified and disseminated through a set of reformed schools. Although traditional cultural values were challenged in the later nineteenth century by the growth of cities as new centres of educational initiative, and by the claims made for science and other modern subjects, these values remained sufficiently powerful to mediate the demands being imposed on schooling from the growth in complexity of a capitalist society. At the same time, bureaucratic and legislative intervention in the period 1897–1904 entailed the development of an educational system which differentiated between the higher elementary (including the technical) sector and the secondary sector, not only in terms of administrative control, but in the type of curricula offered and in pupil intakes and occupational outcomes. Hence the system was able to function in a formal sense by selecting children and allocating them to different occupational levels in the economy.

6. The sinews of society: the public schools as a 'system'

JOHN HONEY

The comparative analysis of educational or social systems across cultures is peculiarly vulnerable to methodological pitfalls. Among the foremost of these is the language we use to describe the key institutions or concepts involved in our analysis, and this is true even when the differences between the cultures concerned are far less stark than those encountered in, say, the exploration of pre-literate societies by Western anthropologists. Indeed, the very closeness of resemblances among the societies of Western Europe which figure in this book increases the need to examine critically the language we use to describe items which we are in danger of treating as being interchangeable between cultures simply because the same names are often applied to them in the different countries involved.

My aim in this chapter is to describe some of the key characteristics of the British 'public' school system between the mid-nineteenth century and the First World War. Few will need to be reminded that the term 'public school' is used in Britain in a special sense which distinguishes it from the public schools of North America – it is in fact the opposite of the publicly provided schools of that country: visitors to England have to come to terms with the linguistic paradox that our 'public' schools are not just private schools, but are indeed the most private of all private schools. But that is not the only semantic obstacle, since my argument presupposes that the term 'public school system', though used in various senses before the mid-nineteenth century, needs to have a special sense reserved to it when applied to British social history after about 1870, and that within that phrase 'public school system' the word *system* itself may have connotations which distinguish it from the specific notion of 'system' which is used in various crucial places elsewhere in this book. Furthermore, as I am to show, the very word 'school' used in this context embodies a set of concepts which is not only new in

British educational history, but needs to be carefully distinguished from those surrounding the use of the word in the context of French or German society in the late nineteenth century, or indeed since.

Originally, the term 'public school' was normally restricted to seven old-established English schools – Eton (1440), Harrow (1571), Winchester (1382), Rugby (1567), Westminster (1560), Charterhouse (1611) and Shrewsbury (1552) – which despite having been founded in some cases for the children of the local poor, had by the early nineteenth century became wholly or partly boarding schools serving a non-local, middle- or upper-class clientele. Two essentially day schools, St Paul's (1509) and Merchant Taylors' (1561), were sometimes classed with them as being 'public' schools. All were in a badly unreformed state in the early nineteenth century and were subject to recurrent serious discipline problems which erupted in sporadic rebellions, especially between the 1770s and the 1820s. The fact is that a boys' school of more than 150 boarders had become, in a disciplinary sense, unviable. France had gone through a similar phase, in the larger Jesuit boarding schools, in the seventeenth and eighteenth centuries, and there were to be many parallels with all these in both European and North American universities in the 1960s.[1] The effect therefore on public opinion in early nineteenth-century England was to make it unlikely that these public schools would survive. The reason why they not merely did so, but expanded into a flourishing and wider 'system', is usually attributed to the reforms associated with Dr Thomas Arnold, headmaster of Rugby School (1828–42) and his disciples, which led to the emergence of a new concept of the 'school', embodying new mechanisms which operated to impart the desired skills and values, and indeed generated new ones. Among these were a new set of roles, and a new status, for headmasters and assistant masters, including a strong pastoral ethic which implied closer boy–master relations; a 'house' system involving self-consciously self-contained boarding houses which made for more effective disciplinary supervision and broke down the unwieldy numbers of boys into manageable units of (typically) 40–60; and a new type of prefect system which gave valued privileges to senior boys in return for their acting as the headmaster's moral agents, so that the 'boy republic' of the boarding school was now more effectively penetrated by the values of the teaching staff, and not just, as previously, by those of the peer group.

Alongside this there was established, especially from the mid-century onwards, the cult of athleticism: whereas games-playing had been unofficial and often unrecognised, compulsory team games, in the organisation of which the boys themselves took substantial responsibility, became a staple of the curriculum, providing a relatively harmless alternative to rebellion. As a result of all these changes in the 'machinery' of school life, a boarding school of over 150 boys had become for the first time viable in a disciplinary sense, and there were to be no further serious challenges to 'law and order' in public schools. There was thus the basis for expansion of the original seven into a much wider 'system' of public schools, with the transformation of numerous existing schools, especially grammar schools (such as the archetypal Uppingham School under Edward Thring between 1853 and 1887), and the establishment of new, purpose-built public schools.[2]

Only after about 1870 can we speak of a 'public school *system*' in the sense which it has come to have in modern British society, and which implies a hierarchy or constellation of schools, most of them mainly or partly boarding schools, who recognise each other as being of a broadly similar type, with a similar ethos and similar 'machinery': interacting at games, rifle-shooting, cadet corps events and similar activities of a kind which by the end of the nineteenth century had come to be regarded as characteristic of public schools and, indeed, definitive of their standing in the system. This was the superstructure; it was served by an infrastructure which mushroomed between 1870 and 1900 – a looser network of preparatory schools for boys aged 7–13, being modelled no longer, as hitherto, on domestic education (the household of the tutor and his family), but on the public schools for which the boys were destined, and imitating much of the 'machinery' of games, chapel, prefects, and the like.

How many public schools were there in the period with which we are concerned? Here we encounter the fact, which has a number of implications for our present analysis, that *nobody actually knew*. There was no clear definition of what a public school was, and which schools had the right to this title (the situation is the same today). A very rough-and-ready working definition is provided by a school's representation on the Headmasters' Conference, but this criterion was of very dubious validity before 1914. However, analysis of the network of relationships furnished by encounters at games and similar activities, which, as we have found, had become characteristic of public schools, yields a set of groupings which might conceivably have been so regarded in the last two decades of the nineteenth century and perhaps the first decade of the present century. This analysis suggests there were perhaps fifty schools whose products from that period could have expected to be regarded as 'public school men', with further groupings of schools – around fifty or so more of them – which had some claim to the title, though there were many in society who would have discounted the claims of these latter schools.[3]

Implicit in the notion of a 'public school system' is the assumption that, now that this community of schools had grown up, it was being widely used. And, indeed, from about 1870 it became the common expectation of the upper and upper middle classes to send their sons away to school, often from the age of 7 or 8 – the young Winston Churchill was sent off to preparatory school at the age of 7 in 1882. This resulted in a generalised transfer of function from the family to the school which is unique among modern societies, and it is the more remarkable, first because it was a transfer from the family to an institution designed to generate powerful values and loyalties separate from – even opposed to – those of the home; and secondly, because the period when this process of transfer began to become general coincides with the existence of three powerful deterrent factors which ought to have inhibited it: the incidence of killer epidemic diseases to which boarding schools were particularly vulnerable, serious problems of sex which the headmasters loudly proclaimed they were unable to cope with, and the prevalence of conditions of brutality (bullying and corporal punishment), hunger, physical hardship and general squalor, all of them known about by the parents, who preferred, however, to turn a blind eye.

That parents persisted in sending their sons to these schools underlines the crucial importance to the pupils' life-chances of the public school system after 1870. So what did they think they were getting for their money? Certainly little of value in terms of a useful curriculum. Latin and Greek dominated the schools in 1870 and only slowly weakened over the following decades. Science was a despised subject which might be taught by men appointed because they were feeble disciplinarians. The general standing of science can be gauged from the fact that of all headmasters of public schools appointed in the century 1860–1960, only some 1–2 per cent were scientists; of the seven 'original' public schools, only one has ever appointed a science specialist as headmaster, and that had to wait until 1981. Wellington College was founded as a public school for the orphans of army officers in 1859 and had many pupils planning a military career. Its founders, including Prince Albert, planned a progressive curriculum including science, but its first headmasters, classicists from conventional public schools, killed this scheme and turned it into a conventional curriculum dominated by Latin and Greek (which to the majority of boys meant little) plus cricket and rugby football.

To understand what the public school system really existed to produce, we need to understand the distinction between *content* and *process* in the curriculum – the difference between *what* was taught and the *manner* of the training, indeed the whole environment where it took place. In the case of these schools the total *process* (based only partly on a subject content, mainly Latin grammar, which had little inherent utility in late nineteenth-century British society) was designed to produce a new type of social personality, by processes of 'hardening' or 'toughening', in a two-stage cycle: starting as a defenceless junior in a preparatory school, fighting his way up the hierarchy of privilege and power symbolised by a prefect and fagging system, caps, badges and precise gradations of dress, then reaching the top of the preparatory school, and exercising responsibility as a prefect or games captain; then going on at 14 to his public school and starting the whole process all over again at the bottom, learning to endure humiliation and physical pain, to come to terms with public opinion and to know one's place, rising to be a house prefect, school prefect or games captain, and arriving at the end with that quality of self-confidence and poise which came to be the hallmark of the public school man. In pre-literate societies, specialised *rites de passage* grew up to fulfil similar kinds of function; in advanced Western societies, military academies are among the few institutions offering a remotely similar experience. Some universities, in Europe and elsewhere, have had traditional forms of initiation, which suggested a similar experience of 'process'; but none of them offered anything like Britain's ten- to twelve-year double cycle of character-building and social moulding, nor was so large a proportion of a whole class or caste involved.[4]

While we are engaged in comparisons, we need to take note of major differences in the concept of the 'school' between Britain on the one hand and France and Germany on the other. What we are doing is comparing the ability to effect changes in pupils' attitudes and values, knowledge and skills, of institutions whose contact with these pupils might be limited to perhaps four to five hours a day for perhaps five or five-and-a-half days a week, in continental Europe, with those in Britain, where, by contrast, 'school' involves mainly boarding schools, where active secondary socialisation takes place for many pupils for up to 100 hours a week, in a self-contained community enclosed within physical and social boundaries, whose characteristic 'machinery' of roles, relationships and activities provides for a whole range of functions which in other countries take place outside school, for example sport, religion, music and other cultural pursuits. And this provision is offered within an atmosphere of intense communality, capable of generating powerful emotions associated with the school itself. What is more, membership of this community is operable not just during one's schooldays, but *for life*, because of the emergence in the latter part of the nineteenth century of the phenomenon of the 'old boy', the alumnus bound to the school by lifelong links which might include games-playing activities, financial benefactions, annual dinners and the provision, in the form of their own sons, of new generations of pupils. For the father of the writer Evelyn Waugh, for example, these links were a powerful force after he left school; moreover, he once confessed that every night of his later life he dreamt he was back at school. Probably in no other country in the world has the conception of the 'school' been so fully and so powerfully developed, to the point of creating an institution of enormous pretensions and self-consciousness, ready to take upon itself tasks in relation not just to the formal schooling but to the whole lives of the pupils. Indeed, this relationship might in some cases be more than lifelong: we have evidence of specific schools being used as vehicles for the expression of forms of family consciousness over several generations; as another example we note how some late nineteenth-century products of the public school system, on being raised to the peerage, took their title from the name of their 'public' school, in preference to their own name or (as was more common) some territorial connection.

As is well known, the public school system came to exercise a crucial influence in British society. This is one of the senses in which I refer to those schools as the 'sinews of society'. 'Old boys' of specific public schools helped each other into jobs, into commissions in the army, into membership of clubs and into the social circles of the privileged. It has been estimated that, of all Conservative Party MPs elected in the four Parliaments of 1905, 1909, 1928 and 1938, two public schools alone – Eton and Harrow – had been responsible for the schooling of proportions of these men ranging between 30 and 43 per cent – a formidable percentage of such Conservative MPs. And most of them would, of course, have been receiving their schooling in the period 1860–1914. (Nor did this kind of representation disappear: of those offered places in Mrs Thatcher's Cabinet formed in 1979, one-third came from Eton or Harrow.)

'Old boys' of specific public schools recognised each other by wearing distinctive old school ties, but there also grew up the generalised caste of 'public school men' who similarly helped each other into jobs. A minor industry of research has grown up around the attempt to measure the preponderance of 'public school men' generally in various occupational and other elites in British society over the past century. Because of methodological difficulties surrounding the definition of the term 'public school' in a given decade, most efforts of precise measurement have been seriously flawed, but nobody disputes their main conclusion, that in privileged positions in British society generally, and specifically among MPs, the civil service, the judiciary, the officer class and the Anglican episcopate, there was in that period a preponderance of products of public schools. From about 1870 the question 'Where were you at school?' became crucial for appointment to jobs, for commissions in the army, for entry to clubs, and even, in many spheres, for one's matrimonial prospects. Increasing importance was attached to the wearing of 'old school' ties, to the publication of school registers listing 'old boys', and to the citation of schooling among credentials in reference books.

A much readier form of identification than all of these was accent. It was the public school system which after 1870 established and diffused one standard socially and educationally acceptable form of English pronunciation, known at one time among phoneticians as 'Public School English', and later as RP (Received, i.e. approved, Pronunciation). In France, Germany and many other countries there are degrees of discrimination against regional accents (I do not here refer to dialects, or *patois*, with distinctive grammatical and lexical features), but nowhere has such discrimination in favour of one 'standard' been so complete as in England since the later nineteenth century as a result of the development of the public school system, and the connection of that system with Oxford and Cambridge. From the 1920s this responsibility for the maintenance of a national standard of acceptable accent passed to the newly created BBC, and despite its cautious attempts to promote more tolerance of non-standard accents, it is still the case today that accent is one of the foremost indicators of social class and of 'educatedness' in Britain, and is also a major but seldom openly discussed factor in British political life.

How far, then, was the public school system a closed system? Superficially it certainly seemed so: a set of mainly boarding schools charging expensive fees, entry to which was preceded by attendance at expensive preparatory schools. In fact there was a small area of opportunity for the sons of parents who were not rich to enter the system. Nearly all the public schools in the period we are concerned with offered entrance scholarships which could give a substantial remission of fees. As the qualifying examinations were essentially in classical subjects, most of the competitors equipped themselves by a preparatory school training, which was often expensive; only a tiny minority attending leading public schools came from really humble homes, though at some schools the sons of Anglican clergy or of army officers could be educated relatively cheaply. But the public school system had a degree of openness in one respect – the imprecision of definition about which schools belonged. Though the typical 'leading' public school was an expensive, entirely or predominantly boarding, school, there were also a few 'leading' public schools which were entirely or substantially day schools, at which the son of a shopkeeper or a less prosperous professional man could be educated for perhaps not much more than £4 a year, and the later careers of such pupils showed that they enjoyed all the privileges in after-life of having come up through the public school system.[5] Furthermore, the lack of definition about which schools counted as public schools allowed a further degree of openness in that it was possible on the strength of a relatively cheap education at a school whose claims to public school status were very marginal, to claim some, at least, of the privileges of being a 'public school man', even if an Old Etonian, say, would not have been very impressed.

This process was assisted by the penetration of formulas associated with the public school system into every corner of English society. Former pupils or masters of public schools 'colonised' the headships and teaching staffs of grammar schools, as they did also the inspectorate, the teacher-training institutions and, after 1902, the new local education authorities; even the Borstal system of reformatory schools for delinquents was created by public school men on public school lines. The development of the public school system had given rise to a new literary genre – the novel or magazine story of boarding school life, starting with Thomas Hughes' *Tom Brown's Schooldays* (1857), based on Rugby School. The effect of a vast output of book and periodical literature upon its enormous readership, most of whom had in their own lives no connection with this kind of schooling, was to make knowledge of the 'machinery', ideals and values, and folklore of the public school model into public property.[6] It was therefore to some extent open to 'outsiders' to imitate it; and especially if they were successful in acquiring the manners, and above all the accent, of the public school product, they could enjoy some of the benefits of the system.

The privileges to which the system gave access were also, to some extent, the reward of attendance at either Oxford or Cambridge, the two universities which were in some respects an extension of the public school system, though they were not coterminous with it. By the 1880s it had become a social handicap at Cambridge and Oxford not to have been at a public school, and the school one attended (especially if it were a leading public school) became one of the key facts about one's identity which one's friends would tend to remember and refer to. Indeed, this kind of information was beginning to become so important that after some 600 years Oxford University's matriculation registers suddenly began in 1894 to record the previous schooling of matriculants. At Balliol College one of the dominant influences on admissions policy from the 1870s onwards was J. L. Strachan-Davidson (later Master from 1907 to 1916), who had not himself been at public school but who in 1895 made explicit his ideals for the social composition of the college: 'The main current [of college life] always has consisted, and to my mind always must consist, of English public school boys.'[7] Keble College, founded in 1870, was probably at the opposite end of the spectrum of academic and social prestige. Yet Table 6.1 illustrates the preponderance at both these colleges of public school men among entrants in the five years 1895–9. During the same period a significant proportion at both colleges, however, had no advantage whatever of 'public school man' status, and there were intermediate categories whose claim to that status was either definitely, or at least fairly, doubtful. Alongside the 82.4 per cent of undisputed 'public school men' at Balliol – mostly from Eton, Harrow, Rugby and Winchester – were a group of nearly 6 per cent, which included a former elementary school pupil-teacher, a product of a humble 'higher-grade' school, and old boys of little-known grammar schools. The corresponding proportion at Keble was 11.1 per cent.[8]

What produced the reforms which brought the public school system into being? There are those who explain this by reference to a response to Non-conformist demands for change. My own analysis views the various pieces of 'machinery' as developing experimentally – and haphazardly – in response to the 'law and order' problem; and one development, compulsory organised games, came partly because of the need to take the steam out of

Table 6.1. *Entrants to two Oxford colleges, 1895–9, in percentages excluding entrants from overseas and entrants from other universities*

	A	B	C	D	E	No. of students
Balliol	82.4	7.1	2.1	1.7	5.9	239
Keble	55.7	17.3	5.9	10.0	11.1	289
Combined	67.8	12.7	4.2	6.3	8.7	528

Source: Figures in columns A to E show the percentage of entrants direct from schooling in Britain who had attended the following categories of school: Column A represents the three groups comprising the 50 schools which most obviously constituted the public schools community in that decade (Groups I–III set out in Honey, *Tom Brown's Universe*, p. 264, and in Simon and Bradley, *Victorian Public School*, p.30); Column B represents schools with more dubious claims to public school standing in that period (Group IV Schools plus 'Long-List' public schools in Honey, *Tom Brown's Universe*, pp. 264, 268); Column C represents schools with negligible claims to such standing; Column D is of schools definitely not public schools. Column E is for entrants claiming to have been educated 'privately' (see *ibid.*, p. 282 for the implications), or about whose schooling there is no record.

indiscipline, and partly because of specific fears about sex: 'Send the boys to bed tired, and you'll have no problem.'

Attempts to explain the development of the system in terms of its functionality have to come to terms with the neglect of science, technology and commerce throughout the 'establishment' educational system of the public schools and Oxford and Cambridge in the nineteenth century and the first half of the twentieth century, a neglect which deprived the potential leaders of a technological and commercially based society of any real understanding of how these fundamental elements worked. It is easy for us to see this in dysfunctional perspective on the basis of the economic and social assumptions of the 1980s, but before 1914 our forefathers may have had more justification than they have been given credit for in the priorities they operated. The demands of governing an overseas empire put a high premium on the moral qualities, the predictability, the social acceptability of the 'public school man'. Even within Britain the preference for gentlemanly abilities, as represented by a public school education, over high technical ability for entrance to the professions, may have had its functional point. Among solicitors and bankers financial rectitude and general moral probity were at least as important as mental arithmetic, and it may not be without significance that public school education increased in importance at precisely the time when faith in the financial soundness of one traditional out-group prominent in banking – the Quakers – was shattered by spectacular bank failures.

Thus the neglect of science and technology which we have noted was due not merely to a feeling that these studies were not appropriate to the education of a gentleman, but to a conviction that technical expertise by itself was not enough. So we note, for example, that by the closing decade of the nineteenth century major British firms like Shell and ICI (or their then counterparts) had created their own supply of properly trained scientists to remedy the lack of recruits to key managerial posts from more traditionally educated public school and Oxbridge products. These firms got them from Continental institutions like Zurich Polytechnic, and they got them from English provincial universities and from Scottish ones. Then in 1892 Oxford, and in 1899 Cambridge, set up their placement agencies (Appointments Boards) to channel their graduates into industry, technology and commerce, and within a few years they had curbed this stream of trained Continental and non-Oxbridge graduate scientists into Shell and ICI by persuading such firms to take on large numbers of Oxford and Cambridge *classicists* – who bore, of course, all the outward and visible signs of membership of the public school gentlemanly elite – and so confirmed the devaluation of technical and professional expertise.[9] The Foreign Office and the Home Civil Service recruited by competitive examination, in which public school men acquitted themselves well, but so did candidates from other schools; in the entry to professional and technical (as opposed to administrative) branches of the Home Civil Service public school and Oxbridge men were less prominent. But in the Colonial Service and, even more, in the Sudan Political Service, where admission was by interview and relied heavily on Oxford and Cambridge dons who had a 'wide acquaintance among Public School Masters' acting as 'talent scouts', there was an overwhelming preponderance of public school men.[10]

At its worst, the public school system can be seen as constituting a network or freemasonry whose members supported each other and covered up for each other, at times even against the national interest. At its best, the public school system was a freemasonry of another kind, guaranteeing certain shared values and standards of acceptable conduct on a nation-wide – even Empire-wide – basis, and this is another sense in which I use the term 'the sinews of society'.

Changes in nineteenth-century British society involving a shift from manufacturing to trade, from land to capital as the basis of personal fortune and social status, and from the provinces to the metropolis and other major urban centres, all generated strains, tensions, anxieties and uncertainties in which the public school system was seen as able to provide new avenues for the acquisition of status, and offer a new mechanism of social cohesion. Its strength lay in its flexibility and in its very lack of firm definition. Though apparently based on social exclusiveness, it provided at its margins a degree of openness which allowed for the exploitation of the system by the lower middle classes, especially the less well-off professional classes. Though the leading public schools achieved a degree of rationalisation of their age range and their curricula in the Victorian period, they operated in ways which transcended the Taunton Commission's categorisation of schools into three grades by leaving age, since their curricular objectives were fundamentally different from those of schools outside the public school system. Though it appeared to offer status in return for academic success, in fact the system had very little to do with scholastic certification at all: headmasters deprecated the judging of their schools on the basis of examination results, and indeed a good proportion of pupils only entered upon their careers by passing examinations for which they were prepared, after leaving their public schools, by crammers.

What the 'process' did claim to certify was character, safeness, reliability; by this method the established classes could protect their interests against the invasion from the classes below them by specifying the criteria on which newcomers would be allowed to compete, criteria in which, because they were not based specifically on academic achievement, the newcomers would have no special advantage, criteria which would ensure that the newcomers were easily assimilable to the mores of the establishment. Thus the consequences of social mobility, potentially so dangerous when on so large a scale, were kept under control. In the course of all this, the 'gentleman ideal' which had so long dominated the conception of 'educatedness' underlying the whole of English secondary and higher education, had been transformed, from one rooted in classical learning leavened by Christianity, to one in which the dominant features related to a process of character-building whose stigmata assured lifelong membership in an identifiable and mutually supportive elite. The price of the relative permeability of Britain's aristocracy and governing classes, which was involved in the use of the public school as a means of mobility, was the identification of gentrified new wealth with those attitudes and values we have noted which disparaged commerce and technology. By contrast, other Western European countries whose aristocracies allowed no comparable filter mechanism or 'social sieve' (to use F. M. L. Thompson's term)[11] enabled a distinct and functional technological and commercial ethos to develop and flourish.

I end with a final linguistic point, this time involving the word 'teacher' (or, in the context of the public school system, 'schoolmaster'). It was a central assumption of the teaching process up to the nineteenth century that 'the student can become the master' – this is what I call the principle of 'identification', whose corollary is the demotivation of working-class pupils in elementary schools. The public school system exploited this principle by ensuring a supply of 'gentlemen' to be public school masters – many of the best products of the system went back and taught – and it did so by creating rich rewards for the top public school headmasters and assistant masters. A top headmaster around 1860 might earn the equivalent of £100,000 a year in our (1980s) money values, and a leading housemaster a third of that. Ten years as headmaster of Harrow would put you on your way to being a millionaire in today's terms. The whole school-teaching profession benefited from this reflected social status, and also from the strong professional ethic of 'vocation' and self-dedication developed in the public school system. Alongside the big salaries in the major schools, there were many lesser public schools where able men would forgo the much greater rewards that their qualifications and abilities might have earned them in other occupations, in order to live out a life of service.[12] The compatibility of relatively high social status with the activity of teacher lent connotations to the English word 'schoolmaster' which ought to prompt us to treat with caution any facile correspondence with the 'teachers' in comparable educational systems elsewhere in Western Europe. How the French and German teaching professions fared in terms of salary, social status, and general professional ethic would seem to be a suitable subject of comparative study.

7. Structural change in English higher education, 1870–1920

ROY LOWE

English higher education underwent a complete transformation in the period 1870 to 1920. At the outset provision was unsystematic and, for many social groups, sporadic. The four small existing universities catered for so few of the population that it was left to a plethora of Mechanics' Institutes, Literary and Philosophical Societies and adult schools to provide any sort of post-school facility for the mass of the people. During the fifty years after 1870 the process of growth by which this crisis was relieved involved the creation of a clearly defined and widely recognised hierarchical structure. To what extent this marked a conscious attempt at the segregation of social classes, and to what extent an inexorable response to external pressures, is uncertain, but it is possible to attempt a description of the hierarchies which were established.

In this analysis agencies of higher education must be considered as part of a developing system, in a relationship not only with the emergent secondary and elementary schools but also with the growing industries and professions. Central to the analysis attempted here is a consideration of how far this process was part of the rigid stratification of society by which dominant social groups used the educational system to preserve their position, and the extent to which this was alleviated by a meritocratic function.

At the apex of this emergent system stood the Oxbridge colleges. An important element in the dynamic of change was the fierce determination of those within the two leading universities to ensure that the pre-eminence of these institutions was not eroded. The tokens of that pre-eminence were a continuing strong commitment to a classical education and the maintenance of strict control over admission to the student body.

So fierce were the external pressures for change that there was, naturally enough, a continuing controversy concerning both what should be taught and to whom. Apologists for Oxbridge point out the extent to which traditional curricula were supplemented by new subjects during this period, but, in reality, every proposal to modernise Oxbridge met with a strong groundswell of conservatism. When, in 1907, an appeal was launched at Oxford to finance teaching in modern subjects, particularly the sciences and modern languages, it was emphasised that

in providing for the endowment of new subjects of a scientific or modern character, the object of this appeal is, while bringing Oxford up to date, not to destroy, but rather to conserve, its old traditions as a university pre-eminently of the 'humane' studies and literary culture.[1]

Similarly, when J. L. Myres, in 1911, proposed a course in Modern Greats, he met a fusilade of criticism. The comment from G. Beardoe Grundy was typical:

Easy paths to knowledge lead to that worst kind of ignorance which knows nothing well, while pretending to complete knowledge . . . If a man has not brains enough to master Greek sufficiently for the purpose of Lit. Hum. he ought not to be put to the high studies demanded by the examination. The university cannot, without degrading its studies, legislate for those who have had serious defects in their previous education.[2]

This conservatism is explicable in part by the fact that this was the period when the major professions looked increasingly to the ancient universities for entrants who had received either a liberal education or a training in the fundamental sciences. Medicine, the law, architecture and the civil service all began to recruit unprecedented numbers of Oxbridge graduates. Although the new appointments boards of Oxford and Cambridge succeeded in steering many graduates into industry, it must be remembered that many of these graduated in subjects with no immediate links with industrial skills, and that almost all of them went into managerial positions of one sort or another, thus reinforcing an industrial hierarchy.[3]

The more recently founded civic universities all aspired to the status and prestige which was universally afforded to Oxbridge. Their ambitions were summarised in the prospectus of the University of Birmingham, drawn up shortly after the grant of a charter in 1900. 'It is clear', claimed the Birmingham dons,

that the Chamberlain ideal for the Midland University has always been a school of general culture, specialising in the facilities for training applied scientists. It is not a technical school; there was already a most excellent one in Birmingham before the university was erected. It is for training 'captains of industry', not the rank and file, or even the non-commissioned officers.[4]

This determination to participate in a competitive scramble for status, which was shared by the other civic universities, and indeed by technical institutions with far less chance of fulfilling their ambitions, was a crucial element in the dynamic of change and helped to precipitate the rigid structuralisation of higher education. It is hardly surprising that institutions sponsored from the profits of a fiercely competitive industrial system and dependent for their well-being and even survival upon attracting students, should succumb to this competitive style from the outset.

What these civic colleges did achieve was to distance themselves from the technical colleges, although in many instances their curricula encroached upon the preserves of those colleges. Equally, they were unable to achieve recognition as first-grade institutions of higher education – this accolade was reserved for Oxbridge, and never truly threatened. Thus, by 1914, a rigidly hierarchical system of higher education had emerged in England.

What made the impact of this development so powerful was the fact that it was geared to a similar hierarchy of secondary schools. The tripartite division foreseen by the Taunton Commissioners in 1868 was, in the event, implemented in a rather different form during the following forty years, with the 'public' schools, the endowed grammar schools and the post-1902 municipal secondary schools becoming the three clearly identified tiers of secondary schooling. Central to this stratification, as to that of higher education, was the notion that able scholars might be promoted on merit through the deployment of a scholarship system. This rationale, which was deployed throughout the period under review, was suspect from its inception. One letter to Joshua Fitch, a Secondary Schools Commissioner, on the Exeter schools indicated the prejudice which from the outset threatened the impartial operation of a scholarship system:

the creation of exhibitions from elementary schools will not in my opinion give these exhibitions to the poor.

As a rule I take it the poor are of inferior intellect. I take it that the lowest stratum of society is of inferior intellect, or else it would not continue the lowest stratum, and that intellect is hereditary like any other quality.[5]

Within Oxbridge, too, there was some resistance to the opening of access such as was advocated by Mark Pattison. James Bryce, writing to Henry Sidgwick immediately after the publication of *Suggestions on Academical Organisation* in 1868, asked:

Have you seen Pattison's book? It is the clearest and finest thing any of our people has put forth. But all the regular Liberals call out that it is Utopian, some that it is self-interested. Certainly we may fear that if other things have not produced a learned class in England, endowments will not.[6]

Equally, there were those within Oxford who saw the need to dovetail the curriculum to that of the group of schools from which the university would draw. In the protracted debate on the need for geographical studies within the university, which culminated in the appointment of Halford Mackinder to a Readership in 1899, the needs of the Empire were often cited. But, significantly, H. E. Rawlinson, President of the Royal Geographical Society, emphasised in 1871 that

Geography will become, very shortly, a large and clearly defined part of education in all the Endowed Schools of England, that is to say in the very schools whose boys form the great majority of those affected by the proposed scheme of examination.[7]

On this ground he thought it worthy of addition to the curriculum of the university. Equally, when geography was formally established in the closing years of the century, it was only after the syllabus had been trimmed to meet the demands of traditionalists, such as W. R. Anson of All Souls College, Oxford, who argued that 'if geography is to take its proper place here it must have its root in the Studies of Classical and Modern History'.[8]

It was clear that changes were under way in the secondary schools to which the universities must respond. As early as 1870 the point was emphasised by John Percival at the annual conference of the National Association for the Promotion of Social Science, which was to become an important forum for the discussion of higher education. Percival's remarks are sufficiently pertinent to be worth quoting at length:

It is this threatening hiatus between the liberal training of our universities and the modern school, as the creation of city life and its requirements, that I see as one of the chief dangers of English education at this time . . . You are no longer content that your boys should spend their time to the age of eighteen in learning portions of a small number of Latin and a still smaller number of Greek authors, something of Latin and Greek grammar and Latin composition, and a smattering withal of elementary mathematics; and yet this is all our universities even profess to exact or enquire about, before a student is admitted to their walls.

They shut out from their influence a whole class of schools, which have sprung up in obedience to what seems a national want, but which can never grow to anything like full educational stature . . . without some such encouragement as the university alone can give. I speak of the modern school . . . Who frequent our universities? Who are those that come under their influence? Not the men who are directing the life of Manchester, Newcastle, Liverpool, Bristol or Birmingham, but the sons of country gentlemen, or men destined for certain professions, or a few sons of the wealthier merchants and manufacturers; whilst the names of Oxford and Cambridge are strange names to the mass of those who are guiding our industrial and commercial enterprise . . .

Who can fail to lament the want of real living connections between our old universities and the great commercial and industrial centres? A great step will have been taken in this direction if the universities should so reform themselves as to remain closely connected with all middle class schools even those of modern aims and tendencies.

I hope also to see Oxford and Cambridge planning various faculties in every great city, and thus flourishing . . . firmly rooted in the very midst of our industrial and commercial enterprise.[9]

It is significant that Percival did not foresee the creation of new universities as a desirable response to this crisis, but anticipated that the Extension Movement, by which Oxbridge dons visited the provincial cities, could meet the national need. This emphasis, which Percival shared with many influential contemporaries, was to help doom local developments to inferior status.

Significant, too, is the response made to those remarks in discussion by the Rev. Nash Stephenson, who emphasised what was to become a key consideration in any discussion of university reform, the risk of dilution:

I have a misgiving as to the wisdom of opening up a scheme for the advancement of the working classes which might prove illusory, and of raising hopes which could never be realised. There must be 'hewers of wood and drawers of water' . . . If some persons ought to govern the minds of others who looked up to them for guidance, they ought not to open illusory expectations which in the end might inflict injury rather than confer good.[10]

It is in this way that the class exclusivity of the university system was justified.

In this atmosphere it is hardly surprising that change within the existing universities, when it did come, was limited in scope. Indeed, even Mark Pattison, an apologist for university reform, argued in 1876 that unless the English middle classes first reformed themselves, the schools and universities could do nothing for them. For him, intellectual philistinism was the English disease; he lamented

the wretched destitution of all intellectual nourishment in which the middle classes of England grow up; the absence in middle-class homes of all intelligent interests; the incapacity for ideas which characterises them; the outer darkness in which their self-complacent existence is passed, while the inexhaustible riches of the several worlds of sciences, of literature, poetry and art are unopened to them, is a modern phenomenon which has now attained the proportions of a social blot . . . The schools will not be improved while the homes remain what they are.[11]

Thus part of the rationale which underpinned the pre-eminence of Oxbridge was the preservation of a gentlemanly ideal in a society evincing increasingly barbaric tendencies. At a conference on secondary education in 1893 the President of Magdalen College stressed that the universities

must teach those things which have a really educating and elevating effect and teach them in a manner which is really educating and elevating . . . They should ultimately set the standard of the secondary schools . . . all the boys from such schools, nay, all English citizens, should be gentlemen.[12]

But, if the diffusion of cultural values was to be an important function of the universities, reinforcing the significance of a humane education in the liberal arts, it was important, too, that this democratic duty was not taken too far:

> It would be no kindness, no real boon to education or the country if the universities were either to neglect or starve learning and science in the interests of education, or again were to lower their standards and intellectually cheapen their degrees, for the sake of admitting and passing through their midst a number of students from secondary schools. They must hold high the intellectual standard.[13]

This liberal education was justified on the grounds that Oxbridge catered for a particular social group, and this view was shared by critics and apologists alike. On the one hand, Bishop Gore, fighting in 1907 for a Royal Commission on Oxford, complained that 'our university . . . is a playground for the sons of the wealthier classes . . . not in any serious sense a place of study at all'.[14] Among his opponents was Lord Curzon, whose *Principles and Methods of University Reform* argued that changes of too sweeping a nature were unnecessary:

> It is as desirable that Oxford should educate the future country squire, or nobleman, or banker, or member of parliament, or even the guardsman, as that it should sharpen the wits of the schoolmaster or the cultivated artisan . . . We have in our old universities a mechanism for training the well-to-do to a sense of responsibility, and a capacity for public affairs which it would be the height of folly to throw away.[15]

Thus the call of national duty was invoked to justify Oxford's continued ministration to the elite.

In the event, during this period classical and humane studies were deployed to strengthen the bond between the old universities and the more prestigious secondary schools. The outbreak of war in 1914 saw the pre-eminence of a literary education, offering a route from 'public' school to Oxbridge and thence to the civil service and major professions, reinforced rather than weakened.

Against this background the existing universities attempted to meet the burgeoning demand for higher education through the provision of Extension lectures on an occasional basis. Initiated by James Stuart of Cambridge between 1867 and 1873, it was from the outset foreseen that this movement would bring the universities into contact with social groups they had so far neglected:

> University Extension leads directly . . . to a reconsideration of our course of study. We educate at this place chiefly and almost exclusively clergymen, barristers and country gentlemen to the profession of medicine, to that of a solicitor, to the military and civil service of the state. To those commercial and industrial pursuits which now engage large and increasing numbers of educated men we contribute little. And even of the three classes mentioned above, a large and increasing proportion do not now seek education at this or the sister university. The object of the 'Extension' movement has been to see whether we could not open the gates of the university wider without injury to its proper functions and character.[16]

This note, penned in about 1872, was to prove prophetic; by the 1890s a mass movement had emerged. Its offshoot was the Workers' Educational Association, which was to become the major 'compensatory' route to higher education for the working classes during the first half of the twentieth century. Although the apologists for this system, men such as Albert Mansbridge and R. H. Tawney, emphasised the extent to which it opened a broad 'highway' to the universities for social groups previously excluded, in reality the outcome was that Oxbridge, in particular, was spared the need for extensive internal reform. Further, the WEA was consciously used during the Edwardian period to head off the pressure which was generated by Ruskin College, newly founded in Oxford, for genuine reform of the University. Ruskin, as an independent college catering for working men with a curriculum centred on the social sciences, posed a direct challenge to the University. As early as 1905, within six years of its foundation, discussions were under way among the Oxford professoriate on how to channel this new college.[17] In the event, attempts to emasculate its work failed and it became necessary to sponsor the Workers' Educational Association as an organisation offering teaching more closely aligned to the University model. It is this consideration which helps explain the tone adopted by Lord Curzon, the Chancellor of the University, when he addressed himself to the problem of University Extension. Curzon was one of the Oxford apologists for whom Extension lecturing was vital, allowing them to claim that Oxford was catering for not only 'those who wish to remain in their order, but desire a university education as a means of raising themselves within it', but also for

the many who hope by means of a university education to rise in the social as well as in the intellectual scale . . . The distinction between the two classes is fundamental. The university will fail in its duty to the nation if it does not endeavour to provide with equal anxiety and liberality for both: but it will require to provide for them by different means.[18]

Thus, for Curzon, the role of the University Extension was critical, since it enabled Oxford to be seen to be catering for social groups it had previously ignored, and could be used therefore to pre-empt demands for sweeping internal reform. Curzon went on to detail his scheme for non-collegiate places, University Extension and tutorial classes, the incorporation of Ruskin and the foundation of a Working Men's College in some detail, and, in a passage which was a direct attack upon what Ruskin College was attempting, emphasised that the curriculum 'should not be confined exclusively to Sociology and Economics since it is doubtful if of themselves these are capable of ensuring a liberal education'.[19]

This hesitance of Oxbridge to cater for the needs of the 'high industrial phase' of development left a lacuna which the embryonic civic colleges were only too keen to fill. Sponsored in the main by industrialists and enthusiasts who keenly proclaimed the need to train the elite of the industrial work force, these colleges took the pure and applied sciences as their province from the outset. Industrial chemistry at Manchester and Leeds, mining at Newcastle and Birmingham, metallurgy at Sheffield, shipbuilding at Newcastle, brewing at Birmingham: by the 1890s the provincial colleges had established an impressive list of specialisms orientated towards the industrial needs of their own areas.

The result was the recruitment of a new clientele, drawn mainly from the localities of the Redbrick university colleges and largely representative of the new middle classes thrown up by this second-phase industrialisation. Direct evidence on the social background of students at differing universities is as yet fairly slight, but there are several pointers which suggest contrasts between the pre-existing universities and those newly established in the industrial towns.

First, they experienced different patterns of growth. While the number of students at Oxford, Cambridge, London and Durham grew eightfold between 1861 and 1931, the student capacity of the new provincial university colleges was nearly thirty times as great in 1931 as it had been in 1861. The growth of technical education in non-university institutions was even more striking: this sector was minute in 1861 (less than 2000 students at one estimate) but rose to almost 1.8 million by 1921, remaining thereafter above the one million level. The vast majority of these students were part-time. These figures have been worked out in greater detail elsewhere, but they suggest, even in their raw form, that the newer institutions were catering for the needs of the new industrial areas and may have drawn largely from them.[20]

There is some evidence, too, that contemporaries thought this was the case. In 1895 the Bryce Report drew attention to the fact that 'Oxford and Cambridge are now largely recruited from sections of society which have had long-standing hereditary connections with them.'[21] This was seen as evidence of a

separation between the older universities and a branch of Secondary Education which is daily growing in importance . . . Several witnesses laid stress on the imperfect connection between the university [Oxbridge] and many secondary schools of the modern type . . . There is very little contact between the higher and lower grade of secondary education in this country. Thus the headmaster of the higher grade elementary school at Leeds, at which boys and girls are prepared for the universities, stated that he 'cannot get boys to go to Cambridge, and has had no boys express a desire to go to Oxford'.[22]

The Bryce Commission investigated the previous schooling of students at four contrasting universities, and the returns (see Table 7.1) suggested very

Table 7.1. *Previous places of education of undergraduates, and scholarships awarded*

	The seven major 'public' schools	HMC schools	Schools not rep- resented at HMC	Private tuition	Training college	Technical school	Pupil- teacher centre	Public elemen- tary school
Oxford	469/125	866/434	313/11	292/12	6/0	5/0	4/2	9/3
Cam- bridge	266/66	838/366	391/135	354/26	15/3	18/10	15/8	10/6
Durham	0/0	28/12	33/10	52/7	1/0	0/0	0/0	4/0
Victoria	18/1	220/37	403/105	71/12	2/2	44/25	9/8	71/43

Source: From Bryce Report, *Secondary Education* (London, 1895), vol. 9, p. 426. In each case the number of students is given first, and the number of scholarships after the stroke.

clearly that the Victoria University, comprising Manchester, Leeds and Liverpool, had a recruitment base which contrasted with its older counterparts. Strikingly, almost two-thirds of the student body of the Victoria University was recruited from modern secondary schools, from technical schools or from the elementary sector, which for this purpose included the higher-grade schools. The Bryce Report commented favourably on the Leeds Central School, which had limited aspirations for its pupils:

The classical education aimed at was limited to such requirements as would be needed for the Victorian or London matriculation, and the degree it prepared for was the BSc rather than BA. What was true of the Leeds School was true of many other schools of the same type.[23]

Several factors ensured that, at their inception, these colleges had little chance of rivalling the existing universities in prestige. Much teaching was part-time and the bulk of it below degree level. The annual returns made by the Redbrick universities to the Treasury show that, as late as 1901, some 45 per cent of the student population were on part-time courses. When the first returns were made, in 1893, only a handful of the students in these new civic colleges were completing degree courses. At Manchester, where 123 students graduated from a student body of over 1000, the proportion was unusually high. Most colleges had fewer than 20 graduates. This is explained by the fact that, although some recruits made their way from newly reformed grammar schools, for many these civic colleges offered a part-time rounding-off of an elementary school education, especially during the 1890s as the new higher-grade schools came into their own.

Thus the seeds of a segmented system, by which different sectors of higher education catered for different social groups, were sown before the turn of the century. In the swift expansion of the late nineteenth century, though, there was still some confusion between the role of technical colleges, polytechnics, mechanics' institutes and the new university colleges, as all claimed some responsibility for technical education.

During the first years of the twentieth century this hiatus was resolved as the civic universities distanced themselves from the 'technical' sector and thus, whether consciously or not, became the natural outlet for the products of reformed grammar schools and municipal secondary schools. This occurred through similar changes taking place in both sectors at the same time.

At the schools' level, developments are fairly well documented and are dealt with elsewhere in this volume. In brief, the structuralisation of secondary education, which was speeded by the attempts of the Endowed Schools and Charity Commissioners to construct a tripartite system after 1869, continued through a period of sustained growth into the first years of the twentieth century. The high-prestige 'first-grade' schools, comprising the 'public' schools and some local grammar schools, aspired at least to keep their pupils to the age of 18, to link with the major universities and to offer a broad, humane curriculum as a preamble to university work. Below them the 'second-grade' schools, although reluctant to accept this label, devised curricula centred far more round modern and scientific subjects and, by the turn of the century, were beginning to stand in a clear relationship to the civic universities, an increasing proportion of whose entrants were recruited from this source. By 1916 it was possible for the committee reporting on *Scholarships for Higher Education* to assume that the vast majority of university entrants made their way via secondary schools.

The Secondary School Regulations in 1904, promulgated by R. L. Morant, threatened to blur this hierarchical divide by imposing a broad curriculum upon all secondary schools administered by the Board of Education (effectively, all those below 'public' school status). Thus, the new municipal secondary schools which appeared after 1902 were obliged to follow a curriculum virtually identical with that of the vast majority of long-established grammar schools.

If one outcome of this was to turn the face of the English secondary schools away from technical education for the foreseeable future, another was to keep them in step with the civic universities. For here, at precisely the same historical moment, similar developments were under way. During the first decade of the twentieth century the newly chartered civic universities, securely established as institutions of higher education, turned increasingly to the problem of redressing curricular imbalance. In brief, they retreated from the full-blown 'scientism' which had been used to justify their establishment, towards the 'defining institutions', Oxford and Cambridge. In so doing they remained in step with the secondary schools from whom they fed.

It is worth exploring the reasons for this change to gain clues as to its significance for the structure of the system as a whole. Sanderson has suggested that in the north of England the influence of Manchester was critical, diverting institutions in other towns such as Leeds and Sheffield from the technological model. The influence of London external degrees, of grants from central government after 1893, and the demands of teacher training, all seem to have played a part. This latter, in particular, was an element in the segmentation process by which significant numbers passed through the grammar schools into the arts faculties of the civic universities and thence back to the schools as teachers, where they worked to project others along the same road.

An element which appears to have been unconsidered in this analysis is the extent and nature of the colonisation by Oxbridge of the emergent civic colleges. In the *Reports from the University Colleges* made annually from 1894 to the Treasury it is possible to glimpse something of this development. In 1894, the first year of return, it is clear that Cambridge was more successful than Oxford in securing posts for its alumni in the civic colleges: at Birmingham five Cambridge men had a single Oxford graduate as a colleague, at Newcastle the ratio was six to one. Elsewhere the two major universities were more evenly represented, although Cambridge still tended to preponderate. But these Oxbridge products, although only a minority of the staff, formed in each case a significant proportion of the graduates appointed. The civic colleges did much work below degree level and, during the 1890s, many of their teachers were non-graduates. Newcastle, for example, had 18 non-graduates and 20 graduates, of whom 7 were educated at Oxbridge. By the turn of the century, when the reversion to the arts was about to accelerate, this Oxbridge domination was even more marked. In this year Birmingham submitted a return showing 18 non-graduates and 17 graduates (3 London, 9 Cambridge and 5 Oxford) as its staff complement. The proportions were similar elsewhere.[24]

Hardly surprisingly, it was the most influential posts in the provincial universities which fell to Oxbridge. In 1894, of 13 professors at Liverpool, only 4 were not from the two ancient universities. By 1901 the appointment of two more Cambridge men to chairs had only sharpened this distinction. This example is striking, but far from untypical. Indeed, there is clear evidence that the Oxbridge 'establishment' saw appointments to the new universities as a kind of gift which was theirs to bestow. The correspondence between Henry Sidgwick and James Bryce is informative:

You may know that the Principalship of Owens College is vacant by the resignation of A. W. Ward. Do you know of anyone at Cambridge likely to be a good man for it? . . . Functions really very important, chiefly administrative, but a man of wide outlook and general intellectual eminence desire [*sic*]. One on the literary side rather than on the scientific is needed, because in Manchester science is sure to take care of itself: it is the humanistic side that needs careful cultivation.[25]

This from Bryce to Sidgwick in 1897; two years later it was the turn of Sidgwick to raise similar issues in discussion of the Birmingham venture:

As regards Birmingham do you think as I remember you thought in the case of Owens College – that science will take care of itself, and the important thing is to take care of literature? Because, if so, I should be inclined to suggest S. H. Butcher . . . He is a brilliant scholar of the non-pedantic kind, a good speaker, an attractive personality with a fine air of distinguished culture about him. He is the best possible available man; at least assuming that my brother Arthur would be considered too old.[26]

Ironically, the man appointed to Birmingham, Sir Oliver Lodge, shared with Bryce and Sidgwick a lifelong interest in spiritualism, such were the vagaries of the late Victorian 'old boy network'. Against this background it is hardly surprising that the civic professoriate sought to build their new Zion in the image of the Oxbridge colleges they had so recently left behind them.

It is interesting to consider the response to Oxbridge of this blurring of roles at and after the First World War. On the one hand, there were those radicals, such as R. H. Tawney, who were ready to see the closer identification of the civic universities with Oxbridge as a part of the process of democratising higher education. He told the 1922 Commission on the Ancient Universities:

It is of capital importance that capacity (wherever it exists) should move freely to the work for which it is best suited. One condition of that movement is easy access to higher education, and any obstacle which makes such education difficult to obtain results in a grave waste of the nation's human resources. There is an immense reservoir of talent in the elementary schools which is not yet drawn on.[27]

Further, Tawney argued, the growth in secondary education, which would foreseeably double from the 8 per cent of the population for whom it then catered, could only sharpen this demand:

There is a general belief among thoughtful working people that higher education in general, and Oxford and Cambridge in particular, had been organised in the past too largely for the convenience of the well-to-do classes, and that, though a certain number of able boys pass to them, no very persistent and strenuous efforts have been made to remove the financial obstacles. The workman in a mining village or cotton town sees his clever boy prevented from going to university by lack of means, while the son of his employer, even if not conspicuously intelligent, appears to be admitted without difficulty. The ill-will which results is not negligible. Few things would do more to ease the tension between classes than the knowledge that higher education, including university education, is easily accessible to every able boy.[28]

But, for many, what Tawney discerned as an ideal appeared as an increasingly real threat; for them it was important to emphasise the distinctiveness of the ancient universities. Ironically, it was the Vice-Chancellor of a provincial university, George Adami, who did this most forcefully in 1922:

From their very eminence, irrespective largely of the extent of the stipend, Cambridge and Oxford will always attract teachers and investigators of the first class. Utilise these, not in training the Toms, Dicks, and Harrys of the under-graduate world, but in influencing and advancing the selected best products of the Empire. If universities are to be overcrowded with undergraduates, let it be the provincial universities. It is their duty to minister to the localities in which they are placed; they receive local grants and local benefactions. When Oxford and Cambridge were the only English universities, then of right men came to them from all quarters. It was this that made them national but this particular need exists no longer. It will raise the tone of the provincial universities if they receive a greater proportion of public school boys.[29]

Equally, though, the civic universities were to be kept in an inferior relationship to Oxbridge, since Adami envisaged a system which would 'give every encouragement to select any promising graduates of the provincial and imperial universities to come into residence' at Oxbridge. This view was echoed at the time by C. K. Webster, the Professor of Modern History at Liverpool, who pleaded that Oxford and Cambridge might become 'purely graduate universities drawing their students from amongst those who have acquitted themselves best at the modern universities'.[30]

This rationale could only be sustained if it were supported by the deployment of meritocratic scholarships. It is appropriate, therefore, that Adami, a significant but relatively neglected figure in the early twentieth-century landscape, should have been one of the leading advocates of competitive examinations. An eugenicist, and a leading enthusiast for racial improvement, George Adami used the Consultative Committee of the Board of Education between 1920 and 1924 to popularise selective scholarships. He was one of the authors of the seminal 1924 Report on this subject. But it must be emphasised that the Board of Education was alerted to the need for a more efficient scholarship system into higher education before Adami's involvement. As early as 1916 an Interim Report had emphasised the need to draw 'by whatever means, the better talent from the rural districts and from the rural labouring class for higher education'.[31] In this process scholarships were to be the catalyst. It is significant that, in this Report, the Consultative Committee of the Board of Education defended the structure of the existing scholarship system, involving closed awards from the 'public' schools to Oxbridge, and argued for its augmentation rather than its replacement:

If the Local Education Authorities took a completely independent line in their methods of award they would cut off their pupils from the advantages offered by

Oxford and Cambridge, and effect a thorough severance between the public schools and the old universities on the one hand and the new universities and the grant earning schools on the other. Such a severance is not to be desired.[32]

In these terms a 'tracking' system sustained by closed scholarships to Oxbridge and local awards to the civic colleges was defended in 1916.

The classic study by G. S. M. Ellis on the access of poor students to the universities confirmed that, for much of the nineteenth century, scholarships offered no more than 'a narrow gate through which the poor child may infrequently have reached the university'. More significantly, the rise of the new universities, which coincided with the reorganisation of secondary schooling, led to a particularly close relationship between these universities and the new secondary schools: 'The comparatively low range of fees, and the economical standard of living which is becoming a tradition within them, have made them [the new universities] relatively more accessible to the children of poor parents.'[33] This view was confirmed by Glass and Gray, who showed that the proliferation of scholarships immediately before the First World War did offer poor students a chance of aspiring to the ancient universities, but that in reality alumni of the 'public' schools (and particularly those of the 15 most expensive public schools) entered the race for scholarships at an enormous advantage. Of the 432 scholarships offered by the Oxbridge colleges in 1913–14, 374 (86%) were awarded to 'public' school pupils, 27 (6%) to alumni of endowed grammar schools and 29 (7%) to pupils of municipal secondary schools. In brief, 'public' school boys had 12 times the chance of winning an Oxbridge scholarship than their contemporaries in the state sector.[34]

It seems, therefore, that, although the period under review witnessed a vast extension of the scholarship system, this did not represent a whole-hearted attempt to democratise higher education; rather, this situation was thought to be defensible on the grounds that different universities had differing functions and served separate social groups, a fact which was to be at least tacitly acknowledged in the working of competitive examinations.

Similarly, at the school level, it was accepted – albeit grudgingly – that a differentiated system of secondary education would necessitate unequal access to higher education. The comments of C. E. Theodosius, a secondary schools inspector, on the grading of education in Bristol, made in 1907, are revealing:

I have recently had occasion to bring to the notice of the Bristol LEA a defect in their educational organisation which had hitherto escaped notice and which I have some reason to believe exists in other large towns. It may be briefly described as a breakdown in the 'educational ladder' at the top.

The old grammar schools of every grade, with all their faults, flattered themselves that they never let the really brilliant boy escape notice, and that every nerve was strained to bring his work to a university scholarship standard. The number of distinguished men who were educated at some of our humbler grammar schools is a confirmation of this claim . . . I suppose it is generally recognised that our new municipal secondary schools are and must remain second grade schools; that the normal leaving age will be 16 or 17 and that the staff will continue for some time at any rate, to consist of elementary teachers who have obtained a London BA or BSc in the interests of their professional work, i.e. by men and women who have ceased to be students at the age of 19 or 20, instead of, as in the first grade schools, by teachers who have had a regular university course, and have only taken up their profession at the age of about 23. It may therefore be assumed that these schools cannot, as a rule, attempt anything like a university scholarship standard of work. The result of this is that our secondary schools must be definitely graded, as indeed they are in practice.[35]

These remarks reflect the 'orthodoxy' preached by the inspectorate in the years before 1914 and are further evidence of a fortuitous dovetailing of the modern schools with the Redbrick universities, where, as the Bryce Commissioners pointed out, the age of entry was commonly 16 or 17, in contrast with Oxbridge, where the age of entry could be 'roughly stated at 19'.[36]

Thus a picture emerges of an educational system which by the time of the First World War had become segmented at various levels, the better to serve the needs of a differentiated society. Distinctive types of secondary school were linked to a hierarchical system of higher education in different ways. The swift growth and transition of the late nineteenth century had only briefly challenged these hierarchies; the adjustments of the early years of the new century served merely to confirm them.

If the period from 1870 to 1914 emphasised the unassailability of English elite institutions despite swift technological and social changes, it was also marked by close parallels between secondary and higher education. Most strikingly, the elite universities and schools (Oxbridge and the 'public' schools) remained aloof from, and relatively unscathed by, the social transformation which impelled traumatic changes at the second level (within the local grammar schools and civic university colleges). Throughout the period controversy centred upon the design and structure of this sector and the role of a technological education within it, rather than upon the refurbishing of elite institutions.

Further, at this more contentious second level, the first years of the twentieth century saw strikingly similar developments, involving a reversion from the modernism of the late nineteenth century towards a more prestigious 'humane' education.

These parallels suggest, at least implicitly, that schools and universities were not simply responding to the same pressures but were making adjustments which confirmed their roles in a clearly structured system. The extent to which these trends involved the clear establishment of a watertight 'tracking' system, by which particular types of school led exclusively to specific areas of higher education, is uncertain. But the evidence assembled here certainly suggests that such a process was under way. At the very least it is possible to conclude that one important element in the dynamic of change was an acute awareness among the English upper and middle classes of the importance of social hierarchies.

Part III
Debate and concluding discussion

8. The debate on secondary school reform in France and Germany

JAMES ALBISETTI

The contributions to this volume by Detlef Müller and Fritz Ringer point out the remarkable similarities in the structural reforms of French and German secondary education introduced in the first years of the twentieth century. The following essay will attempt to demonstrate that the processes by which these reforms were reached also reveal very striking parallels, and to show that they involved issues beyond those associated with the reproduction of the cultural capital of the bourgeoisie.

Well before the appearance of either Müller's *Sozialstruktur und Schulsystem* or Ringer's *Education and Society in Modern Europe*, several historians of French education had analysed the secondary school reform of 1902 in terms very similar to 'systematisation' and 'segmentation' as defined by these two scholars. Antoine Prost, for example, had argued that the theoretical equality of the four tracks created in that year was not realised in fact, that 'the sections without Latin remained the inferior sections, primarily as a result of their recruitment'.[1] Prost's views were echoed in Joseph Moody's survey of French educational history and in Theodore Zeldin's magisterial history of modern France. Viviane Isambert-Jamati conducted a more thorough investigation of this theme and came to basically the same conclusion. Without making direct reference to Müller's work, Patrick Harrigan has argued that the French secondary schools of the 1860s recruited pupils from a wider social base than has been traditionally assumed, implying that they played much the same 'comprehensive' function that Müller ascribes to the *Gymnasien* of this period.[2]

Too exclusive a concentration on the social origin of pupils in the various tracks, however, distorts our understanding of secondary school reform in the late nineteenth century. In both France and Germany the educational authorities faced a number of different, and at times contradictory, challenges in this period, and experimented with various responses to them before arriving at the relatively long-lasting solutions adopted around 1900. Using a framework borrowed from my book on the German reforms,[3] this chapter will compare these responses to common challenges.

The demands of the present

Ringer is correct to stress the difficulty of linking educational reforms to specific changes in the economy. Yet one should not neglect the fact that in France and Germany after 1850 increasing numbers of critics asserted that the classical schools had failed to keep up with the changing scientific, technical, industrial and commercial realities of life. Such critics emphasised two separate problems the secondary schools needed to solve: the provision of a better grounding in scientific methods and subject matter for pupils going on to medical, technical or scientific studies at university level; and the arming of the early leavers and graduates who entered commerce and industry with the rudiments of the skills that their jobs would require.

In France special preparatory classes for the Ecole Polytechnique and the military academy at St Cyr had existed even before 1848, a tacit admission that the classical *lycée* on its own did not prepare pupils for all future studies. In 1852 Hippolyte Fortoul, Napoleon III's Minister of Public Instruction, took a further step towards a formal division of the *lycée*, introducing a 'bifurcation' after the *quatrième* (at about the age of 14) into literary and scientific tracks, with pupils taking some classes in common but having separate *baccalauréat* examinations. This was designed both to produce more graduates with a solid grounding in natural science and to stem the flood of pupils into the newly authorised Catholic secondary schools. Bifurcation came only after pupils had taken four years of Latin and three of Greek, and thus did little to help the early leavers who entered commerce and industry. Yet by restricting medical, scientific and technical studies to holders of the scientific *baccalauréat*, Fortoul endeavoured to eliminate inadequately prepared students in these fields. In 1858, however, opposition from the medical profession led to the restoration of the right to study medicine to graduates of the literary track, a retreat that proved to be the beginning of the end for bifurcation. Other problems also arose, including a shortage of science teachers and unsatisfactory results in the classes both tracks took in common. In 1863 Victor Duruy delayed bifurcation until after the *troisième*; a year later he abolished it altogether.[4]

Duruy's restoration of a single-track *lycée* meant that one curriculum again had to satisfy the needs of all potential students. The consequence of this decision was a series of changes in the *lycée* curriculum over the next 15 years that diluted the ancient languages with more 'modern' subject matter. In 1863 Duruy had already moved the beginning of instruction in modern languages from the *troisième* to the *sixième*; two years later he abolished the requirement that pupils should write compositions in Greek. In the early 1870s Jules Simon retained the goal of a modernised *lycée*: as he put it, 'we must raise our children for our time and our country, but we must not separate our age and nation from the tradition of the Latin races or the human tradition'. Simon left office before he could add more class hours for history, French and modern languages, and reduce the time devoted to Latin compositions and verses; but a new curriculum issued in 1880 brought about much of what he had wanted. Latin was delayed until the *sixième*, Greek until the *troisième*; Latin compositions were dropped from the *baccalauréat* examination. At the same time, the sciences received a modest increase in class time, and some instruction in modern languages was begun in the elementary classes before the *sixième*.[5] Despite these efforts to adapt the *lycée* to the needs of the times, however, Duruy and his successors found it necessary to continue preparatory classes for the Ecole Polytechnique. Beginning in 1893, the medical faculties added a year of basic instruction in the sciences for *lycée* graduates not sufficiently prepared for the study of medicine.[6]

The Prussian *Gymnasium* experienced a similar increase in time devoted to modern subject matter at the expense of the ancient languages. In the late 1870s many professors of science and medicine had complained publicly about the poor quality of students coming from the *Gymnasien*. These complaints led the educational authorities to issue a revised curriculum in 1882, cutting nine credit hours for Latin and two for Greek, while adding four hours each for science and French and two for mathematics. This reform enabled the *Gymnasium* to retain for the time being its monopoly over preparation for medical study in the new regulations for the certification of physicians issued in 1883.[7]

These modest reforms of the *lycée* and the *Gymnasium* in the early 1880s did not prevent the emergence in that decade of more far-reaching attacks on the classical tradition. These attacks combined pedagogical concerns with the desires of an apparently increasing number of parents to free their sons from Greek and Latin. In France, Raoul Frary argued in *The Latin Question* that 'the needs of one generation are not those of the preceding one', and warned that 'the cult of beauty should not make us neglect the cultivation of the useful'. Noting 'the multitude of indifferent and bored pupils that the law and social custom force to parade before the altar of the classics', Frary demolished, at least to his own satisfaction, all the traditional justifications for studying Latin and Greek. He expressed particular concern about the pedagogical consequences of basing instruction on subjects the purpose of which young pupils could not grasp. From this perspective as well, a secondary education centred on modern languages, history and science was preferable.[8]

In Prussia the nine-year *Realgymnasien*, with no Greek, less Latin, but more science and modern languages than the *Gymnasien*, had offered an alternative to parents since 1859. Enrolment in these schools tripled between 1860 and 1880, encouraged in part by the opening of sections of the philosophical faculties to their graduates in 1870 and by the hope, ultimately disappointed, that medical studies would also soon be opened.[9]

The 'special secondary education' created by Victor Duruy in the 1860s did not offer an alternative to the classical track that was equivalent to the *Realgymnasium*. It replaced not the scientific track of the bifurcated *lycée*, but rather the various non-classical courses which had grown up in many *lycées*. Duruy saw special secondary education as aiming to reinforce existing social divisions 'in that it would counter the tendency of young men to emigrate from the countryside and would keep young men who would ultimately take jobs in the commercial and industrial sectors from overtaxing the classical curriculum'.[10] Before 1880 special secondary education lasted only four years and offered its graduates no career privileges. It did prove popular, however, especially in the *collèges* of provincial towns and cities, and by the mid-1870s was enrolling more pupils than the lower grades of the public *lycées* did. Most pupils did not complete the four-year course, choosing to enter family businesses or other careers after finishing their years of compulsory schooling. Recognition of this fact contributed, in 1881, to the division of the course into a three-year cycle for all 'special' pupils and a second cycle of two years for the minority who wanted to continue their schooling beyond the compulsory age.[11]

Even after this extension of its course, special secondary education did not present as clear a threat to the classical track as did the nine-year *Realgymnasium*. Yet in less than twenty years it came, according to Alexandre Ribot, 'to menace the positions of classical education'. Through a process that Ribot considered 'curious',[12] the special curriculum was extended in length and made more literary than technical in orientation, along the way being rechristened 'modern secondary education' and gaining its own *baccalauréat* with significant privileges. How and why had this happened?

The overburdening question

The transformation of special into modern secondary education has continued to confuse recent historians. Theodore Zeldin argues that the aspirations of the clientele of special secondary education did not dictate such a change. C. R. Day explains the transformation by pointing to the hostility of the educational authorities to the practical goals of the special secondary course, which did not conform to their vision of what secondary education should be. Ringer attributes what he calls this 'generalist shift' primarily to the 'socio-cultural aspirations of teachers and parents', but does not explain why these aspirations were satisfied by the government.[13] It is clear that the demands of critics such as Frary played a major role in the creation of a modern track.[14] More important, though, were contemporary changes in the *lycée*, which amounted to a rejection of the single-track secondary school re-established by Duruy in 1865. The indisputable cause of this rejection was the growing fear that *lycée* pupils were dangerously overburdened with school work.

Accusations that the classical schools put an excessive strain on their pupils had surfaced in Germany during the 1830s and 1850s, and in France in the 1840s.[15] In neither country, however, had there ever before been as widespread or as sustained an interest in overburdening as arose in the last third of the nineteenth century. In France the first major blast in this campaign against the *lycée* came in 1867, shortly after Duruy had abolished bifurcation. In a book entitled *Homicidal Education*, the poet Victor de Laprade accused the schools of maintaining a regimen 'absolutely contrary to nature, which lowers the vital force and enervates the constitution of both the individual and the race subjected to it for too long'. He insisted that children were less carefree than in earlier days and called for a new concern and love for youth. Laprade suggested a survey of the physical condition of the educated classes, saying that medical authorities confirmed every day the immense increase in the number of 'nervous' disorders. He considered 'the dream of the Ecole Polytechnique' to be 'a curse for youth' in France and asked how many great geometers it produced compared to the number of young men who remained 'neuropathic, consumptive, rachitic and imbecilic'. Laprade feared for the future of France because 'the weakening of the physical constitution of the race is soon carried over into the intellectual realm'.[16]

After military defeat in 1870 gave greater credibility to such fears of French degeneration, similar sentiments were expressed even by the former Minister of Public Instruction, Jules Simon. He noted that the public generally paid attention only to the successful candidates for the *baccalauréat* or the *grandes écoles* and not to the 'number of children who leave the *collège* broken and in ill health'. Simon considered Duruy's single-track *lycée* to have demanded too much and lamented that his own successors had retained his plans for more time for history and modern languages without accepting the cuts he had proposed, so that pupils 'who formerly were overburdened are now crushed'.[17] Similar complaints multiplied in the 1880s. For example, Octave Gréard's study of secondary education began by asking whether 'the burden that youth is put under is not beyond the effort it is wise to demand of it'. Even after major reductions in classroom hours, Paul Bourget could say in the 1890s that nothing more than a visit to 'a French *lycée* with its barrack-like buildings, hemmed-in playgrounds, the

promiscuity of its dormitories, the bare ugliness of its studies and classrooms
. . . is needed to show you that the young men there brought up must be
physically impoverished, nervously overstrained, robbed of joy and spon-
taneity'. For Edmond Desmolins the result of French secondary education
was 'to compromise our vitality'.[18]

Duruy's abolition of the requirement to write Greek compositions had
been designed to ease overburdening; so had the delay in the start of Latin
and Greek that was introduced in 1880. As public concern grew, the Conseil
Supérieur de l'Instruction Publique launched an investigation of the problem in July 1884. Three years later the National Academy of Medicine
conducted a similar inquiry.[19] This debate on overburdening in France was
carried on in extremely vague terms compared to discussions in Germany at
the same time, where critics of the *Gymnasium* brought forward statistics on
the high percentage of unfit one-year volunteers, on the rising age of the
average graduate and on the increasing rates of mental illness, nearsighted-
ness and suicide among secondary pupils. Yet much of the public accepted
overburdening as an established fact, much to the later horror of Alfred
Binet, who wrote *Mental Fatigue* in 1898 to publicise the rudimentary and as
yet inconclusive efforts to measure intellectual stress, which had been begun
in the 1890s by German psychologists and physicians.[20]

That the authorities did believe in the reality of overburdening is shown by
the sharp reduction in classroom hours made in the *lycée* curricula of 1885
and 1890.[21] In contrast to the reforms introduced between 1865 and 1880,
these reductions did not touch Latin and Greek at all. Although the 'social
meaning' of the ancient languages did not depend on a precise level of
teaching, educators apparently believed there was a certain level below
which these could not be cut if their pedagogical goals were still to be
achieved. The loss in class hours for modern languages, sciences, history,
French and drawing marked an unmistakable retreat from the single-track
lycée envisioned by Duruy and Simon.[22] As Ringer points out, an upgrading
of special secondary education followed each of the reductions in modern
subject matter at the *lycée*, including the introduction of a modern *baccalauréat* that by 1898 was producing 24 per cent of all *bacheliers*.[23]

In Prussia fears about overburdening, especially as voiced by Emperor
Wilhelm II at the school conference of 1890, led to the loss of about two
hours per week of classes in new curricula for all secondary schools issued in
1892. In contrast to the changes in the *lycée*, however, the *Gymnasium*
suffered further cuts in Latin and Greek in order to allow more time for
German, drawing and physical education. In response to a demand from the
Emperor the school conference had resolved that the *Realgymnasium*
should disappear, while *Oberrealschule* graduates were to receive most of
the privileges that modern secondary education had won in France. The
effort to eliminate the semi-classical schools proved abortive, but the

Prussian system of secondary education as envisioned by the conference would have closely resembled the French structure of 1891.[24]

Concern with overburdening also generated unprecedented interest in both pedagogy and sport in the secondary schools. During the nineteenth century *lycée* teachers had received minimal pedagogical training; as Hippolyte Taine wrote, 'the future professor leaving the Ecole Normale at the age of 24 with his new *agrégation* has not yet taught a class, except during two weeks at a Paris *lycée*'. French critics of overburdening often attacked the excessive specialisation of *lycée* teachers, seeing even Germany, where teachers usually taught two subjects, as a model worthy of imitation.[25] The growing interest in pedagogy is illustrated by the number of major works on the history of education and teaching which appeared in the late 1880s, the introduction of a course on the science of education at the faculty of Toulouse in 1888, and the changing picture of teacher–pupil relations that Viviane Isambert-Jamati has found in the annual speeches given at *lycée* ceremonies.[26] Yet, as the Ribot Commission heard from many witnesses, this new interest could not make up for the lack of formal training. The reforms of 1902 required future secondary teachers to take a course in pedagogy, and beginning in 1904 Emile Durkheim held a chair in this field at the Ecole Normale.[27]

Another proposed remedy for overburdening lay in improving physical education and sport. In France during the 1860s and 1870s interest in better physical training had stemmed primarily from concern about military preparedness. As Jules Ferry put it, schoolboy gymnastics was 'a patriotic endeavour'. Duruy also urged greater attention to gymnastics and military drill; but Simon could still comment in the early 1870s that gymnastics had been 'treated like modern languages; we lose an hour a week pretending to teach them, but in reality do not teach them at all'. A decade later Michel Bréal echoed Simon in praising the superior physical training in German schools, even though it had 'more of a military aspect than ours does'.[28] With the fears about overburdening rising in the 1880s, interest in fitness for its own sake became more common; the first sports clubs began to appear outside the schools. In 1888 Pierre de Coubertin, the future leader in the revival of the Olympics, convinced Simon to become the chairman of a Committee for the Preparation of Physical Exercises in the Schools. The following year a government commission repeated this call for improved physical education.[29]

That these continuing exhortations had little effect becomes more understandable when one realises that gymnastics were performed in street clothes and that few *lycées* had gymnasia, playing fields or shower rooms. Sports clubs did exist at about half the public secondary schools by 1900, but they attracted only a small percentage of pupils. To remedy the persistent neglect of fitness, the Ribot Commission recommended that physical education should be 'organised seriously'; it even suggested that it should 'have a place in the final examinations'. In the first decade of the new century, however, sport was still making little progress in French secondary schools.[30]

The French interest in pedagogy and physical fitness had direct parallels in Germany in this era. Beginning in 1890, future Prussian secondary teachers had to spend a 'seminar year' in pedagogical studies and teaching practice after completing their work in the universities. The new curricula of 1892 raised the time devoted to physical education from two hours to three or four hours per week, with a recommendation that some of the time be devoted to games. Yet the popularisation of sport advanced only slowly in the 1890s.[31] Thus, in the realm of official decrees, Prussia led France by a decade in introducing better pedagogical training and physical education as a means of combating overburdening. The evaluation of the impact in the schools of these decrees, however, would require studies that are more specialised than those that are as yet available.

The 'ballast'

When Léon Bourgeois explained the creation of modern secondary education to the Ribot Commission, he pointed to three main factors. Two have been mentioned: many clients of the *lycée* had demanded a secondary education without Latin and Greek; and many had also complained that the government had piled on too many subjects in the classical schools. Bourgeois' third reason was that many teachers of the ancient languages had urged that pupils without a taste for Latin and Greek should stay out of the traditional *lycée*.[32] Bourgeois' comment echoed Duruy's justification of special secondary education – that it would prevent the overtaxing of the classical curriculum – but suggested that the modern track could not attract such pupils unless it offered greater privileges.

This interest in excluding from the classical schools what the Germans called the 'ballast' and the French often referred to as the 'lame' appears to support the notion that the systematisation of secondary education around 1900 served to accentuate social segmentation. If the operative assumption of the authorities was that the less interested and less talented pupils in the *lycée* were also those from lower social classes, Müller's thesis would apply very well to France. Yet if this was the official assumption, the sharp reductions in class hours in 1885 and 1890 make no sense: why ease overburdening in order to keep unwanted pupils in the classical track? One wonders, in fact, if the chief victims of overburdening were not the less talented sons of upper middle-class parents. That after 1902 only 19 per cent of the candidates for the *baccalauréat* chose the Latin–Greek option indicates that the 'ballast' of uninterested pupils in the classical track must have included many boys from among the traditional clientele of the *lycée*.[33]

Despite the fact that special secondary education absorbed most of the growth in French secondary enrolments after 1863, there was increased concern in the 1880s and 1890s about a 'ballast' in the *lycées*. Frary saw a 'multitude of indifferent and bored pupils' in the classical course, and Edouard Maneuvrier, in 1888, estimated that the 'lame' comprised two-thirds of the pupils. Hippolyte Taine clearly exaggerated when he suggested, in the early 1890s, that nine out of ten pupils were wasting their time in the *lycée*; but, as Bourgeois' remarks to the Ribot Commission indicate, the 'ballast' did concern the French educational authorities at the time of the reforms of 1890 and 1891.[34]

The rapid expansion of the new modern track, to the point where by 1898 it had as many pupils starting as the classical, suggests that this problem had been solved; so does the fact that in that year there were fewer pupils in the first three grades of the classical track than in the final four grades.[35] Yet critics continued to complain about the drag on classical studies exerted by uninterested pupils. Leading defenders of the traditional *lycée* gradually came to see that only by further sacrificing its monopoly over desirable privileges could the classical track free itself from this 'ballast' and maintain a curriculum heavily slanted towards the ancient languages. In 1898 Georges Fonsegrive proposed that granting equal privileges to graduates of the modern track would enable the *lycées* to offer 'serious Latin studies'. Ernest Lavisse told the Ribot Commission that this reform would allow the re-establishment of a 'frankly classical' course.[36] Describing the reforms of 1902 to an American audience, Gabriel Compayré wrote:

Up to the present time there was in the classes of our *lycées* too large a number of pupils who followed, with no profit, instruction for which they were not fitted. They encumbered the classes, where they formed a kind of *corpus mortuum* and embarrassed the teacher, whom they reduced to this dilemma, either not to take them into account, considering them a negligible quantity, or if he wanted to be of service to them, to lower his methods of instruction and check the progress of those of their fellow pupils who could and would go on.[37]

In the future, Compayré believed, 'the chosen few who remain loyal to the old humanities will hereafter comprise only good scholars, earnestly bent on studies which they will have sought out of their own free will, and in which they will be capable of succeeding'.[38] From the point of view of the teachers it is not clear that 'good scholars' meant 'boys from better homes'.

In Germany the existence of the *Realgymnasien, Oberrealschulen,* and six-year *Realschulen* did not prevent the growth of a similar concern about a 'ballast' in the classical schools. Especially during the 1880s, the Prussian government devoted a great deal of effort to trying to lure or drive the 'ballast' out of the *Gymnasium* and into the other schools. Yet the Ministry of Education failed to obtain privileges for *Realschule* graduates in the middle-level civil service or for *Oberrealschule* graduates in the technical fields of the upper civil service until after the school conference of 1890. The modern track grew substantially during the next decade, but growth came much more at the expense of the semi-classical track than at that of the *Gymnasium*, and thus did little to remove the problem of the 'ballast'.[39] As in France, defenders of the ancient languages in Germany came to realise in the 1890s that only by surrendering the *Gymnasium*'s near-monopoly over preparation for the universities could the traditional curriculum be saved and the 'ballast' diverted into the modern schools. The *Gymnasium* Association reached this conclusion only on the eve of the school conference of 1900.[40] In neither country, however, did the classical track after the turn of the century become more 'frankly classical': as long as it aimed to prepare graduates for medical and scientific studies, no further reductions in modern subject matter could be made.[41]

The abandonment of single tracks leading to the universities was not welcomed by everyone, particularly not by those who regretted the destruction of a common educational experience for all future students and professionals. In Germany this position was adopted by the Association for a Comprehensive School (*Einheitsschulverein*), founded in 1886, which favoured a modernised *Gymnasium* accompanied by shorter modern schools, in essence a system like the French *lycées* and special secondary schools as of 1881. In France the most prominent advocate of retaining a single-track *lycée* was the conservative sociologist and philosopher Alfred Fouillée. In his *Education from the National Viewpoint*, published at the time of the upgrading of 'special' into 'modern' secondary education in 1891, Fouillée argued that having two tracks would force boys to choose too early in life what career they would pursue. He feared that the choice would fall more often to the modern track, thus cutting off many future members of the elite from the Latin tradition. To retain a single track, Fouillée was willing to jettison obligatory Greek and to claim that the 'ballast' would not be better off without Latin, nor the Latin classes without the 'ballast'.[42]

A minority of school reformers in both countries favoured a different method of dealing with the 'ballast'. Admitting that a single secondary track was no longer possible, they none the less wanted to delay tracking by several years through a common foundation for all secondary education, which would not include the ancient languages. This idea never triumphed completely in Prussia, but delaying Latin until the fourth year of secondary school did become a local option in 1900.[43] The cycles created in France in 1902 did not serve quite the same function, because the modern first cycle did not prepare pupils for the three upper tracks with Latin, but the Latin first cycle was a common foundation for these three options in the upper grades.

The academic proletariat

The most powerful opposition to the granting of privileges to the semi-classical and modern tracks in order to lure the 'ballast' out of the classical schools came not from supporters of a comprehensive track or advocates of a common foundation, but from members of the professions being opened to graduates of the less prestigious schools. In Prussia resistance from civil servants, lawyers and physicians had been crucial in preventing the extension of privileges to *Realgymnasium* graduates in the 1880s and 1890s, and it did not disappear even after the Emperor's decree of November 1900.[44] In France physicians had opposed Fortoul's bifurcation in the 1850s and, as George Weisz has recently shown, they vigorously opposed the reform of 1902 as a measure likely 'to exacerbate professional overcrowding and to lower the precarious social standing of doctors'.[45]

That opening the universities to graduates of semi-classical and modern schools would produce an unemployable and politically dangerous academic proletariat was a common fear on both sides of the Rhine in the late nineteenth century. In the mid-1880s Bismarck equated an academic proletariat with Russian nihilism and castigated over-ambitious German parents who were trying to raise their sons above their station. Only after a levelling-off of university enrolments in the early 1890s did official concern about overcrowding subside sufficiently for equal privileges to be granted, in 1900.[46]

In France, concern about the overcrowding of the professions was more widespread in the 1890s than it had been in the 1880s. Although secondary enrolments per age group were virtually stagnant from 1880 to 1914, the number of *baccalauréats* per age group rose by about 50 per cent between 1876 and 1898, and more *bacheliers* chose to enter the universities. As a result the student population rose from 11,200 in 1876 to almost 30,000 in 1901, or from 4.7 to 12.0 students per thousand of those aged between 19 and 22. Three times as many medical degrees were granted between 1896 and 1900 as had been between 1861 and 1865.[47]

Such expansion lent credibility to works such as Henry Bérenger's *The Intellectual Proletarians of France*, which, despite its reliance on undocumented statistics, did much to popularise concern about the overcrowded professions. Bérenger asserted that half the physicians in France did not earn an adequate living and that many lawyers did not begin to earn money until their mid-thirties. He also claimed that ten times as many engineers as France needed were being produced and that each year about 100 new *agrégés* and 1000 new *licenciés* were competing for 200 to 300 openings in the secondary schools.[48] Other Frenchmen who were worried about the academic proletariat included among the *déclassés* not only the unemployed or underemployed, but also the *bacheliers* who did not gain access to the *grandes écoles* of their choice and the large number of pupils who failed the *baccalauréat*. Alexandre Ribot's estimate of a failure rate of 32 per cent was lower than many figures cited in the contemporary literature.[49]

A foreign observer of French secondary education at the turn of the century blamed the growing academic proletariat on 'the feeling of caste' which prevented the *bachelier* from 'turning to mercantile or commercial pursuits'.[50] Jules Simon agreed, suggesting that the graduate who failed to win a place in a *grande école* 'was too vain, and had nourished too many illusions, to accept material occupations'. According to Frary, classical education did 'not prepare young Frenchmen for any productive profession'; for Gustave LeBon, the *lycée* fitted a boy for 'absolutely nothing but public functions'. Both Frary and LeBon echoed Bismarck's criticism of ambitious parents pushing their sons into the classical schools, even though the stagnation of enrolments in this period makes the notion of the lower orders crowding into the *lycées* patently unbelievable.[51]

Another factor blamed for swelling the ranks of university students in this period was a change in the French conscription law which took effect in 1891. The revised law fixed the length of service at three years for 70 per cent of French youth and one year for the rest; against the objections of the Chamber, the Senate insisted that this 30 per cent should include all university students, who now would not have to pay for their own maintenance as 'volunteers', as their German equivalents did. According to one senator the new law led to the universities being flooded with 'innumerable postulants, eager for studies without a future, and all aspiring for membership in that fortunate intellectual elite which will exempt them from two years in the barracks'.[52]

The granting of limited university privileges to graduates of modern secondary education did not attract as much attention as a cause for the overcrowding of the professions as might have been expected in the light of the rising number of modern *baccalauréats* in the 1890s. The conservative Fouillée, eager to restore a single-track *lycée*, did emphasise how the new modern track had added to the academic proletariat. Ernest Lavisse, however, told the Ribot Commission that there was no proof that opening the medical and legal professions to graduates of modern secondary education would produce more severe overcrowding in these fields.[53]

If contemporaries disagreed on the causes of the academic proletariat, political conservatives – and many liberals – in both countries agreed on the dangers it posed. To Frary the *déclassés* were 'the most dangerous of discontents'; for Bérenger 'the souls of the intellectual proletariat are fatally inclined to either servility or revolt'. Paul Bourget believed that the graduate left the *lycée* 'either a functionary or refractory, crushed or revolted . . . wasting himself either in feeble platitudes or in destructive insanity'. LeBon, in his *Psychology of Socialism*, developed an elaborate explanation of why the Latin races were particularly susceptible to socialism, stressing that 'the host of graduates, licentiates, instructors, and professors without employment will one day, perhaps, constitute one of the most serious dangers against which society will have to defend itself'.[54]

The Ribot Commission, influenced by these fears about the academic proletariat and by pressure from lawyers and physicians who wanted to restrict their professions to graduates of the classical *lycée*, recommended by a majority of one vote not to open medical and legal careers to graduates of modern secondary education. The educational authorities overrode this recommendation, however, and granted access to the universities to graduates of the modern track and the new Latin–Sciences and Latin–Languages tracks, which were similar to the *Realgymnasium*.

In the view of George Weisz, this reform constituted 'a very deliberate attempt to make higher education more accessible'.[55] His interpretation suggests, in contrast to the views of Prost and Isambert-Jamati, that the privileges granted to the less prestigious tracks were expected to be used and that the segmentation which might continue or develop at the secondary level would not prevent a greater social mixing in the universities. When one considers that of the candidates for the *baccalauréat* in 1910 only 19 per cent came from the Latin–Greek track, with 25 per cent from Latin–Languages, 22 per cent from Latin–Sciences, and 34 per cent from Sciences–Languages, it is clear that before 1902 the lure of privileges is all that had kept many pupils enrolled in the classical *lycée*.[56] As Ringer's data indicate, the reform of 1902 did not so much broaden recruitment into the secondary schools as encourage more of the young men in the schools to complete a *baccalauréat* and enter the university.

The results of the Prussian reforms of 1900 were rather different. In 1911 the classical *Gymnasium* still produced 66 per cent of secondary school graduates, although its proportion of total enrolments had fallen to 46 per cent. This greater loyalty to the classical track, however, did not prevent a rapid rise in the inclusiveness of Prussian secondary education, from 2.7 per cent in 1900 to 3.2 per cent in 1911. The *Gymnasium* did not lose enrolments as the French classical track did, but the expansion took place almost entirely in the other schools.[57]

The national heritage, patriotism and civic training

One other aspect of secondary school reform in the late nineteenth century reveals further striking similarities between German and French developments: the changing role of the national heritage in education. Before

German unification the *Gymnasium* had not devoted much attention to German literature and history. By the 1880s, though, many people had begun to demand that this situation should come to an end. As in many other areas Wilhelm II did express the national mood when he told the school conference of 1890: 'we must raise young Germans, not young Greeks and Romans!' Numerous reformers suggested that German studies should form the new core for a humanistic secondary education, while others considered increased attention to German history a necessary means for preparing young men to handle their future political tasks. The Kaiser went further, insisting that instruction in German history should foster patriotic and anti-socialist views. Through a Cabinet Order of 1 May 1889 and his participation in the school conference he succeeded in having these goals included in the guidelines issued to elementary and secondary teachers.[58]

France's much longer history of political unity and literary greatness did not translate into a significant role for French culture in the *lycée*. In the early 1870s Simon increased the hours devoted to French in order to aid in 'vanquishing the greatest enemy of our colleges, boredom'. Yet, as Theodore Zeldin reports, 'it was only in 1880 that a larger selection of French set books was prescribed – Bossuet, Pascal, Voltaire. Only in 1885 was the study of nineteenth century authors permitted, but "with prudence"; only in 1890 was the injunction to prudence dropped'.[59] Even between 1880 and 1885, when French had its highest number of class hours, Michel Bréal bemoaned the neglect of the *chansons de geste* while praising the treatment of medieval epics in the *Gymnasium*. Frary also lamented the neglect of the Middle Ages, which he saw as a more important source of modern French culture than either Athens or Rome.[60]

A revised *lycée* curriculum in 1854 had given more importance to the history of France, but when Duruy took office he found the pupils in the philosophy class woefully ignorant of 'the political, economic, and social condition of France and the world'. He introduced new studies in the last year of the *lycée* which were designed to be 'the ideal instrument for instilling patriotism in the nation's youth'. In some quarters, however, Duruy was accused of forcing teachers to become 'adulators of the Empire'. When an investigation in 1871 still found a 'serious ignorance of history' among advanced pupils, Simon increased the hours allotted to this subject; but he shied away from the treatment of contemporary affairs. A Parliamentary Commission confirmed his stance, but 'allowed the principal events between 1815 and 1848 to be taught in the secondary schools, provided that everything that might arouse controversy be eliminated'.[61] History lost class hours in both 1885 and 1890, however, and on the eve of the First World War Albert Malet of the Lycée Louis-le-Grand could still lament that pupils preparing for the *baccalauréat* 'had the liberty not to know one of the essential parts of our national history, the formation of France by the Capetian kings'.[62]

Even in matters of political and social indoctrination, secondary education in the Second Reich and the Third Republic did not differ drastically. The French elementary schools after 1870 became notorious breeding grounds of chauvinism, with even liberals like Lavisse producing textbooks that extolled military virtues, praised France's services to the world, and provided very little information about other countries.[63] Conditions were not very different in the secondary schools, despite the claim made in the 1890s by Charles Langlois and Charles Seignobos that France did not 'seek to use history, as is done in Germany, for the purpose of promoting patriotism and loyalty'. In 1897, when candidates for the modern *baccalauréat* were asked what the purpose of studying history was, 80 per cent answered, in effect, 'to exalt patriotism'.[64]

The regime looked to history and social science to provide a basis for a republican morality that could substitute for the religious teachings of its clerical opponents. By the 1890s the republicans had united behind the ideology of 'solidarity', which has been described as 'an extension of the fraternitarian French Revolutionary tradition from civil and political to social rights'. Yet 'solidarity' also contained explicit anti-socialist themes similar to those espoused by Wilhelm II. Emile Littré, an important solidarist theorist, wrote that education 'as a means of popular enlightenment . . . would loosen the hold of socialist doctrine'. Léon Bourgeois insisted during the wave of anarchist bombings in the 1890s that democracy could not 'stand still between fear and violence', but must solve the social problem by an education that would 'establish links of solidarity among the citizens'.[65]

The effects of this ideology on pedagogical practice were predictable. Official guidelines accompanying the *lycée* curriculum of 1880 indicated that 'French history, in particular, should elucidate the general development of the institutions from which modern society has emerged, and should inspire respect for, and attachment to, the principles on which this society rests.' It is not surprising that Fouillée urged the schools to teach the necessity of private property from 'a social, national and international point of view'; but the more democratic Alfred Croiset also advocated teaching a doctrine of social evolution that would demonstrate that 'sudden revolutions are impossible'.[66]

Republicanism also did not seriously challenge the validity of secondary schools designed to serve only a small fraction of the population.[67] Although some witnesses before the Ribot Commission did speak of the desirability of a common elementary school through to the age of 12, little was done to break down the barriers between the *lycées* and the mass of elementary pupils. The decree of 1902 did structure the secondary course to follow four years of elementary education, but the government continued to provide financial support for the private elementary classes attached to the *lycées*, something not done in Germany.[68]

Conclusion

This brief survey of the debates over secondary school reform in France and Prussia reveals a pattern of similar responses to common challenges, especially the impossibility of teaching all desired subjects in one secondary curriculum. That neither government ever proposed a single track with options shows not only a wish to protect the exclusivity of the classical track, but also the power of deeply rooted traditions. To dismiss all concern about overburdening, the 'ballast' and the academic proletariat as 'ideology' would be as wrong-headed as to insist that these issues did not often mask conservative social goals.

9. On 'systems' of education and their comparability: methodological comments and theoretical alternatives*

JÜRGEN SCHRIEWER and KLAUS HARNEY

The main interest of this volume for historical scholarship on education lies in its attempt to test, by means of historical comparisons, the explanatory power and the potential for generalisation of certain complex models that have recently been developed in educational sociology and history with the aim of interpreting the structural changes and the social functions of European educational systems. This purpose should be seen in the wider context of increasing interaction between the social sciences and history. As a result of a growing historical awareness among sociologists and of an increasing attention to theory among historians, we are increasingly under pressure to examine the theoretical foundations, the credibility and the range of our explanations in order to avoid methodological pitfalls. In this connection the comparative method is acquiring a new and central significance as the most promising way to achieve the analytical separation of the general from the particular that is required by meaningful historical interpretation. For, as Manning Nash once vividly put it, 'the value of contrasting . . . culturally and historically disparate societies is akin to the role of litmus paper in bringing out the special ingredients of different social mixtures'.[1]

In the context of a renaissance of comparative historical work the studies collected in the present volume concentrate on the structural changes in secondary and higher education in England, France and Germany in the late nineteenth and early twentieth centuries. They clearly point to impressive parallels, which have not been shown so precisely before: (i) the temporal centrality of the key period (roughly 1850–1920) for the rise of modern educational systems, whose primary structural characteristics persisted for decades or even up to the present, (ii) the largely parallel way in which

* Translated by Nelson Wattie and edited by Fritz Ringer.

educational institutions that arose contingently were organised into coherent, all-embracing systems, and finally (iii) the remarkably comparable way in which these systems affected social selection and reproduction. While testifying to the heuristic fertility of the comparative approach, the particular viewpoint of this volume has already had an unusually stimulating effect on primary research (e.g. a detailed examination of the development of English endowed grammar schools during the nineteenth century) and has made phenomena visible that had been neglected because of nationally limited viewpoints (e.g. the significance of state intervention in the history of British education).

But the purpose of the volume goes beyond the presentation of new findings or points of view. Its most important aim is to offer comprehensive socio-historical interpretations of national developments. In what follows we wish to make some comments concerning these theoretical claims of the book. Combining methodological commentary with the development of conceptual alternatives, we would like to point out potential directions for further research.

Theoretical models, socio-historical interpretations and the method of comparison

If the comparative method is to achieve the degree of explanatory coherence which has been unanimously claimed for it by the protagonists of comparative historical research on education,[2] then two conditions must be met. The first concerns the methodological design of comparative analyses or, more precisely, the distinction to be observed between comparison as a social scientific method and comparison as a universal form of human thought. Comparison in the latter sense is characterised by so-called 'simple' or 'one-level' techniques, that is by procedures that relate the objects of comparison to each other with regard merely to their factual aspects and, in so doing, restrict their scope to a single level of analysis determined by fields of homologous features. Such simple comparative operations lead to statements about similarities and dissimilarities in the compared objects, that is to the clarification of distinctive characteristics (e.g. the specific traits of the French *grandes écoles* in contrast to the traditional European university pattern), to the construction of classes or categories (e.g. the centralised state-supported and state-administered educational systems in France and Germany), or to the identification of parallel developments or tendencies (e.g. similar processes of 'systematisation' in all three educational systems in the late nineteenth and early twentieth centuries). The statements that result, however, remain at a merely descriptive level; in themselves they have no evidential value as arguments relating to theoretical concepts, hypotheses or explanatory models.

Comparison as a systematic social scientific method, by contrast, relies on so-called 'complex' or 'multi-level' techniques. These are much more sophisticated procedures for establishing relationships. They are based on hypothetically assumed connections between diverse variables, as postulated in theories or in explanatory models (e.g. in Müller's model the relationships between systems of entitlements, qualifications crises and the increasing differentiation, typification and structural division of the school system), and are guided by such theoretical hypotheses in their respective design and execution, for, starting from hypothetically assumed connections between variables identified at different levels of analysis, they aim at searching out their empirical references, which can be observed in the form of co-varying sets of phenomena embedded in varying cultural contexts, and then at setting these relationships into relation with each other. To put it more concisely, comparison as a method does not consist in relating a series of observable facts to each other but in relating relationships or even whole patterns of relationships to each other. Only in this elaborated form does the comparative method in the social sciences attain the affinity to theory construction which has been attributed to it since Durkheim; similarly, it is only in this elaborated form that it fulfils the functions of testing, elucidating or criticising models of explanation.

This brings us to the second of the preconditions mentioned above. If comparison is effectively to be practised as a social scientific method, theories or theoretical frameworks structuring its design and execution are required, for the possibility and the analytical perspective (the 'whither') of a comparison can only be determined within the terms of a problem formulated precisely in advance and conceptualised according to appropriate theoretical models, not to historical self-definitions of social groups. Only on this basis will it be possible to establish the comparability of the empirical–historical phenomena observable in varying cultural contexts in such a way that they act as functionally equivalent indicators of theoretical constructs. The transition from historical narration to comparative analysis, therefore, is not a matter of an unproblematic continuum. Rather, the much greater need for the latter to be related to theory follows from the imperatives of the 'logic of comparative inquiry'.[3]

The overall structure of this book, with its sequential arrangement of theoretical models, historical studies informed by them, and concluding comparative evaluations, seems to come some way towards meeting these requirements of the comparative method. If one reads more closely, however, problems become apparent on the level of *methodology*, of *systematic conceptualisation* and of *interpretive theory*, and these tend to restrict the book's value as a comparative analysis.

To begin with, it is a disadvantage both methodologically (affecting the structural premises for comparison) and theoretically (affecting the chances of convincingly testing conclusions) that the three theoretical models of Müller (systematisation), Ringer (segmentation) and Steedman (defining institutions – in Chapter 4) are outlined separately, rather than integrated into one more general system. Even after the concluding discussions, it remains an essentially open question whether the relationship between these three models is a matter of partial incongruity, of necessary complementarity or of *ad hoc* interchangeability. The difficulty is aggravated by the general mode of interpretation practised by the authors. Since most of them stress overall similarities instead of national variations, and since most of them share the common assumption that educational systems, irrespective of all idiosyncratic properties of institutions in different national contexts, primarily perform the function of social reproduction, the problems of compatibility that arise from empirical–historical differences and from interpretative inconsistencies are always bridged over with statements at a high level of generality. As limitations of space prevent us from examining the whole range of these problems in detail, we shall focus our remarks firstly on Müller's model of 'systematisation' and secondly on the basic assumption common to all three models.

Although Müller develops an explanatory model of some complexity, he confines it to the unique case of Prussia and does not work out its actual theoretical implications. The elements of historical narration and generalisable explanation are fused in such a way that they can hardly be distinguished from each other. From a methodological point of view this makes it difficult to use Müller's model in order to structure a comparative study. From a theoretical point of view, however, this very difficulty makes it interesting to test its validity by means of comparison: 'The Bochum team needed analysis in more than one cultural and national context in order to test their hypotheses and increase their understanding of social processes analysed historically.'[4]

The purpose of Müller's model is to grasp the socio-logic which controlled the structural change in the Prussian school system taking place during the second half of the nineteenth century, that is the transformation, marked by processes of increasing differentiation, typification and structural division of educational opportunities, from a relatively open range of multifunctional schools, which had a socially heterogeneous intake and fostered social mobility, into a highly selective hierarchy of class-related school types, university courses of study, and regulations for admission to the professions, which were structurally adjusted to one another at each level. The model that is offered to explain this transformation combines arguments of varying degrees of generality: (i) the presupposition based on the works of Bourdieu that there is a general and decisive connection between school systems and the reproduction of social classes; (ii) the complex effects of the relatively 'progressive' or 'democratic' structure of the early Prussian school system and of its system of entitlements (i.e. encouraging the educational aspirations and upward social mobility of children from non-academic classes, and thereby producing successive cycles of academic overcrowding); (iii) the coincidence of one such overcrowding crisis with the more general economic and social crisis of the 1870s to 1890s (the Great Depression), or, more precisely, the particular way in which a conservative coalition of the aristocracy, the bourgeoisie and the academic professions *in Germany* sought to cope with the cumulative crisis by pursuing policies of an anti-liberal and social-protectionist kind; and (iv) additional factors specific to the historical circumstances, such as the efforts of the Prussian state, which had coalesced from heterogeneous regions, to unify its administrative systems, or the impact of Prussian fiscal reforms on the financial resources of municipalities and secondary schools.

Apart from the fact that the process of system formation took a different course in France, the English case with its partly similar structural changes is a good test of Müller's model, if only because certain determining factors important in Germany (Prussia) are not found in England (e.g. powerful centralised administrative authorities or formal leaving qualifications provided with state-guaranteed entitlements). One might expect, therefore, that in England external demands for stabilising and reproducing social status would be far more successful in establishing a consistently class-related hierarchy of school types, precisely because they were not filtered through central administrative authorities. And in fact Hilary Steedman's study of the endowed grammar schools, which refers explicitly to Müller's hypotheses, reveals at first sight a surprisingly similar configuration: the transformation of a relatively undifferentiated set of institutions with a heterogeneous social intake before 1869 into two distinguishable groups of schools with different curricula, different leaving ages, staffs and clienteles, and different opportunities of access to high-status positions.

In fact the different ways this structural change manifested itself in the two countries can be seen to correspond consistently with their underlying contextual conditions. In place of the administrative definition of school types by the Prussian state authorities, there was, in England, an open 'market competition' between the schools based on an interaction between parental demand for successful schooling and institutional response to it. In place of the establishment of a hierarchical system of school types at a fixed distance from each other, there was, in England, an open process of redistribution between the poles of the 'rising' (i.e. successful Oxbridge scholarship) schools and the 'sinking' (i.e. unsuccessful or 'struggling') schools. In place of the formal linking of school types to hierarchies of employment and social status in the Prussian system of state-guaranteed entitlements, there was, in England, an informal conversion of social hierarchies into educational hierarchies as a consequence of the successive introduction of open competitive examinations for the civil service (from 1856 onwards).

On the other hand, these aspects of the English case do not add up to an overall pattern that is fully equivalent to Müller's account of 'systematisation' in Prussia, for if one considers the other contributions on England as well, the polarisation described by Steedman turns out to be only one phase in the transformation of the English system, limited both in time (1867–97) and in its institutional range (endowed grammar schools), and not an overall process that completely defined *the modern* system of education in England. It is necessary to complete Steedman's findings by adding features specific to the English pattern as a whole. First, contemporaneous with the process of polarisation, substantial areas of functional, organisational and curricular overlap were becoming apparent between the 'sinking' grammar schools, which were less successful in competing for pupils, and some of the institutions of technical and elementary education, which were coming up as their new rivals from a lower level in rapidly increasing numbers (e.g. science classes, day science schools, higher-grade elementary schools, etc.). Second, structural change did not come to its climax in England until the beginning of the twentieth century, when it was supported both by a coherent administrative infrastructure organised at the turn of the century (1899, Board of Education; 1902, local education authorities) and by powerful motives aiming at ideological and cultural integration, while also responding to alarming deficiencies in secondary education (Reeder). Finally, this last phase was characterised by a pattern of change quite contrary to previous tendencies: on the one hand, the three subsystems of secondary, technical and elementary education were being *clearly separated* in their administration, organisation, curricula, overall philosophy and function; on the other hand, and complementary to this, the tendency towards curricular *standardisation within* each subsystem was no less clear. Following upon the regulations of 1904, 1907 and 1918, the 'earlier tendencies towards horizontal segmentation' (Reeder, p. 149) were increasingly inhibited in England, and a *single* academic type of school emerged as the only form of public secondary education. This standardisation, which clearly contrasts with the class-related differentiation of school types in Germany, took the form of a curricular adaptation to the educational institutions of the upper classes, which had been taken over from earlier times and which, because of their prestige, were able to act as standard models (i.e. the 'public' schools for the secondary range and Oxbridge for the new civic universities – as Roy Lowe points out, the pattern of change and the stages of development in higher education were on the whole very similar to those in secondary education (Reeder)).

Seen against this background, the limited range and the non-transferability of Müller's model can be recognised. Its limitations not only reveal the theoretical need for an alternative explanation; they also highlight the negative impact on systematic comparison of a 'systems' concept that is not given a theoretically adequate definition, neither in Müller's presentation nor in other contributions to this volume. The two problems, that of interpretive theory and that of comparative methodology, are closely connected.

Indeed, instead of explicitly defining the term 'educational system' theoretically, and thereby making actual comparison possible, virtually all of the authors use the term more or less as it was used in the sources by the social groups and actors under examination. As a result, the 'systemic' nature of a nation's network of formal education turns out to be primarily conceived of in terms of administrative government control and of the co-ordination of parts (subsystems) into a whole. Under the cover of this kind of terminology, historically rich in meaning but with its theoretical significance undefined, reductions of substance occur with regard to the very nature of the topics under consideration. For what the authors really analyse are not the processes involved in the *formation of educational systems* (precisely), but the processes involved in the *structuring and restructuring of parts of such systems*. After all, Müller's model of 'systematisation' is basically concerned with structural change in the field of *secondary* education. The almost total exclusion of primary education, however, means that a point of reference indispensable for determining the 'systemic' nature of an educational system is ignored. As a result, if only because they are relying on a 'systems' concept that is itself systematically abridged, the authors are forced to fall back on explanatory models stressing 'exogenous' factors (such as social classes and their reproduction).

As an alternative, it is possible to suggest an explanation that stresses 'endogenous' factors (such as intra-systemic relationships) as well.[5] This follows from a concept of 'educational systems' grounded in sociological systems theory and in the related concepts of 'meaning' and 'inclusion' (outlined below). In the light of this theoretical alternative one could explain the structural changes in the educational system of late nineteenth- and early twentieth-century England as being the inevitable processes of internal differentiation (creating subsystems) and specification (delimiting distinctive spheres of action by removing ambiguities and determining specific contents) within a particular functional subsystem of society – for education – which had just been constituted by 'inclusion'. For one must bear in mind that the basic process of inclusion concomitant to the formation of the educational system was taking place in England in the very period under consideration, in parallel with the simultaneous process of inclusion within the political system: the extensive electoral reform in 1867, the organisation of a public system of primary education from 1870 onwards, the institution of universal compulsory education after 1880, and the final acquisition of literacy on the part of the younger generations after 1900. Whereas the internal differentiation and specification of the system generally are the inevitable complements to the basic process of system formation itself, the particular forms taken by them in particular contexts are contingent upon historical circumstances. In the case of England they were determined *inter alia* by the existing institutions (above all the 'public' schools) and by contemporary motives of political and cultural integration. And even here, intra-systemic factors played a major part, especially the teachers (see Honey on the 'colonisation' of secondary education by 'public' school alumni, and Lowe on that of higher education by Oxbridge graduates) and the 'educational establishment' (i.e. the members of the new central education authorities shaped by, and aiming at, traditional humanistic liberal education).

Quite apart from the fact that this alternative model of explanation can be applied in the same way to German developments, it is a consequence of our comparative argument that Müller's model can be read primarily as an account of determinants specific to a unique historical context. It can then be used to explain not the basic process of structural change as such, but its specific variant in Germany. The major circumstances which can then be seen as effective in Germany are the following: (i) the range of institutions which had been carried over from the historical past and had to be subjected to respecification after being incorporated into an overall system; (ii) the successive cycles of academic overcrowding which had been stimulated by the state system of entitlements (while in England the problem was rather the lack of efficient secondary education); and (iii) the particular ways of perceiving and restrictively coping with the Great Depression in Germany, which had arisen from specific social and political traditions (while in England and France the Depression seems to have had little or no effect on the development of education).[6]

A further feature of the interpretive approach of the book worth discussing in some detail is the assumption, common to all of the authors, that highly developed educational systems primarily perform the function of social reproduction. This assumption, too, raises problems of both a methodological and a theoretical kind. To begin with, the repeated pointing-out of broad similarities cannot be regarded as a satisfactory feature of comparison, as long as very considerable institutional differences remain unexplained. Comparison is here carried out merely in the sense of the 'universal form of human thought', not in the sense of the 'quasi-experimental method' of the social sciences, and its evidential value and explanatory force are therefore slight. More concretely, the more the basic assumption asserting the reproduction of social hierarchies and cultural capital is applied without distinction to all the national contexts under consideration, the less able it is to explain the particular, context-bound forms these processes take on. Merely emphasising general similarities, therefore, means getting round the requirements of comparative inquiry and, at the same time, reducing its explanatory potential.

If the reproduction thesis is actually to structure a comparative study, a kind of systematic translation must relate the general level of theory to that of middle-range constructs, which in turn will make it possible to identify functionally equivalent indicators in various historical contexts by a methodical procedure open to review. For if the findings of the comparative social history of education are not to be limited to the repetition of general similarities, this field of study should be able to explain precisely why, for example, secondary education in Germany was shaped into a hierarchy of clearly differentiated institutions with differentiated curricula, while the English pattern was characterised by institutional and curricular adaptation to a single standard model. It should then be able to make informative and explanatory statements about the consequences of such variations. Here one must recall Ringer's comparative analysis in *Education and Society*, in which the specific features of the English case are clearly pointed out. Emphasis is laid, for instance, on the surprising finding that 'the most blatantly aristocratic of the three major European systems of the nineteenth century [could] change so fast' towards 'a comparatively "democratic" distribution of access chances'. As major determinants of this divergent pattern of social selectivity Ringer mentions institutional arrangements that make a clear contrast with the German hierarchy of school types; above all, these are 'the absence of clear curricular segmentation' and a rigorously generalised selection based on achievement, from which upper middle-class children were not protected, as Müller found they were in the German *Gymnasium*.[7]

Only if one succeeds in this way in establishing varying historical manifestations of the general reproduction hypothesis will it really be possible to build up a line of comparative argumentation which can convincingly confirm, elucidate or criticise given models of explanation. The example quoted also makes it clear that Ringer's 'segmentation' concept suggests promising starting-points for the necessary translation from the level of general hypotheses to the level of verifiable constructs, for its very advantage is that it includes conceptual connections with the indicators 'inclusiveness' (i.e. the ratio of overall utilisation of formal education by a given population or its relevant age groups) and 'progressiveness' (i.e. ratios of differential utilisation of formal education by the social strata of a given population). It is unfortunate, however, that most of the contributors neither took up nor elaborated the potentialities of this conception. This is one reason among others for the dominant impression on the reader that the aim of relating the mass of historical facts and processes to the general reproduction thesis is not achieved in a convincing manner.

Finally, it should not be overlooked that the overall interpretative approach suggested by this theory itself involves a kind of foreshortening. This follows from present-day preoccupations with claims and programmes for social reform and from the fact that the social sciences tend to see themselves partly as vehicles of social criticism. Unmistakably, this point of view has affected researchers in the social history of education and has been projected onto the past. It is virtually inevitable, then, that this kind of perspective on historical research involves a preference for 'exogenous' explanations, as can be seen in this book and elsewhere. Yet the fundamental fact of universal school education cannot be grasped in this way in its overall historical and societal implications, for these are not confined to issues of stratification and social reproduction. Indeed, the very fact of universal education or, to put it more precisely, of 'modern educational systems', can only be adequately understood if the explanatory models employed are integrated into an embracing sociological theory.

'Systems' and 'system formation': outlines of an alternative model

In the following we wish to point out an alternative approach of this kind. In doing so, we refer to the renewal of general sociological theory being carried out by Niklas Luhmann on the basis of general systems theory, and to the transfer of his generalised model of social systems to historical studies in the fields of education and of the sociology of knowledge.[8] In our view the decisive advantage of employing this kind of theoretical model lies in the avoidance of some of the problems that have become obvious in the above commentary. Problems of *comparative methodology* are avoided by recourse to theoretically defined concepts that are not context-bound and are hence suitable for comparisons. Problems of *systematic conceptualisation* are avoided by acknowledging in a non-reductive way the 'systemic' nature of educational systems. Problems of *interpretive theory* are avoided by extending the range of explanatory references and taking into account both the autonomy of systems and their dependence on the outer environment.

In the classical philosophical tradition, which has shaped the idea of 'system' used in most contributions to this volume, a 'system' was conceived of as a whole that consists of parts and relations between parts. General systems theory replaces this model with one that focuses on the difference between the system and its environment. In the case of social systems this difference is constituted by a selection of meanings. Social systems are essentially systems focused on meaning; their borderlines are the borders of areas of meaning. In general, therefore, it is possible to speak of social systems when the experiences and the actions of several human beings refer to each other on the basis of common meaning, and when such a network of meanings established via communication dissociates itself from an outer environment. The function of social systems constituted in this way by the selective focusing on meanings is to establish structured potentialities for comprehending and manipulating the complexity of the world, which would otherwise hopelessly overtax the mental receptivity of man.

The opportunities to structure historical analyses which such a 'systems' concept can provide, despite its abstractness, are demonstrated in an exemplary manner by one of the contributions to this book. We refer to John Honey's careful examination of what makes the 'public' schools system a 'system', for it cannot adequately be grasped as a particular system distinguishable from other schools by merely describing administrative definitions or organisational features. It can be fully characterised only in terms of selections of meanings and of communications channelled by meanings, that is in terms of a 'similar ethos' and of regular 'interactions'.

Historically, 'systems of education' as particular functional subsystems of society are rather modern forms of societal organisation. They cannot be conceived adequately unless the general concepts of systems theory are complemented by concepts related to a theory of socio-cultural evolution. Social systems in general increase their capacity to cope with environmental complexity by internal differentiation into subsystems. This kind of system differentiation must be seen as the reduplication of the difference between system and environment within systems. The degree of internal complexity and the particular forms of internal differentiation of social systems are dependent on evolutionary change. Modern European societies are characterised by the change of their primary scheme of differentiation from stratification to functional differentiation. In functionally differentiated societies, subsystems develop as a consequence of the selective focusing of interactive and communicative processes on special societal functions: 'Salient examples are the political function of providing for collectively binding decisions, the economic function of securing want satisfaction within enlarged time horizons, and the religious function of interpreting the incomprehensible.'[9] Since all of these functions are equally important at the level of society itself, none of the subsystems so constituted can lay claim to a necessary primacy (as Bourdieu's theory implies); at most, there are primary roles for individual functional subsystems which are temporary and vary in successive historical periods.

After functional subsystems of society for politics, for the economy, for science and for religion had already evolved, an increasing range of opportunities and possibilities for building up a particular subsystem for education – as a special function to be fulfilled at the universal level of society – began to emerge towards the end of the eighteenth century. This process found its major starting-point in the already existing differentiation of complementary roles, that is, above all, the differentiation between service roles (such as teachers) and service-receiving roles (such as pupils). And it was carried through by setting free the very dynamism inherent in these asymmetries and by making universal the service-receiving roles in particular. This process is called 'inclusion'. Consequently 'inclusion' is the most obvious indicator of the historical transition from stratification to functional differentiation. In place of a structured hierarchy of unequal subsystems based on social classes, the primary scheme of societal organisation is now in principle the equal access of *everybody* to *every* subsystem, as voter, patient, plaintiff, pupil, etc. Therefore 'inclusion' and the 'selective focusing of interactive and communicative processes on special societal functions' are the decisive features necessary for theoretically defining 'educational system' and 'system formation', *not* the historically context-bound features of administrative standardisation or organisational co-ordination.

Inclusion involves processes both of growth and perfectioning, and of internal differentiation, and these are complementary to each other. It is a significant feature of the differentiation process that the emergent educational system, during the initial stage of inclusion, is rather decentralised and open in its organisation, and that its services are called on not by the lower but by the middle and upper classes. The more the continuing process of inclusion advances, the more acute is the need for internal differentiation and specification, and at the same time for the removal of mere ambiguities and unregulated competition. Such processes of internal differentiation and specification can be conceived of as ways of coping with divergent expectations and relationships: with the system's autonomy and its dependence on the environment, with its functional orientation towards the encompassing societal system and its output performances in inter-systemic relationships, with inclusion and selection, with qualifying for universal communication in society and inculcating differential 'habitus' specific to certain groups or classes.

These divergent relational dimensions, on the one hand, draw attention to the system's own functional imperatives; on the other hand, they delineate breaches where the educational system is sensitive to, and dependent on, the impact of its environment. The observable outcomes of the intra-systemic operations of mediation and processing are, therefore, configurative patterns which necessarily vary with changing historical and socio-cultural contexts. We call them the 'schemes of internal articulation' of educational systems. Ultimately, this is what Müller's model of 'systematisation' really refers to. From a theoretical point of view, therefore, the system's need for internal articulation is the general theme of the present volume; and explaining the varying schemes of system articulation observable in different nations is its main perspective for comparison.

Finally, the concept of system articulation is the level of concreteness of our alternative model, to which Ringer's concept of 'segmentation' (elaborated, as compared to earlier versions, with the notions of 'meaning', 'habitus' and *Deutungsmuster*) can be seen to be a fruitful complement. The concept of segmentation seems to offer the methodological possibility of detecting *divergences* in the development of school systems, and of thus uncovering not the unity but the specific variety of functional differentiation in varying national contexts. In Ringer's analysis the distinction between class and status, taken over from Max Weber, provides the background for a line of questioning about the degree to which this class–status difference engenders horizontal or vertical segmentation and becomes less visible with increasing inclusiveness, etc. Incidentally, such categories can lead to viable comparisons only when applied on the basis of theoretically clarified relations of similarity and difference. This condition is met in the case of such categories as segmentation, class, status, etc. because they are designed from the beginning for the observation of relationships within determinate contexts.

At a trans-contextual level the issue is the increasing autonomy of the special function of 'education'; in particular contexts the issue is the systemic articulation of this function. National historical developments constitute the context (though other contexts could of course be imagined in principle), in which the increasing autonomy of education must be articulated, and in which schemes of articulation can be observed (e.g. the interlocking of bureaucratic and educational careers, occupational differentiation along the borderline between class and status, etc.). Following Durkheim's distinction between unity and diversity in education, one can attribute the diversities given in schemes of articulation to the diversity of the 'milieux' in which they are formed.[10] And it may turn out, for example, that the hierarchic structuring of school systems is possible *both* through bureaucratisation – i.e. non-conflictual forms of distributing success in Mannheim's sense – *and* through the conflictual dynamics of status competition, as in the English case.[11] Only the comparative sorting-out of such differences in the integration of 'milieux' can generate useful analytical approaches to the question that is central to the present volume, namely to what extent various forms of internal articulation in educational systems are correlated with their contributions to social reproduction.

10. Systematisation: a critique

JAMES ALBISETTI

The notion of the 'rise of the modern educational system' or, in more general terms, of 'systematisation' in the sense used by Detlef Müller involves several implicit assumptions which require greater justification or clarification than they have received in this volume. In contrast to Fritz Ringer's concepts of inclusiveness, progressiveness and segmentation, 'systematisation' refers to a process occurring in time. Especially when one speaks of the *rise* of a system, there is an implication that this process has a fairly specific beginning and ending. Yet the discussions in this volume of the systematisation of English, French and German education do not adequately establish such time limits.

A second implicit assumption inherent in the concept of systematisation is that some X, whether Hegel's cunning of reason, Marx's economic substructure or Carlyle's hero in history, was the driving force behind this process. Yet most contributions to this volume either sidestep the question of causation or provide contradictory statements about the role of conscious human agency in the rise of the modern educational system. For example, Roy Lowe comments that he is 'uncertain' about the extent to which structural change in English higher education 'marked a conscious attempt at the segregation of social classes' (p. 163), but then devotes a significant portion of his chapter to quotations from individuals which point to such a conscious attempt.

The role of human intentions in this process is particularly important because of the general tone of indictment that underlies most discussions of systematisation and social reproduction. If all that is involved is description of an anonymous or even inevitable process, more neutral language is needed. This problem can be illustrated in the contributions of Müller, who, despite suggesting that scholars should refrain from moral judgements about the defensive strategies employed by the academic bourgeoisie to protect its social status, makes such judgements himself when he uses terms such as 'apparent rationality' to describe the Prussian educational system around 1900. Such condemnations, which imply, but do not reveal, a knowledge of what a 'truly rational' system would have been, rest on his thesis that the effect of school reforms in the late nineteenth century was 'to replace a system which promoted social mobility and involved educating school children in socially heterogeneous groups by types of schools designed to reproduce specific classes and social groups'.[1] The validity of this thesis, and with it any justification for the harsh terms in which systematisation and segmentation are discussed, will be the third area examined in this essay.

With regard to the chronological limits for 'the rise of the modern educational system', it is clear that one cannot expect scholars to demonstrate that at time A there was no system at all and by time B an immutable system had emerged. Yet for the notion of systematisation to be meaningful, they must show that decisive changes occurred within a limited time span and that these persisted in their basic outlines for significant periods. Müller and other contributors to this volume argue that such decisive changes did take place. In an unpublished paper Ringer has made the clearest statement about the survival of the new structures: 'Further changes in the organisation of European secondary and higher education between about 1920 and 1960 substantially modified, but did not fundamentally alter, the structures that had emerged by around 1910.' Yet both the decisiveness and permanence of the changes are open to question.

For England Brian Simon suggests that the Royal Commissions of the 1860s laid the basis for the later systematisation of secondary education towards the close of the nineteenth century. Yet the creation of the separate Clarendon and Taunton Commissions to study different groups of schools serving different social classes suggests that this basis already existed in the period before 1860. Without trying to decide whether the Education Acts of 1918 and 1944 were 'substantial modifications' or 'fundamental alterations' of English schooling, one can still ask whether the secondary school system of 1950 did not differ more from that of 1910 than the latter did from that of 1870.

Similar questions can be asked about France. If, as Ringer notes, the secondary schools of the mid-1860s revealed 'a perfect example of socially vertical segmentation', one wonders what decisive changes in this area the reforms of 1902 introduced. Three of the four secondary tracks created in 1902 did last for several decades, but the elimination of curricular differences between private and public elementary classes in the 1920s and the introduction of free secondary schooling in the 1930s brought changes to French education which can be seen as having greater significance than the earlier 'systematisation'.

The permanence of the Prussian reforms of 1900 is less open to question, though even here the elimination of private elementary classes during the Weimar Republic and the many measures introduced by the Nazis illustrate the further evolution, if not mutation, of the system. Less clear, however, is the decisiveness of the reforms of the late nineteenth century, particularly when one takes literally Müller's assertion that 'the structural change in the Prussian school system . . . was completed by 1892'.[2] As early as 1832 Prussia had had separate regulations for *Gymnasien* and *Bürgerschulen*, and from 1859 on it possessed versions of the classical, semi-classical and modern schools which would persist well into the twentieth century. Matthew Arnold believed that the Prussia of the 1860s already possessed a well-articulated system of secondary schools, one that was, 'in its completeness and carefulness, such as to excite a foreigner's admiration'.[3] The most decisive reform of this system did not occur by 1892, but only after the school conference of 1900, with the granting of the right to matriculate in most areas of the Prussian universities to *Realgymnasium* and *Oberrealschule* graduates.

The question of causation in the rise of the modern educational system involves very basic historiographical issues. In many ways it epitomises the controversies between traditional historians and the practitioners of what has been called 'historical social science' or 'social science history'. This volume cannot resolve these controversies, but at least it can avoid additional ambiguities and open contradictions. Müller has written that 'system formation with its accompanying social consequences . . . was not the result of strategic conservative planning' (p. 24). Heinz-Elmar Tenorth and others have pointed out how this position forces Müller to portray the 'system' as developing itself. Yet in an earlier article on the problem of the overcrowded professions in Germany in the late nineteenth century, he argued that propaganda about this 'qualifications crisis' was a 'consciously employed defensive strategy on the part of the ruling social classes and political groups'.[4] In the discussions of English and French education as well, one is too often left to wonder whether individuals, classes, economic developments or forces of spontaneous generation were responsible for 'systematisation'. Although educators and political leaders did not always achieve their intended goals, their contributions to the process of systematisation must be investigated in a more thorough fashion.

The critical tone employed in most analyses of the social consequences of educational systematisation invites more general discussion. Most recent studies of the social origins of pupils and students appear to rest on the assumption that, to use Ringer's terminology, increased inclusiveness and progressiveness, and decreased segmentation, are desirable trends. I know of no scholar who suggests that the educational system he or she has studied was too inclusive or progressive, or that it was insufficiently segmented.[5] By not setting any limits to such trends, these scholars seem to advocate a pure 'meritocracy' where family background plays no role in educational and employment opportunities. Yet no one says explicitly that where 1 per cent of the adult population practises medicine only 1 per cent of doctors' children should follow their parents' career, or that 100 per cent inclusiveness to the age of 20 or beyond is the ultimate aim. As long as mobility is always too little and segmentation always too great, one does not obtain an adequate picture of what these scholars consider to be the maximum possible, desirable or permissible degree of mobility.

Critics of educational systems that tend to reproduce existing social classes appear to share Müller's belief that an educational policy that would 'facilitate social mobility' is 'a democratic school policy'.[6] Yet Ringer, in his unpublished essay, has commented that 'mobility may not be the best road to democracy even in principle'. It is clear that achieving absolute equality of educational opportunity, much less equality of educational outcomes, would involve a level of coercion on pupils and parents that is incompatible with most Western notions of democracy. It would seem to be incumbent on Müller and others to specify more fully the relationship between freedom and equality in the notion of democracy that underlies their work. In doing so, they might recall that in biology, where the metaphor of reproduction originates, the alternative is not equality or mobility, but extinction.

Implicit in most discussions of the role of educational systems in social reproduction is an unstated assumption that some high, but never achieved, level of social mobility is 'natural' or 'normal', and that what needs to be explained are the obstacles blocking its achievement. A rather different perspective emerges – perhaps unintentionally – in a recent article by Hartmut Titze. In examining university enrolments in Germany in the late nineteenth century, Titze mentions 'a *naturally* large proportion [of doctors' sons] in the medical faculty because of self-recruitment'. Among sons of secondary teachers, he finds a self-recruitment rate of from 25 to 43 per cent to be 'comparatively low'.[7] Such comments invite social historians to consider whether their task should not be to explain not the limits to mobility, but what mobility does occur.

Titze's work on enrolment trends in the various university faculties also casts doubt on the extent to which the government manipulated the qualifications crisis to achieve social and political ends. His data reveal a very rational and informed economic self-interest operating among students in the late nineteenth century. Poor job prospects discouraged less affluent students from pursuing certain fields; good job prospects attracted larger numbers. That this was true even in the study of Protestant theology may raise some interesting questions about the nature of the 'calling' that motivated German pastors in this age; but, in general, Titze does not indicate that governmental deception was needed to divert less wealthy students away from overcrowded fields.

Even at the Prussian secondary schools there is little evidence that what social segmentation did exist among the three tracks after 1900 was the result of the kind of governmental deception Müller describes. Graduates of the *Realgymnasium* and the *Oberrealschule* did have to take supplemental examinations in ancient languages in order to study certain fields, but by 1913–14 37 per cent of medical students and 29 per cent of law students were coming from these schools. When one considers how openly Bismarck in the Reichstag, Gossler in the House of Deputies, Wilhelm II at the school conference of 1890, and the semi-official *Norddeutsche Allgemeine Zeitung* on many occasions expressed the government's interest in reducing both the overcrowding of the professions and the 'ballast' in the *Gymnasium*, it is difficult to grasp how parents who were concerned enough about their sons' education to send them to secondary schools would not be aware of the privileges attached to the different tracks after 1900. As Ringer has suggested, the vigorous debates over secondary school reform in the late nineteenth century caused the social significance of educational segmentation to reach an unprecedented degree of consciousness and visibility.

The rapid flight from Greek in France after 1902 suggests that the granting of approximately equal privileges to other tracks allowed parents and pupils to escape a classical curriculum they had not wanted in the first place, but had been forced to accept as the price of university admission. This same phenomenon can be observed in Prussia, where, during the 1860s and 1870s, *Realgymnasium* enrolments had expanded much more rapidly than the population, sustained in part by the opening of sections of the philosophical faculties to their graduates in 1870. Only the refusal, in 1883, to open the medical faculties reversed this trend, leading to a decline in enrolments which lasted until the reforms of 1900. Although the flight from the classical track after 1900 was less marked in Prussia than in France, the surge in *Realgymnasium* and *Oberrealschule* enrolments and the rise in inclusiveness from 2.7 to 3.2 per cent between 1900 and 1911 indicate that systematisation allowed many pupils to escape from an unwanted *Gymnasium* curriculum and brought more young males into the secondary schools.[8]

The most crucial question to be asked about the systematisation of secondary education around 1900, however, is whether it did in fact 'replace a system which promoted social mobility and involved educating school children in socially heterogeneous groups'. No one has argued that these allegedly 'comprehensive' secondary schools of the mid-nineteenth century promoted mobility to such an extent that they led large numbers of boys from the lower-middle classes into the French, English or German universities. On the contrary, the universities of 1910 recruited students from a much broader social base, including the white-collar middle class, than did their predecessors of 1850.[9] At the university level systematisation could be said to have increased mobility, even if it increased segmentation at the secondary level.

The extent to which the secondary schools of 1850 educated their pupils in socially heterogeneous groups is also open to doubt. Simon remarks briefly that this was the case in grammar schools before the Endowed Schools Act of 1869, but does not make the same claim for the 'public' schools. Müller notes the existence in many *Vormärz Gymnasien* of separate classes or tracks designed especially for boys not expected to remain in school past the age of compulsory schooling, and admits that existing social status was usually the decisive factor leading parents to choose such programmes. He also suggests that the wide diffusion of *Gymnasien* throughout Germany before 1850 resulted primarily from the interest of bureaucrats, officers, pastors and teachers in having schools which could prepare their sons for the universities. If lower-class pupils were welcome in the lower grades of these schools, or in special classes, largely because their tuition payments reduced the cost of secondary education for the upper classes, it is highly doubtful that what social mixing did occur served the democratic goals of a comprehensive school. A few talented boys may have been encouraged to continue an education that their parents would not have chosen otherwise, but it is difficult to see that the *Gymnasium* of 1850 provided for greater equality of opportunity than the secondary schools of 1910 did.[10]

Similar ambiguities exist in the evidence that has been used to demonstrate that the French *lycée* around 1850 recruited pupils from more diverse social backgrounds than its successor around the turn of the century did. Robert Anderson has argued that the *lycées* of the mid-nineteenth century were 'favourable to social mobility', but noted at the same time that 'the schools contained a large number of pupils who were getting either a fragmentary classical education or an education which was not truly secondary at all'. Patrick Harrigan, basing his views on an extensive survey of pupils taken in 1865, insisted that 'in its clientele, French secondary education was more democratic than the contemporary political or social system', but he also noted that municipal *collèges* of this era, perhaps like English grammar schools, 'could satisfy the uniquely limited ambitions peasants and artisans had for their children'. Both Anderson and Robert Gildea have demonstrated the continued existence during this period, despite official opposition, of many short 'modern' programmes attached to *lycées*, which were similar to the special classes discussed by Müller.[11] It thus appears that the French secondary schools of 1850 also did not provide the kind of equality of educational opportunity which is usually associated with a comprehensive school.

The crux of these various criticisms of the concept of systematisation is that it has not yet been proved that the reforms of German, French and English education around the turn of the century involved structural and social changes of such a magnitude as to justify the singling-out of this era as a crucial turning-point in the historical developments of the last two centuries. With specific reference to Germany the 'qualifications crisis' of the 1880s does not appear to have been of the epoch-making importance Müller has attributed to it. As Titze has noted, the government's fears about the overcrowded professions at this time 'for more than a decade . . . hindered the development of sober policies directed toward long-range modernisation,' but the qualifications crisis did not do much more.[12]

One final criticism must be made: the virtually complete neglect of gender discrimination and of girls' schools in the discussion of the 'rise of the modern educational system'. Opposition to greater educational opportunities for women during this period was much more virulent than the hostility to letting boys from lower social groups into the secondary schools and universities. Even in areas where girls' education impinged directly on boys' schools, such as in the reallotment of endowments by the Endowed School and Charity Commissioners in England, these facts go unmentioned.[13] If changes in female education were included, the evolution of Western European schools since 1900 or 1910 would appear much more as a 'fundamental alteration' of the system that existed at the turn of the century.

11. Segmentation: a critique*

HEINZ-ELMAR TENORTH

Barely liberated, especially in Germany, from the task of cultivating the pedagogical tradition, the scholarly history of education was long in danger of abandoning itself to other disciplines. Inspired primarily by the theories of the social sciences, the history of education was almost reduced to an adjunct of the history of industrialisation,[1] interpreting education as an epiphenomenon of economic development. At the same time, moved by contemporary political conflicts over equality of opportunity, the history of education came close to using questions about the origins of inequality as a focus for retrospective prophecies, and of thus limiting itself to the history of the prevention of social mobility through education.[2] It is therefore no accident that the concept of segmentation, presented here primarily by Fritz Ringer, grows out of the critique of such reductionist models as those of the economic functionalists. In fact it is based on the thesis that the role of the educational system in the development of world views is probably more important than its role in social mobility.

Yet this departure from commonly favoured interpretations by no means moves the concept of segmentation into the camp of conservative pedagogues, for Ringer certainly does not neglect the processes in which class societies are reproduced, nor does he nourish the illusion that the autonomy of the educational system could be interpreted, in idyllic fashion, as an autarchically pedagogical evolution, far removed from all social processes. On the contrary, the concept of segmentation commits the history of education to a specific analytical programme and, at the same time, to broader questions of social theory and social history – primarily to reflections upon the history of knowledge and of world views, to research on traditions and ideologies, and to investigations on the internal articulation

* Translated by Fritz Ringer.

and hierarchic structuring of the middle classes. The concept also permits cross-culturally comparative studies. Finally, supported by findings about the congruency and incongruency of educational patterns and class patterns, it leads to reflections about the specific, 'ambivalent' structure of modernity.

In view of its openness, breadth, and variety of perspectives, the concept of segmentation deserves further discussion. Indeed, it also *requires* such discussion, because Ringer himself introduces the concept in a rather incidental way, as a 'statistical property' of educational systems, and then works at minimising the systematic significance of his assumptions. In the first part of this chapter I shall therefore introduce the explicit assumptions and systematic implications of the concept; in the second part I shall draw primarily on representative findings and themes in German educational and social history to call attention to a few research desiderata that can be identified with the concept. The critique is meant as an internal one, as encouragement to the originator of the concept to develop his often implicit theory of educational history more fully – if such an expectation can be imposed upon a historian.

Segmentation: the concept

The concept of segmentation was first introduced by Ringer in his comparative study on *Education and Society in Modern Europe*.[3] Along with 'inclusiveness' and 'progressiveness', segmentation there appears as part of the 'statistical properties' used to describe and to analyse modern educational systems, against the background of modern expectations with respect to educational systems. None the less, the concept of segmentation takes on meaning, not as a statistical indicator, but as a complex interpretive device for the structure, development and importance of educational systems. This is not surprising since Ringer himself conceded as early as 1979 that there is no 'single statistical index' for the decisive phenomenon of 'horizontal segmentation', that is for the 'disjunction between the hierarchies of education and of class'.[4] The statistical representation of segmentation, no different from that of inclusiveness and progressiveness, is achieved primarily through indices of recruitment and of educational access chances for various age groups and social strata. Even 'the limiting case of segmentation'[5] is therefore identical with the point of departure for mobility studies, with the question of participation in advanced education, and with the separation between those parts of the population that receive such education and those that are excluded from it.

Yet Ringer does not limit the concept of segmentation to these equality of opportunity issues, but moves beyond them into the internal structure of curricular sequences within secondary schooling on the one hand and, on the other, into the interrelationships between curricula, segments of the social structure, and the structure of social role conceptions. Altogether, segmentation refers first to those internal structures of secondary schools ('tracks') that can be distinguished not only in their curricula, but also in the social composition of their student recruitments, and that represent the relationship between social and educational hierarchies – in their horizontal or vertical segmentation. Secondly, with regard to the social structure, segmentation means that hierarchies can be distinguished within the middle classes, as defined by their holdings of property and/or their participation in advanced education. In a comparative context this makes visible such characteristic differences in middle-class roles as that between the German educated upper middle class (*Bildungsbürgertum*) and the French *bourgeoisie*.[6] Thirdly, segmentation refers to the structure and function of knowledge in society, to the difference between modern and traditional beliefs, and to the divergence in the respective significance of such knowledge for the legitimation of educational structures, for the construction of self-images by social strata, for hierarchies of prestige and for the emergence of 'cultural patterns of interpretation' (*kulturelle Deutungsmuster*). Viewed in a systematic way, the concept of segmentation thus entails explanatory claims in the three dimensions of education, social structure and knowledge systems.

Indeed, Ringer's work is always guided by the aim of pointing at the interdependence of these three dimensions in the historical process. Hence the significance for Ringer of the French sociologist Pierre Bourdieu, whose sociology of education – in the attempt to explain the role of habitus – also assumes a great variety of connections and who distinguishes an economic, a social and a cultural form of 'capital'.[7] Unlike the sociologists of education, however, the historian Ringer also uses his concept to structure and periodise the historical development of educational systems, of social structures and of patterns of interpretation, in their interrelationships. His thesis is that educational structures that can be described as segmented were fully formed by the end of the nineteenth century, that these structures have preserved the traditional meanings of educational articulations and processes into our own time, but that they have also satisfied the needs of the older and younger professions for qualifications. As a result, the initially separated hierarchies of class and status, of power and prestige, have approached each other, so that the incongruencies between educational systems and social structures have converged in modern class societies. This account of the structures and developmental patterns of modernity incidentally reveals that Ringer has been inspired not only by Bourdieu, the contemporary master, but also by Max Weber, the traditional patriarch of sociology.

Differing from Ringer's own modest interpretation of his concept (in the Introduction to this volume) – that it is primarily descriptive and does not offer 'a theory of educational change' – I would point to his actual work and to the way it interconnects themes and events, systematic structures and cognitive dimensions. I would here discern a quite systematic, theoretical conceptualisation of the development of educational systems and of the social structures that shaped them and made them possible. To be sure, one can ask whether the theory has been worked out in a sufficiently explicit manner, and one can ask, further, whether it has the explanatory potential for individual nations and cultures that Ringer disclaims at the systematic level, but factually reasserts in his analysis of national developments.

I would also find the theoretical character of Ringer's concept confirmed by the fact that he succeeds in using his assumptions to integrate the other theories in this volume. Müller's concept of systematisation thus appears as an intepretation, in which the formation of educational structures that have been analysed as segmentation is shown to be a correlate of the formation of the bourgeois class society. Hilary Steedman's account of 'defining institutions' can be understood as a more general interpretation of a developmental pattern that Ringer concretely terms 'the generalist shift' in Germany and France. Ringer here points to the mechanism in which modern, younger educational programmes and institutions assimilate the norms established and perpetuated in the classical schools, norms based on such nationally divergent patterns of meaning as *Bildung* or *culture générale*, which are preserved in the key institutions of the respective educational systems: the German *Gymnasien*, the French *lycées* or the English 'public' schools.

A reading of the contributions to the volume makes clear an underlying theoretical idea about educational and social change that is generally shared by Ringer as well. The history of educational systems is viewed sociologically as support for the interpretation of the modern school as a middle-class institution. This thesis, which can be confirmed for the present as well, holds to the insight that the school as an institution can be traced primarily to middle-class consciousness – both as regards its curricula and its values, its goals and behavioural models, and therefore also its clientele and its patterns of recruitment and of opportunity. Sensitive to the changing situation of the middle class, the school reflects the fact that its particular characteristics are made possible by the division of power and influence within society and that, at the same time, the status and prestige hierarchies of middle-class life are created and sustained by the educational system. Ringer remains committed to this well-known and much-cited explanation when, arguing historically, he finds the decisive determinants of educational history not in technological changes or in economic processes, but in configurations of social power and interests, and in inherited patterns of experience and forms of thought. The middle classes are understood as the ruling powers in society and as the representatives of the dominant culture;

the educational system appears as the locus in which world interpretations –
taken over from the aristocracy and then reinterpreted – are transmitted
along with normative life styles and value systems. Even the 'history of
educational distribution' is consistently interpreted as 'in some measure' a
'history of ideas', so that Ringer accurately characterises the guiding theme
of his work as the 'social history of the middle classes'.[8]

One could therefore almost consider the fact that Ringer interprets the
congruency or incongruency of education and society most often as a
relationship between cultural and economic hierarchies as a relapse into an
uncritical economism. His periodisation provokes an analogous criticism,
since he reads the sequence of specific phases in the history of education as
paralleling the stages of industrialisation. But these seem to me mere
remnants of a – now no longer supportable – theory that sought to explain
the specific structure of modernity (and not only its origins) primarily
through the concept of the class society – despite the insight into the
fundamental difference between class and status, and prestige and power,
on which modern societies are based. As a historian of knowledge, Ringer
should be aware, after all, that while mentalities cannot be studied in
isolation from the social place of their origins and functions, they nevertheless do not depend uniquely upon these conditions, whether in their social
and temporal validity, or in their dynamics. In any case the specific
structures and dynamics of ideologies and patterns of interpretation in the
historical process can be grounded in the venerable assumptions of the
German Ideology only by way of a methodologically almost uncontrollable
multiplicity of intervening variables, and even then to little effect.[9]

Such fundamental questions, grouped around the difficult task of
adequately comprehending the ambivalence and openness, the structural
contradictions and systematic possibilities of modernity, I can here leave
aside, along with the question as to whether the specific concern with the
middle classes might perhaps be better served by a class theory after all.
These questions may be broached by such studies in educational history as
those collected in this volume, but they cannot be clarified in this context
alone. Further the value of studies in the history of education must be
determined primarily in the context of work in their own field. In what
follows I want therefore to refer to the history of education, and primarily to
events and processes in German history up to the early twentieth century.

Segmentation: the German case

If one considers the history of German education, one is reminded, even
while fundamentally accepting the concept of segmentation, that the curriculum on the one hand, and the social origins of students on the other, may
indeed provide important indicators for the analysis of the educational

system, but that they are not the only typical or the invariably decisive factors. For the history of secondary schools in Germany in particular, other characteristics are important; these Ringer does not exclude, but he does not weigh them heavily either. Particularly important for the social control of the schools was their financing and their local supervision. The conflict of interest between the state and the municipalities, and the differences of interest between groups of teachers with respect to their training, salary and means of corporate self-management, these are characteristics of educational systems and of their development that could be fruitfully compared as well. Among regional variations the problem of religious affiliation should not be ignored since differences in this respect were by no means ephemeral. Here is a variable that affected the formation of educational aspirations, and hence the different school populations, and that probably had great weight historically for Germany – but also systematically for comparisons between Germany and France. In any case this factor had so much weight that it should not be reduced to the opposition between tradition and modernity. Lastly, and separately from the issue of curricula and with a focus upon the school populations, I would also assign greater importance than some of Ringer's measures apparently do to the role of academic certificates and 'entitlements' (*Berechtigungen*), which were probably nowhere as important as in Germany.

   The certification system and its dynamics should be seriously considered when the historical findings of this volume are further discussed, partly because the three protagonists of theory construction, Müller, Ringer and Simon, seem unanimously to assume that in the process of system formation the structure of class relationships remained intact, along with the dominance of the traditionally leading institutions within the educational system. Ringer adheres to a historical variation of this general thesis when he interprets the equalisation of university access achieved by the modern segments of the German secondary system around 1900 as a victory of the *Gymnasium* (in Chapter 2), partly because it 'prevented an inflationary "devaluation" of the *Gymnasium Abitur*' (p. 67). In providing evidence and indicators for the continuing social exclusiveness and the surviving privileges of the *Gymnasium*, Ringer limits himself to the period before 1914 (in his statistics) and to the Weimar Republic. But it is very questionable whether the indicators internal to the educational system that he uses really demonstrate the stabilisation of privileges. If one thinks in terms of the long time intervals that are characteristic of the history of education, then the equalisation of the secondary schools around 1900 probably signified the beginning, instead, of an inflationary development in access to the *Abitur* and to university study. As a result of this inflationary development traditionally educated strata were unable as early as the late 1920s to ensure the social status of their heirs in a conclusive way. The systematic reduction of privileges can be even more clearly detected in such extra-educational indicators as the declining difference between the incomes of those educated and those not educated at universities. Perhaps the politics of the trade unions were primarily responsible; but without the inflationary devaluation of academic certificates through the widening of institutionally defined access to advanced education, this development would scarcely have been possible.[10] The relationship among classes, and thus the structure of the social hierarchy, may have remained stable; but for German social history the transformations of the social structure that accompanied successive crises, particularly at the end of the Weimar period, were more important.

During this process of massive social ascent and descent within the middle classes the internal structure of the school system, too, changed in its specific significance. In the differentiation of the educational system, as Ringer has already shown for the French case, the addition of new segments could also raise and meet new expectations. In this transformation of the educational system its functionality increased for individuals, for the structure of schooling and for society. And one has to ask whether historians, too, should use other methods and other sources in a supplementary way in order to understand the peculiarly dynamic role thus taken on by the educational system.

Against this background I would see research deficits, to begin with, in the realm of personal interactions within schools. Historians of education should approach these questions not with the intention of nourishing fashionable attitudes about the history of everyday life (*Alltagsgeschichte*), or in order to portray an idyllic province of pedagogy, but with the theoretical purpose of studying the construction of the habitus as a process, and not only in its products. Especially in Germany, the history of education falls far short of showing the mechanics of its school system in the way that John Honey, in the English example, has taught us to see the machinery of the 'public' schools. But in the German state schools, too, one is sure to find at least modified forms of the phenomena of school cultures, of life styles, and of connections between schools, school clienteles and society, that affected careers as they did in England.

Given the lack of research, I can here provide only an example from literature – to use the opportunity for a somewhat melancholy marginal notation, rather than for the presentation of as yet inconclusive proofs. Nevertheless, in the children's book *The Flying Class Room*, which first appeared in 1933, the author Erich Kästner describes an intractable controversy between pupils of different secondary schools. Having recourse to the old categories of educational history, Kästner stylises the controversy as a conflict between 'Realists' (modern secondary students) and 'Gymnasts', that is between pupils in the traditional segments of the educational system. Thoroughly in sympathy with the 'Gymnasts', Kästner lets one of the pupils describe the roots and structure of the conflict: 'That the modern school students are at odds with us is sort of prehistorical. It is supposed to have been exactly the same ten years ago. It is a conflict between the schools, not between the pupils. The pupils only carry out what the chronicles of the schools prescribe.'[11] Research in the history of education would make a more clearly professional contribution to a history of the construction of mentalities if it investigated these forms of identity formation through schooling more precisely.

Furthermore, the field of school organisation should not be neglected. For the period after 1900, however, the focus of interest would no longer be the internal conflicts of the middle classes, but rather the defensive battles of delimitation against the rising lower and lower middle classes. I would interpret the organisational politics of the educated middle classes in Prussia around 1900 and after as indications of a new but soon consolidated unity of the middle classes. The decreasing significance of internal conflicts within the middle-class camp was partly reflected in the fact that the protectionist school associations dissolved or decayed after the accreditation of the school types they had protected. Typical for the period that followed were associations that were dominated by the teaching profession, groupings like the 'secondary teachers' convention' (*Oberlehrertag*) of the philologists, in which the teachers of all secondary schools formed a unified organisation regardless of former differences among school segments. As representatives of their clients, but also in their own interests, these teachers discovered a new opponent to be fought, not in the middle class, but in Social Democracy and its educational efforts. The marginal disadvantages experienced by modern secondary school pupils within such specific university courses of study as theology, which Ringer stresses, found no echo in the politics of associations and remained without consequence in educational policy as well.

I do not want to deny entirely the existence of conflicts within the middle class; in the form of controversies over educational theory, they nourished the journals and occupied the teaching profession. But they lost their socio-structural significance (after 1900), if only because the class conflict grew sharper and educational boundaries more problematic. At the level of legitimation, ideology remained important, but primarily in that it generalised the myth of social ascent through education. It thus pushed the expansion of secondary education to a point at which the *Gymnasium* in fact recovered the comprehensive school function that it had inevitably lost after 1830 or 1840, a loss which, according to Müller, had secured the privileges of the educated upper middle class and the mechanisms of its social reproduction. The continuity of debates over educational policy, the unchanging character of ideological conflicts in education, and the persistence of their themes is due in large part to the professionalisation of thought about the educational system. Conflicts over educational processes are thus partially transferred out of the educational system and delegated to the research system. There, professors of education, and of the history and sociology of the educational system, continue to quarrel over the historical dimensions of a problem, the present meaning of which is becoming ever more questionable for those most directly affected by educational processes. The socio-historical consequences of this transfer have remained almost unexplored, so that one cannot yet adequately discuss the impact upon educational opportunity and mobility, and upon the formation of mentalities and structures of knowledge, of this autonomisation of discourse about learning processes.

This raises the final item on the list of research desiderata. In German social history the patterns of interpretation transmitted within the various segments of the social structures – the 'social milieux'[12] – have played an important role, and not only in educational processes or in the educational system. Until 1933, for example, the predominance of the nationalist, conservative camp, which asserted itself within the educational system as well, prepared the ground on which National Socialism could rise to power. The efforts of the Weimar Republic, especially the educational policies of the Prussian state, obviously did not suffice to prevent these developments. This might force historians of education to place several sceptical limitations upon their explanatory claims. Thus it is an open question whether the educational system can do more than transmit and confirm patterns of interpretation that have been produced and elaborated elsewhere. It is also unclear how far the constitution of such patterns is due to historically analysable processes outside the school – in peer groups, on the street, in families, in everyday life. Perhaps historians of education should not only give up their fixation with organised schooling, but should also ask themselves how to change the conditions and structures in which institutionalised education is today produced and transmitted.

In the process one should also analyse whether the mechanisms of educational production really are no more than vehicles for the survival of traditions, for the endurance of organisations, and for the illegitimate domination of the middle classes, vehicles for social facts that must be critically evaluated and revised, as Ringer suggests, in accordance with the self-consciousness of democratic societies and the standards of education. One can accept his criticism of the fatal role of the 'mandarins'[13] in German educational and social history, and yet one has to ask oneself – probably quite in Ringer's own sense – whether the classical theory of education (*Bildung*) did not contain a theoretical and normative demand upon the logic of educational processes that does not lose its validity merely because one can point to its origins in middle-class culture or to the deformation of the classical idea during its decline to a status symbol. The discussion of these questions requires a history of education that is interested in more than industrialisation and equal opportunity, in more than status and prestige, a history of education that is interested, for example, in segmentation.

Concluding comments*

DETLEF K. MÜLLER and FRITZ RINGER

Instead of responding to all of the individual points made by all of our critics, we thought it best to confine ourselves to more general reactions and to comment separately, each of us in his own name.

In criticising the concept of systematisation, James Albisetti formulates a virtually classical objection: 'One is too often led to wonder whether individuals, classes, economic developments, or forces of spontaneous generation were responsible for systematisation' (p. 212). The multiplicity of factors involved in systematisation, their interconnection and interaction, may drive the historian of education to desperation and encourage him to have recourse to tranquillisers in the form of simple explanatory terms: the economic process, state intervention, the dominant class. No less dangerous is the sedative of 'intention', the attempt to expand one's own consciousness by penetrating the intentions, opinions and goals of historical actors. In structural as in narrative history, patterns of explanation can narrow one's consciousness, as drugs do, if they are stripped of complexity and mediation.

But who can master the art of keeping all the explanatory factors in motion like a magician's nine hovering balls? Of course one could play a clever trick on the audience, setting up mirrors to create the impression that nine balls are in motion when only three really are. In their references to Luhmann's systems theory, it seems to me, Jürgen Schriewer and Klaus Harney confront us with such a cabinet of mirrors.

What is accomplished by the theory they offer, a theory in which conflicts are resolved, contradictions smoothed out, and developmental processes schematised? By means of what criteria is one to substantiate, for example,

* Detlef Müller's comments translated by Fritz Ringer.

whether in modern Europe the original stratification of society has been replaced by 'functional differentiation', and functional differentiation in turn by 'focusing on meanings' that 'establish structured potentialities for comprehending and manipulating the complexity of the world' (p. 207)? How is one to distinguish the 'necessary internal differentiation' of systems from reform strategies designed to protect social privileges? In Schriewer and Harney's model the history of institutions is reconstructed in accordance with their legitimations, which then retroactively substantiate their functional evolution. Forms of differentiation are taken out of the social context in which they arose.

In all modern societies, in Luhmann's terminology, one can detect an increasing spread of complementary roles as a consequence of the social differentiation of subsystems. 'Inclusion' can refer to growth and complementary differentiation, and 'inclusion' can also be used to describe the entry of increasing numbers of students into the educational system, as well as, ultimately, into its higher-ranking parts. Neither the hypothesis of systematisation nor that of segmentation excludes the possibility of such processes. On the contrary, both hypotheses assume that some such processes took place. Our research interest, however, was not focused upon social change *in general*, but upon the *specific* forms and consequences of social change. The results of our research contradict global theories of systematisation and of modernisation. Schriewer and Harney's thesis that a hierarchy of unequal subsystems was replaced by universal access to all subsystems, as applied to educational systems over the entire span of the nineteenth and twentieth centuries, is either trivial or false: trivial if the reference is to the whole school system (e.g. the introduction of universal compulsory schooling), false if the reference is to structural change in education (e.g. the structural transformation of the *Gymnasium*).

Systematisation in education was related to developments in other subsystems of society. Like other subsystems, it was affected by bureaucratic rationalisation. The Prussian curricular decrees of 1882, 1892 and 1902 were partly consequences of administrative actions, as were the increasingly precise definitions of school types in Prussian educational statistics. The content of these definitions, and the actual realisation of the types, however, were predetermined neither by a general process of inclusion, nor by the specific terminology of the bureaucracy.

The analytical model of systematisation is designed to identify the processes and traits that formed the educational system during the phase of its constitution and that determined its further evolution. By means of the distinction between the three phases of system emergence, system constitution and system complementation, the various causal factors and the extent of their influence can be analytically isolated and empirically tested. The 'autonomy' of the educational system thus loses its metaphysical character and is resolved into a variety of different historical processes. It was only with its constitution that the educational system acquired the social import-ance that is characteristic of its modern structures, and that made its autonomy possible.

Even at its beginnings the institutionalisation of the modern educational system was shaped by reforms based on inherited patterns. But these patterns still permitted a great variety of possible later developments, so that the several schools or school forms were largely unprotected against the impact of conflicting social interests, of economic market conditions, or of the credentials requirements of university programmes or of occupational groups. In the phase of system emergence the several school forms were increasingly interrelated; they developed distinctive educational objectives and completion criteria of their own, while attending to particular client groups of parents and pupils and seeking to develop school environments suited to these groups. The bureaucratic reining-in of these developments by means of regulations and prescribed curricula, along with the sanctioning of stipulated entrance and completion requirements, gradually narrowed the range of possible further developments and forced the headmasters and teachers of the various schools to join one of the emerging school forms and to adjust to its criteria.

To say that an organisational structure is open is not to make a value judgement. Secondary recruitment was socially broader before the constitu-tion of the system, but the duration of school attendance and the achieve-ment of social mobility depended upon extra-educational factors to a much greater degree. After the structural principles of particular school types were set down, and especially after the constitution of the system, by contrast, the actual completion of a school programme acquired a social importance of its own.

In the phase of system constitution limits were placed upon curricular flexibility *within* schools – upon the multiplicity of educational programmes within a school type and upon curricular diversity among schools – that is upon the multiplicity of educational programmes *within* the educational system as a whole. The structural characteristics of the system were due neither to the number nor to the rigidity of administrative directives, but to the transformation of formerly open school forms into functionally delimited school types. As particular school forms were integrated into an overall system, their legitimating ideologies lost their limited ranges and became parts of a general theory of education in which attention to the educability of the individual was replaced by educational objectives stipulated for social groups (elite education, popular education).

The phase of system constitution can be considered a 'crucial turning-point'. Possible developments were fixed; alternatives foreign to the system were precluded. Girls' schools were integrated into the existing system of boys' schools. Traditional patterns in girls' education changed some existing structures within the system (e.g. primary teacher training), but the integration produced only modifications, not a 'mutation of the system'. The introduction of compulsory common elementary schooling reflected additional legitimatory needs arising from the logic of the system. Thus the processes grouped under the heading of system complementation were fixed by the structural principles of the system. The 'logic' inherent in the institutionalisation and legitimation of the educational system during the phase of system constitution has shaped subsequent developments right up to the present. Expansion and differentiation, curricular patterns, and educational theories were modelled on the assumptions of the system. During the phase of system complementation neither crises nor false paths were precluded, but the range and character of possible solutions were indicated by the system.

Without here trying to discuss what research deficits might have been made up, I cannot accept the demand that one must encompass an ever wider range of problems – Tenorth's 'school interactions', for example. Such a demand reminds me of a spectator who, observing nine hovering balls, promptly calls for twelve.

Detlef K. Müller

I would like to begin these comments by referring once more to the discussion between Detlef Müller and myself over the change in the structure of Prussian secondary enrolments between 1870 and 1914. On the critical side I believe that Müller occasionally gives too much weight to short-term enrolment fluctuations brought about by alterations in the accreditation of the modern secondary schools. Thus in 1870 graduates of the *Realgymnasium* were admitted to the universities to prepare for the secondary teaching certificate in 'modern' subjects. In 1879 this concession was sharply restricted by the provision that they could teach even these subjects only in modern secondary schools. That restriction was removed again in 1886, but then a tactical alliance between *Gymnasium* supporters and sponsors of the *Oberrealschule* at the school conference of 1890 once again put various obstacles in the path of the *Realgymnasium*, which were not removed until a decade later. Since each turn in the fortunes of the *Realgymnasium* altered rates of entry to *all* secondary school types, one must be very careful not to confound the short-term effects of the *Realgymnasium* wars, as I am tempted to call them, with more long-term shifts in the structure of enrolments.

On the positive side I must concede that Müller's comparison of enrolments by grade for 1875 and 1910 (Figure 1.6) is based on more precise data than my prototype for 1870 and 1911 (Figure 2.2). I still believe that my grouping of the *Realgymnasium* with the *Oberrealschule* is justified by the common perception of all non-*Gymnasien* as modern schools (*Realschulen*), as well as by the ultimate convergence of the *Realgymnasium* with the *Oberrealschule* in the compromise of the 'reformed' institutions. Moreover, the proportional differences between Müller's Figure 1.6 and my Figure 2.2 are not very large. Thus I remain convinced that processes of exclusion from the *Gymnasium* were accompanied by countervailing processes of inclusion in the modern secondary schools, as Müller is certainly aware. Nevertheless, Müller's latest diagram does in fact strengthen his case for the existence of *de facto* exclusion from the lower and intermediate grades of the *Gymnasium*, while also providing a good example of the way in which a theoretical debate can engender new and more accurate empirical work.

Some of what James Albisetti writes about the human intentions and other causes behind the processes of systematisation or segmentation I have tried to take up in the Introduction. I can add little, except to repeat that we are not forced to choose between some mysterious X on the one hand, and the invariably realised intentions of individuals or groups on the other.

To Albisetti's charge that there is a kind of egalitarian bias in our work I personally will plead guilty. But the more interesting question he raises in that connection is how much progressiveness or segmentation in an educational system is possible, or desirable, or normal. I quite agree that this is an important and difficult question, and I first tried to deal with it in the Introduction and Conclusion of *Education and Society*.

While there may be *some* biological basis for variations in testable academic ability (loosely, 'intelligence'), such variations are largely random, to the best of our knowledge, with respect to the economic and cultural capital of parents. At the same time, the cultural capital of parents clearly affects the academic ability of pupils in profound and as yet incompletely analysed ways. As a result, academic ability is distributed unequally over the social spectrum, and yet a good deal more equally than access to advanced education. That is why 'meritocracy' and rigorous academic selection are still the only sure road to a more progressive social distribution of schooling. Increased inclusiveness, while desirable in itself and as an independent form of democratisation, has proved an uncertain source of social mobility through education. If one *wants* a more progressive allocation of educational opportunities, as most of us probably do to some extent, then one must also want 'meritocracy' to some extent. Egalitarian attacks on merit principles in the recent past were simply misguided. Thus Albisetti rightly identifies the crucial question about 'meritocracy' when he asks how much compulsion would be necessary or tolerable to alter or erase the 'natural' transmission of cultural capital from parents to children.

But while I agree that we have no clear answer to this crucial question, I do not agree that we need one to pursue our historical studies of systematisation and segmentation, any more than economists need a model of the perfect income distribution to investigate real economic processes. We are on safe ground, methodologically, as long as we realise that our questions about progressiveness and segmentation are always and necessarily comparative questions, that we can properly deal only with changes over time and with similarities and differences between educational systems, exactly as we have tried to do in this volume.

Unfortunately, Albisetti himself has not put his critical questions in a consistently comparative way, and he has also attributed substantive positions to Müller and to myself that we have not in fact argued at all. Thus Müller has claimed only that *Gymnasium* recruitment was relatively open in the early nineteenth century and comparatively closed by the end of the century. About cross-national comparisons he has said only that the *Gymnasium* was more meritocratic and more progressive in its social make-up during much of the nineteenth century than the English 'public' schools and the French *lycées*. My own argument about France has *not* been that the French *lycées* and *collèges* of the 1860s resembled comprehensive schools; nor have Anderson and Harrigan advanced that possibly interesting hypothesis. Rather, Harrigan has argued, in an essentially non-comparative way, that there was an important lower middle-class presence at the French *collèges* of the 1860s, particularly in the 'special' stream. I have argued that segmentation in the French system around 1860 *and later* was more purely *vertical* (less horizontal) than segmentation in the German secondary system. But this is perfectly consistent with my simultaneous claim that French secondary recruitment was generally less *progressive* than German secondary recruitment during much of the nineteenth century, that is until structural changes in the French system from the 1880s on brought French opportunity ratios closer to German levels. I made this latter point partly in order to warn Müller that in France, at any rate, unmistakable processes of exclusion during the later nineteenth century were accompanied by equally unmistakable processes of *inclusion*, which almost certainly brought modest gains in progressiveness as well.

This brings us down at last to the really central objection raised by Albisetti, and by each of our other critics as well. They suspect Müller in particular of the view that systematisation choked off any further expansion of secondary schooling in Germany and elsewhere, and that it thereby also permanently halted all advances towards greater progressiveness in secondary and university education. But since Müller is by no means blind to the evidence, this *cannot* be his real point, and the failure to recognise that begins to seem unreasonable and unproductive. In my Introduction and elsewhere, I have tried to show how and why even substantial increases in inclusiveness may produce little or no increase in social mobility. Without going over that ground all over again, I suggest that it is part of Müller's point. One way to grasp the remainder is to suppose for a moment that neither systematisation nor segmentation had intervened in the development of secondary education during the later nineteenth century. As Müller has urgently tried to make clear, the unimpeded continuation of processes actually at work *within* the educational system would then have led to extraordinary rates of mobility through education, as well as to fierce meritocratic competition within the *Gymnasium* and comparable schools. Systematisation not only prevented that from happening; it also did so by introducing new distinctions and criteria of classification that have profoundly shaped – and legitimated – the hierarchic differentiation of the modern occupational and social system.

Along with pupils firmly intending to enter the learned professions, the Prussian *Gymnasium* of the early nineteenth century took in substantial contingents of students from artisanal backgrounds, who could either leave school to return to the social world from which they came or be inducted upwards into the hierarchy of education by an unusual taste for learning (Albisetti's 'few talented boys'). Apparently, a pervasive expectation of status persistence was not seriously threatened by such cases of selective and even sponsored individual mobility. Perhaps the partial separation of the educational hierarchy from the main avenues to wealth and power helped to sustain these conditions, along with the humble circumstances of the clerical and teaching professions, the usual goals of students from modest backgrounds.

Müller is trying to help explain how this pattern broke down. Both socially diffuse and politically articulate aspirations for greater equality of opportunity may have played a role. So may educational reformers interested in intermediate schooling that seemed to them economically useful or socially ameliorative. Quite clearly, the educational system itself participated in a process of mobilisation. In any case, a stable form of social and cultural reproduction was disturbed just as the educational hierarchy began to interact with the occupational hierarchy in the high industrial context. Among the dominant classes the Great Depression gave rise to protectionist sentiments that helped to transform the expectation of status persistence into a more or less conscious determination to limit and channel mobility. That, roughly, was the context in which systematisation took place and in which segmentation became both more rigorous and more socially visible.

With that I hope to have answered some of Elmar Tenorth's questions, as well as most of Albisetti's. Both Müller and I would have to agree with Tenorth that European school systems did become somewhat more inclusive during our period, and they thereby also raised and partly satisfied new expectations. We can also agree that the more substantial expansion of enrolments per age group in the twentieth century has reduced the significance of segmentation *within* the secondary system, while focusing attention upon the more decisive boundary between the secondary and the primary schools. This, as I argued in *Education and Society*, was the overriding issue of the inter-war period in France as well as in Germany. And of course the internal divisions within the middle class paled in this context. Here, as elsewhere in Tenorth's generally sympathetic commentary, the questions asked are clear and interesting, but they do not pertain to the period or to the analytical problems we have chosen to treat in this volume.

I want particularly to thank Tenorth for his very complete and lucid account of my theoretical efforts. It seems to me, however, that these have already somewhat stretched the limits of the empirical evidence. Without sharing the legendary aversion of the historian to social theory, I feel that a little such stretching is quite enough. My temptation to abandon that viewpoint is not increased, moreover, by what Tenorth writes about the 'systematic reduction of privileges' in the twentieth century, or about the way in which 'the functionality' of contemporary educational systems has 'increased for individuals, for the structure of schooling and for society' (pp. 222–3). These are very large generalisations indeed, and I cannot share the untroubled optimism they reflect.

I have a related problem with the very ambitious theoretical constructions of Jürgen Schriewer and Klaus Harney, for, to begin with, I see nothing wrong with 'the universal form of human thought'. In history as in ordinary life I take the aim of such thought to be singular causal explanation (not the detection of law-like regularities). The most obvious form of causal analysis, surely, is the comparative method of similarities and differences, whether or not it is formalised as 'the "quasi-experimental method" of the social sciences' (p. 204). And I just cannot agree that the use of this method led us to attend exclusively to cross-national similarities that obtained at a 'high level of generality'. On the contrary, the sort of questions we put to our evidence brought us back again and again to differences, which stood out all the more clearly against the background of common trends. Indeed, I cannot imagine serious comparison and causal analysis that would lead to anything else.

As if in compensation, I find Schriewer and Harney's account of Luhmann's general systems theory very hard to accept, primarily because I cannot assign a clear status to some of its propositions. I can imagine pursuing the idea of articulative processes taking place at the borderlines between such 'subsystems' as the educational and the occupational ones. I might even be persuaded to look for commonalities between 'inclusion' in schooling and 'inclusion' in politics, though I am frankly sceptical. But what am I to make of these three sentences, for example?

The internal differentiation and specification of the system generally are the inevitable complements . . . of system formation itself (p. 204).

Modern European societies are characterised by the change of their primary scheme of differentiation from stratification to functional differentiation (p. 207).

The more the continuing process of inclusion advances, the more acute is the need for internal differentiation and specification, and at the same time for the removal of mere ambiguities and unregulated competition (p. 208).

If these are descriptive statements at a *very high* level of generality, then what is the evidence for them? Or if they are functional propositions of the limited sort that can sometimes be translated into causal claims, then what accounts for the 'inevitability' and for the 'need' that are referred to? The 'system' that figures in these sentences is so large that *everything* becomes endogenous to it. It really does seem to be moved, too, by a mysterious X, perhaps by the teleology of the need to 'remove mere ambiguities and unregulated competition' from modern society.

Admittedly, there is a possible reading of Bourdieu's 'social reproduction' in which an equally total functionalism could be implied: in which the workings of class society know no incongruities, in which the distribution of capital is always flawlessly reproduced, and in which legitimating ideologies never lead to contradictions, or to potential criticisms of what they sustain. Suffice it to say, in conclusion, that I would find such a reading quite as problematic as the reinterpretation of Müller's concept of systematisation along the lines suggested by Schriewer and Harney.

Fritz Ringer*

* I wish to thank Detlef K. Müller and Brian Simon for an enlivening series of scholarly and theoretical discussions.

Notes

Introduction

1. Robert Locke, *The End of Practical Man: Entrepreneurship and Higher Education in Germany, France, and Great Britain, 1880–1940* (Greenwich, Conn. and London, 1984).
2. C. R. Day, 'Technical and Professional Education in France: The Rise and Fall of *l'enseignement secondaire spécial*, 1865–1902', *Journal of Social History*, vol. 6 (1972–3), pp. 177–201.
3. For a brief introduction, see Pierre Bourdieu, 'Cultural Reproduction and Social Reproduction', in Jerome Karabel and A. H. Halsey (eds.), *Power and Ideology in Education* (New York, 1977), pp. 487–511. See also Pierre Bourdieu and Jean-Claude Passeron, *Reproduction in Education, Society and Culture*, trans. Richard Nice (London and Beverly Hills, 1977); Pierre Bourdieu, Luc Boltanski and Monique de Saint-Martin, 'Les stratégies de reconversion', *Social Sciences Information*, vol. 12, no. 5 (1973), pp. 61–113; Pierre Bourdieu, 'Les trois états du capital culturel', *Actes de la recherche en sciences sociales*, no. 30 (November 1979), pp. 3–6; and Pierre Bourdieu, *La distinction: Critique sociale du jugement* (Paris, 1979).
4. Having written about the 'generalist shift' in my main contribution to this volume some time ago, I encountered Guy Neave's parallel account of the 'academic drift' more recently, but still before the writing of this Introduction. See Guy Neave, 'The Dynamic of Integration in Non-Integrated Systems of Higher Education in Western Europe', in H. Hermanns, U. Teichler and H. Wasser (eds.), *The Compleat University: Break from Tradition in Germany, Sweden and the USA* (Cambridge, Mass., 1983), pp. 265–8.
5. Fritz Ringer, *Education and Society in Modern Europe* (Bloomington and London, 1979), pp. 232–3, 241–2.
6. See the comments on this aspect of Weber's work in *ibid.*, pp. 14–18.

1. The process of systematisation: the case of German secondary education

1. Friedrich Paulsen, *Geschichte des gelehrten Unterrichts auf den deutschen Schulen und Universitäten vom Ausgang des Mittelalters bis zur Gegenwart* (Leipzig, 1896); Louis Liard, *L'enseignement supérieur en France, 1789–1889* (2 vols., Paris, 1888–94).
2. Fritz Ringer, *Education and Society in Modern Europe* (Bloomington and London, 1979). For the following, see also Harold Silver, 'Comparative and Cross-Cultural History of Education', in H. Silver, *Education as History: Interpreting Nineteenth- and Twentieth-Century Education* (London, 1982); Jürgen Schriewer, 'Vergleichend-historische Bildungsforschung', *Zeitschrift für Pädagogik*, vol. 30 (1984), pp. 323–42; Detlef K.

Müller, 'Sozialstruktur und Schulsystem', in Walter Rüegg and Otto Neuloh (eds.), *Zur soziologischen Theorie und Analyse des 19. Jahrhunderts* (Göttingen, 1971), pp. 213–37; Müller *et al.*, 'Modellentwicklung zur Analyse von Krisenphasen im Verhältnis von Schulsystem und staatlichem Beschäftigungssystem', *Zeitschrift für Pädagogik*, suppl. 14 (1977), pp. 37–77; Brian Simon, *Education and the Labour Movement, 1870–1920* (London, 1965); and A. Baumeister, *Die Einrichtung und Verwaltung des höheren Schulwesens in den Kulturländern von Europa und in Nordamerika* (Handbuch der Erziehungs- und Unterrichtslehre für höhere Schulen, vol. 1, part 2, Munich, 1897).

3. My concept of 'system' is to be distinguished from the usual static version, in which historical processes are ignored. For an example of such static usage, see Talcott Parsons, 'The Elementary and Secondary School as a Social System', *Harvard Educational Review*, vol. 29 (1959), pp. 297–318.

4. Detlef K. Müller, 'Der Prozeß der Systembildung im Schulwesen Preußens während der zweiten Hälfte des 19. Jahrhunderts', *Zeitschrift für Pädagogik*, vol. 27 (1981), pp. 245–69.

5. For this and the following, see Detlef K. Müller, *Sozialstruktur und Schulsystem: Aspekte zum Strukturwandel des Schulwesens im 19. Jahrhundert* (Göttingen, 1977), and an abbreviated edition under the same title (Göttingen, 1981).

6. Talcott Parsons, *Das System moderner Gesellschaften* (Munich, 1972).

7. For structural change in German secondary education during the nineteenth century, see the systematic bibliography in Müller, *Sozialstruktur und Schulsystem*, and especially the following nineteenth-century works and source collections: Brauns and Theobald (eds.), *Statistisches Handbuch der deutschen Gymnasien* (2 vols., Kassel, 1837–39); Paul Schwartz, *Die Gelehrtenschulen Preussens unter dem Oberschulkollegium, 1787–1806 und das Abiturientenexamen*, vols. 1, 3 (Monumenta Germaniae Paedagogica, XLVI, L (Berlin, 1910–12)), esp. vol. 1, chapters 1–3; Ludwig von Rönne, *Das Unterrichts-Wesen des preussischen Staates*, vol. 2 (Berlin, 1855); J. F. Neigebaur, *Die preußischen Gymnasien und höheren Bürgerschulen: Eine Zusammenstellung der Verordnungen, welche den höheren Unterricht in diesen Anstalten umfassen* (Berlin, 1835); E. Bonnell, 'Preussen: Die höheren Schulen', in K. A. Schmid (ed.), *Encyklopädie des gesammten Erziehungs- und Unterrichtswesens*, vol. 6 (Gotha, 1867), pp. 267–335; Ludwig Wiese (ed.), *Das höhere Schulwesen in Preussen: Historisch-statistische Darstellung*, vol. 1 (Berlin, 1864), vol. 2: *1864–1868* (Berlin, 1869), vol. 3: *1869–1873* (Berlin, 1874), vol. 4: *1874–1901*, ed. B. Irmer (Berlin, 1902); Ludwig Wiese (ed.), *Verordnungen und Gesetze für die höheren Schulen in Preussen* (Berlin, 1875, 1886); A. Beier (ed.), *Die höheren Schulen in Preußen (für die männliche Jugend) und ihre Lehrer: Sammlung der hierauf bezüglichen Gesetze, Verordnungen, Verfügungen und Erlasse* (Halle, 1909); W. Lexis (ed.), *Das Unterrichtswesen im deutschen Reich* (4 vols., Berlin, 1904); W. Lexis (ed.), *Die Reform des höheren Schulwesens in Preussen* (Halle, 1902); and O. Heinemann, *Handbuch über die Organisation und Verwaltung der öffentlichen preussischen Unterrichtsanstalten* (2 vols., Potsdam, 1907–9).

8. Pierre Bourdieu and J.-C. Passeron, *Die Illusion der Chancengleichheit* (Stuttgart, 1971); Pierre Bourdieu, *La distinction: Critique sociale du jugement* (Paris, 1979).

9. Müller, *Sozialstruktur und Schulsystem*, pp. 65–84, 611–20.

10. For this and the following, see Müller, *Sozialstruktur und Schulsystem*, pp. 90–189; Detlef Müller, 'Possibilities and Limits of the Prussian School Reform at the Beginning of the Nineteenth Century', in H. N. Jahnke and M. Otte (eds.), *Epistemological and Social Problems of the Sciences in the Early Nineteenth Century* (Dordrecht, Boston and London, 1981), pp. 183–206; Detlef K. Müller, *Datenhandbuch zur deutschen Bildungsgeschichte*, vol. 1 (Göttingen, forthcoming); Detlef K. Müller, 'The Qualifications Crisis and School Reform in Late Nineteenth-Century Germany', *History of Education*, vol. 9 (1980), pp. 313–31; Detlef K. Müller, 'Die Entstehung des modernen Schulsystems im Staat Preussen und den Provinzen Westfalen und Rheinprovinz', in Kurt Düwell and Wolfgang Köllmann (eds.), *Rheinland-Westfalen im Industriezeitalter*, vol. 4 (Wuppertal, 1985), pp. 39–85; Manfred Heinemann, *Schule im Vorfeld der Verwaltung: Die Entwicklung der preussischen Unterrichtsverwaltung von 1771–1899* (Göttingen, 1974); K. E. Jeismann, *Das preussische Gymnasium in Staat und Gesellschaft* (Stuttgart, 1974); A. Leschinsky and P. M. Roeder, *Schule im historischen Prozess* (Stuttgart, 1976); Rudolf Vierhaus, *Deutsch-*

land im Zeitalter des Absolutismus (*Deutsche Geschichte*, 6 (Göttingen, 1978)); Werner Conze, 'Sozialgeschichte 1800–1850', in Hermann Aubin and Wolfgang Zorn (eds.), *Handbuch der deutschen Wirtschafts- und Sozialgeschichte, Band 2: Das 19. und 20. Jahrhundert* (Stuttgart, 1976), pp. 426–94; and Thomas Nipperdey, *Deutsche Geschichte, 1800–1866: Bürgerwelt und starker Staat* (München, 1983).

11. Cited in Rönne, *Unterrichts-Wesen*, pp. 176ff. See also Wiese, *Das höhere Schulwesen*, vol. 1, pp. 622ff.

12. From Brauns and Theobald, *Statistisches Handbuch*, pp. 7–8.

13. See C. Peter, *Ein Vorschlag zur Reform unserer Gymnasien* (Jena, 1874). Peter was headmaster of Pforta from 1856 to 1877.

14. Minister's memorandum of 30 December 1831, cited in Rönne, *Unterrichts-Wesen*, pp. 139–44, esp. pp. 140, 142.

15. Ministerial circular of 13 December 1862, 'Deutscher Unterricht auf den Gymnasien', reprinted as no. 8 in *Zentralblatt für die gesamte Unterrichtsverwaltung* (1863) (henceforth *ZBL*), pp. 18–23, esp. p. 19.

16. Ministerial circular of 20 October 1863, 'Lehrplan für den Unterricht im Zeichnen auf Gymnasien und Realschulen', reprinted as no. 242 in *ZBL* (1863), pp. 580–91, esp. p. 587.

17. Ministerial circular of 7 January 1856, 'Normalplan für den Gymnasial-Unterricht', reprinted as no. 56 in *ZBL* (1859), pp. 162–9, esp. p. 165.

18. From Wiese, *Das höhere Schulwesen*, vol. 1, pp. iv, 25.

19. In Süvern's 1819 'Entwurf eines Allgemeinen Gesetzes über die Verfassung des Schulwesens im Preussischen Staate', the 'town school' occupied an intermediate position between the 'common elementary school' and the *Gymnasium*. See the reprinting of the 'Entwurf' in *Die Gesetzgebung auf dem Gebiete des Unterrichtswesens in Preussen vom Jahre 1817–1868: Aktenstücke und Erläuterungen aus dem Ministerium der Geistlichen, Unterrichts- und Medicinalangelegenheiten* (Berlin, 1869), pp. 15–74, esp. p. 16.

20. 'Genehmigter Plan für die Einrichtung des städtischen Armenschulwesens in Berlin', in L. Beckedorff (ed.), *Jahrbücher des preussischen Volks-Schul-Wesens*, vol. 6 (Berlin, 1827), pp. 169–222. For the development of the *Volksschule*, see J. F. Neigebaur, *Das Volks-Schul-Wesen in den preussischen Staaten: Eine Zusammenstellung der Verordnungen, welche den Elementarunterricht der Jugend betreffen* (Berlin, Posen and Bromberg, 1834); and K. Schneider and E. von Bremen (eds.), *Das Volksschulwesen im preussischen Staate* (3 vols., Berlin, 1886–7).

21. In Berlin during the 1830s net expenditures for the schools were only one-sixth as high as the budget item for the financing of the debt; net school expenditures did not exceed debt costs until 1861.

22. Friedrich Thiersch, *Über gelehrten Schulen mit besonderer Rücksicht auf Bayern* (Stuttgart and Tübingen, 1826); G. Mayr, 'Statistick des Unterrichts und der Erziehung im Königreiche Bayern für die Jahre 1869/70, 1870/71 und 1871/72 mit Rückblicken auf die Ergebnisse der früheren Jahre', in *Beiträge zur Statistik des KR Bayern*, no. 29 (Munich, 1873–5).

23. See Werner Conze, 'Sozialgeschichte 1850–1918', in Aubin and Zorn, *Handbuch*, pp. 602–84.

24. J. P. Müller, 'Erste allgemeine deutsche Realschulmänner-Versammlung zu Gera, 28.–30. September 1873', in *Central-Organ für die Interessen des Realschulwesens* (henceforth *Central-Organ*), vol. 1 (1873), pp. 647–88.

25. E. G. Fischer, *Über die zweckmäßige Einrichtung der Lehranstalten für die gebildeten Stände: Versuch einer neuen Ansicht dieses Gegenstandes mit besonderer Rücksicht auf Berlin* (Berlin, 1806); E. G. Fischer, 'Über die englischen Lehranstalten in Vergleichung mit den übrigen', in *Berliner Gymnasium zum Grauen Kloster, Öffentliche Prüfung, April 1827* (Berlin, 1827), pp. 1–18; E. F. August, 'Zweck, Ziel und gegenwärtige Einrichtung des Real-Gymnasii', in *Cölnisches Realgymnasium, Öffentliche Prüfung, 1829* (Berlin, 1829), pp. 27–34; E. F. August, 'Lehrplan des Realgymnasiums', in *Cölnisches Real-Gymnasium, Öffentliche Prüfung, März 1850* (Berlin, 1850), pp. 19–27.

26. At the *Realschule* in Elberfeld in 1864 fees ran from 96 marks in the lower grades to 120 marks in the upper grades; fees in the Elberfeld *Gymnasium* varied with the parents' tax situation, from 51 marks in the lower grades to 123 marks in the upper grades.

27. 'Bericht der Unterrichtscommission des Hauses der Abgeordneten über Rechte und Stellung der Realschulen', in *ZBL* (1859), pp. 144–62; M. Strack, 'Die Unterrichts- und Prüfungsordnung vom 6. Oktober 1859', in *Central-Organ*, vol. 1 (1873), pp. 199–218; *Akademische Gutachten über die Zulassung von Realschul-Abiturienten zu Fakultäts-Studien: Amtlicher Abdruck* (Berlin, 1870); Qu. Steinbart, *Unsere Abiturienten: Ein Beitrag zur Klärung der Realschulefrage* (Berlin, 1878).

28. For this and the following, see F. W. Nottebohm, *Chronik der Königlichen Gewerbe-Akademie zu Berlin: Festschrift zur Feier des 50jährigen Bestehens der Anstalt* (Berlin, 1871); 'Denkschrift über die Gewerbeschulen', in *ZBL* (1881), pp. 189–212; *Das technische Unterrichtswesen in Preussen: Sammlung amtlicher Actenstücke des Handelsministeriums sowie der bezüglichen Berichte und Verhandlungen des Landtags aus 1878/9* (Berlin, 1879); Walter Parow, *Res, non verba! Bildungsideal und Lebensbedingungen der Oberrealschule im Vergleich mit dem altklassischen Gymnasium* (Braunschweig and Leipzig, 1903); P. Wust, *Die Oberrealschule und der moderne Geist* (Leipzig, 1917); and Herwig Blankertz, *Bildung im Zeitalter der großen Industrie: Pädagogik, Schule und Berufsbildung im 19. Jahrhundert* (Berlin, Darmstadt, Dortmund, 1969).

29. F. Hofmann, *Über die Einrichtung öffentlicher Mittelschulen in Berlin* (Berlin, 1869); J. Tews, *Das Volksschulwesen in den großen Städten Deutschlands* (Langensalza, 1897); A. Sachse, *Die preußische Volks- und Mittelschule: Ihre Entwicklung und ihre Ziele* (Leipzig and Berlin, 1913); W. Heinecker, *Das Problem der Schulorganisation aufgrund der Begabung der Kinder* (Langensalza, 1924); Christa Berg, *Die Okkupation der Schule: Eine Studie zur Aufhellung gegenwärtiger Schulprobleme an der Volksschule Preussens, 1872–1900* (Heidelberg, 1973).

30. The fully developed *Volksschulen* were gradually separated from the rest and formed a new group of higher primary or 'middle schools'. Among some 92,000 pupils in the 372 Prussian *Mittelschulen* of 1911, 11 per cent took Latin and only 13 per cent took no foreign language at all.

31. Compare the curricula programmes of 1882, 1892 and 1901, reprinted in *ZBL* (1882), pp. 234–76; *ZBL* (1892), pp. 199–399 and *ZBL* (1901), pp. 471–544.

32. See 'Allerhöchster Erlaß vom 26. November 1900', reprinted in Beier, *Die höheren Schulen*, pp. 69–71.

33. See Wiese, *Das höhere Schulwesen*, vol. 3, pp. 22–9, 57–8.

34. See *Beiträge des Preussischen Städtetages zur Handhabung der staatlichen Schulverwaltung gegenüber den Städten* (Berlin, 1917).

35. See Müller, *Sozialstruktur und Schulsystem*, pp. 274–97, 764–800.

36. See Müller, 'Qualifications Crisis'; and Hartmut Titze, 'Enrollment Expansion and Academic Overcrowding in Germany', in Konrad H. Jarausch (ed.), *The Transformation of Higher Learning, 1860–1930* (Stuttgart, 1983), pp. 57–88.

37. See Hans Rosenberg, *Große Depression und Bismarckzeit: Wirtschaftsablauf, Gesell-schaftspolitik in Mitteleuropa* (Berlin, 1967).

38. Detlef K. Müller, 'Bildungssystem und Generationskonflikt', *Bildung und Erziehung*, vol. 38 (1985), pp. 231–44; Bernd Zymek, 'Jugendgenerationen zwischen bürokratischem Bildungssystem und charismatischen Erneuerungsbewegungen', *Bildung und Erziehung*, vol. 38 (1985), pp. 231–44.

39. W. Lexis, *Denkschrift über die den Bedarf Preussens entsprechende Normalzahl der Studierenden der verschiedenen Fakultäten* (Berlin, 1891); J. Conrad, *Das Universitäts-studium in Deutschland während der letzten 50 Jahre: Statistische Untersuchungen unter besonderer Berück-sichtigung Preussens* (Jena, 1884); A. Petersilie, 'Die Entwicklung der höheren Lehranstalten in Preussen in statistischer Beleuchtung', in *Central-Organ*, vol. 12 (1884), pp. 78–91; H. Keferstein, *Die Überfüllung der höheren Berufsarten* (Hamburg, 1889); F. Pietzker and P. Treutlein, *Der Zudrang zu den gelehrten Berufsarten, seine Ursachen und etwaigen Heilmittel* (Braunschweig, 1889); H. Matzat, *Die Überfüllung der gelehrten Fächer und die Schulreformfrage* (Berlin, 1889); F. Malvus, *Das heutige Studium und das Studierten-Proletariat* (Berlin, 1889).

40. O. von Bismarck, speech in the Reichstag, 9 May 1884, in *Stenographische Berichte über die Verhandlungen des Reichstags, V. Legislaturperiode, IV. Session* (1884), p. 480.

41. See von Gossler, speech in the Prussian parliament, 28th session, 1889, House of Deputies,

in *Stenographische Berichte über die Verhandlungen des preußischen Hauses der Abgeordneten* (1889), p. 842; von Gossler, speech in the Prussian parliament, 33rd session, 1888, House of Deputies, in *Central-Organ*, vol. 16 (1888), p. 251.

42. See Ministerium der geistlichen, Unterrichts- und Medizinalangelegenheiten (ed.), *Verhandlungen über Fragen des höheren Unterrichts, Berlin, 4.–17. Dezember 1890* (Berlin, 1891); Ministerium der geistlichen, Unterrichts- und Medizinalangelegenheiten (ed.), *Verhandlungen über Fragen des höheren Unterrichts, Berlin, 6.–8. Juni 1900* (Halle, 1901).

43. Friedrich Paulsen, 'Bildung', in W. Rein (ed.), *Encyklopädisches Handbuch der Pädagogik*, vol. 1 (Langensalza, 1903), pp. 658–70; Friedrich Paulsen, *Gesammelte pädagogische Abhandlungen*, ed. E. Spranger (Stuttgart and Berlin, 1912); Friedrich Paulsen, 'Das moderne Bildungswesen', in W. Lexis *et al.*, *Die allgemeinen Grundlagen der Kultur der Gegenwart* (Berlin and Leipzig, 1912), pp. 54–85.

44. Bernd Zymek, 'Perspektive und Enttäuschung deutscher Gymnasiasten 1933 und 1983', *Bildung und Erziehung*, vol. 36 (1983), pp. 335–49; Bernd Zymek, 'Expansion und Differenzierung des höheren Schulsystems im Staat Preußen und seinen Provinzen Rheinland und Westfalen während der 1. Hälfte des 20. Jahrhunderts', in Düwell and Köllmann, *Rheinland-Westfalen* vol. 4, pp. 149–80.

45. On girls' schools, see Müller, *Datenhandbuch*, chapter 2.

46. For an account of the complementation of the system up to the present, see Peter Drewek and Detlef K. Müller, 'Zur sozialen Funktion der gymnasialen Oberstufe', in Herwig Blankertz *et al.* (eds.), *Sekundarstufe II: Jugendbildung zwischen Schule und Beruf* (Stuttgart, 1982), pp. 108–29.

2. On segmentation in modern European educational systems: the case of French secondary education, 1865–1920

1. Fritz Ringer, *Education and Society in Modern Europe* (Bloomington and London, 1979).

2. The best German equivalents of 'access' and 'distribution' would be *Zugang* and *Anteil*. The best German equivalent of 'progressiveness', incidentally, would *not* be *Fortschrittlichkeit*; a 'progressive' educational system, like a 'progressive' tax structure, is one that tends to encourage social mobility. In practice, such percentages as $A5/At$ or $A1/At$ cannot usually be obtained from the available evidence. In their place one can have recourse, at least in principle, to the socio-occupational census (i.e. the percentage of manual labourers in the work force). In place of the distribution ratio one can thus obtain what I call an 'opportunity ratio', a mathematically more general form of the distribution ratio.

3. This should clear up some of the questions raised by Peter Lundgreen, 'Bildung und Besitz – Einheit oder Inkongruenz in der europäischen Sozialgeschichte? – Kritische Auseinandersetzung mit einer These von Fritz Ringer', *Geschichte und Gesellschaft*, vol. 6 (1980), pp. 262–75. By themselves, neither Lundgreen's *Bildungsprofile* nor his *Sozialprofile* mean very much. Segmentation is a kind of internal differentiation; its empirical measure can only be a *deviation*. This is true *in principle*, whether or not the access or distribution ratios are actually calculated. Unlike progressiveness, incidentally, segmentation can almost always be measured *exactly*.

4. Lundgreen seems to think that the inclusiveness of a segment is its most important characteristic, or perhaps its *only* important characteristic. He goes so far as to suggest that an increase in the inclusiveness of a segment should be interpreted as an *increase in segmentation*. If this were taken seriously, segmentation would reach a maximum where students in a given system were evenly divided over two curricular options (French or English as the main foreign language, for example), regardless of whether the two groups of pupils differed in their social origins. A concept of segmentation defined in that way would serve no analytical purpose. Whether or not differences between 'small' segments are significant can only be decided in the light of the interpretive question at issue. In nineteenth-century France, the Ecole Polytechnique and the Ecole Normale were *minute* segments within the system of higher education as a whole. Yet the pronounced social differences between the two schools were quite significant. To be sure, they only affected social roles, relationships and outlooks *within a very small elite* of the highly educated. What is known about graduates of the *Oberrealschule* during the late nineteenth century,

incidentally, derives much of its significance from what it suggests about pupils who left the school before reaching the *Abitur*.

5. Here, again, Lundgreen's interpretation is puzzling. Does he really believe that the *social meaning* of secondary schooling during the late nineteenth century changed with every increase or decrease in the hours assigned to Latin?

6. Karl-Ernst Jeismann, *Das preussische Gymnasium in Staat und Gesellschaft* (Stuttgart, 1974), pp. 164–5.

7. Detlef Müller, *Sozialstruktur und Schulsystem: Aspekte zur Theorie und Praxis der Schulorganisation im 19. Jahrhundert* (Göttingen, 1977), pp. 274–80.

8. The most interesting distribution ratios for the *Oberrealschule* (In column) are: Learned professions 0.26, Primary teachers 0.33, Technical professions 1.8, 'Industrialists' 2.2, Commerce 1.3, Artisans 2.1.

9. Hans-Ulrich Wehler, 'Vorüberlegungen zur historischen Analyse sozialer Ungleichheit', in Wehler (ed.), *Klassen in der europäischen Sozialgeschichte* (Göttingen, 1979), pp. 9–32.

10. Raymond Williams, *Culture and Society, 1780–1950* (New York, 1958).

11. What follows is based in part on Ringer, *Education and Society*; readers may wish to consult the bibliography there, as well as the chapters and appended tables for France, to supplement the necessarily sparse annotation of the present essay. Particularly important on the *enseignement spécial* is C. R. Day, 'Technical and Professional Education in France: The Rise and Fall of *l'enseignement secondaire spécial*, 1865–1902', *Journal of Social History*, vol. 6 (1972–3), pp. 177–201. Particularly important for the French secondary education debate of the late ninteenth century are Georges Weill, *Histoire de l'enseignement secondaire en France, 1802–1920* (Paris, 1921); Viviane Isambert-Jamati, 'Une réforme des lycées et collèges: Essai d'analyse sociologique de la réforme de 1902, '*L'année sociologique*, 3rd series, vol. 20 (1969), pp. 9–60; and, above all, Clement Falcucci, *L'humanisme dans l'enseignement secondaire en France au XIXᵉ siècle* (Toulouse and Paris, 1939), which reproduces substantial portions of key texts.

12. Falcucci, *L'humanisme*, p. 271.

13. *Ibid.*, p. 285.

14. *Ibid.*, p. 288.

15. *Ibid.*, p. 291.

16. *Ibid.*, pp. 297–8.

17. Jules Ferry, *Rapport au président de la République* (decree of 29 October 1881) cited in Antoine Prost, *Histoire de l'enseignement en France, 1800–1967* (Paris, 1968), p. 346.

18. Ferdinand Buisson, *Rapport à la commission mixte* (1887) cited in *ibid.*, pp. 317–18.

19. Falcucci, *L'humanisme*, p. 333.

20. For this and the following, see *ibid.*, pp. 295, 362, 382, 386, 388–9.

21. *Ibid.*, p. 291.

22. *Ibid.*, p. 413.

23. *Ibid.*, p. 383.

24. *Ibid.*, p. 462.

25. Chambre des Députés, Session de 1899, *Enquête sur l'enseignement secondaire*, vols. I–II: *Procès-verbaux des dépositions*, presented by Alexandre Ribot (Paris, 1899). A reading of the testimony in these two volumes has shaped much of the interpretation offered in the present essay; but I am deferring an explicit analysis of this testimony (and of related materials) to a forthcoming publication. See also Alexandre Ribot, *La réforme de l'enseignement secondaire* (Paris, 1900).

26. Ringer, *Education and Society*, p. 328.

3. Systematisation and segmentation in education: the case of England

1. Brian Simon, *The Two Nations and the Educational Structure, 1780–1870*, first published as *Studies in the History of Education, 1780–1870* (London, 1960), esp. chapter 6, pp. 227–336.

2. *Ibid.*

3. For instance, Henry Craik, *The State in its Relations to Education* (London, 1884) and later books in this genre.

4. Sheila Fletcher, *Feminists and Bureaucrats: A Study in the Development of Girls' Education in the Nineteenth Century* (Cambridge, 1980).
5. Such Executive Commissioners were appointed by the Acts concerning both Oxford and Cambridge, the 'public' or 'great' schools, and the endowed grammar schools.
6. Reference will be made to 'England' rather than 'Britain' throughout. Scottish developments differed from English ones and need a separate study, but see Walter Humes and Hamish Paterson (eds.), *Scottish Culture and Scottish Education, 1800–1980* (Edinburgh, 1983). There were also important differences in Wales, relating in particular to the Welsh Intermediate Education Act of 1889. See Leslie Wynne Evans, *Studies in Welsh Education* (Cardiff, 1974).
7. Geoffrey Holmes, *Augustan England. Professions, State and Society, 1680–1730* (London, 1982).
8. For legal judgements affecting education, see David Owen, *English Philanthropy, 1660–1960* (Oxford, 1964). See also Simon, *The Two Nations*, esp. pp. 104–9.
9. Schools Inquiry Commission (Taunton), *Report*, vol. 1 (1868), p. 93.
10. Geoffrey Best, *Mid-Victorian Britain, 1851–1875* (London, 1973), p. 170.
11. Harold Perkin, *The Origins of Modern English Society, 1780–1880* (London, 1969), p. 302.
12. Samuel Bowles and Herbert Gintis, *Schooling in Capitalist America* (London, 1976).
13. Pierre Bourdieu and Jean-Claude Passeron, *Reproduction in Education, Society and Culture* (London and Beverly Hills, 1977).
14. Joan Simon, *Education and Society in Tudor England* (Cambridge, 1966); Foster Watson, *The English Grammar Schools to 1660: Their Curriculum and Practice* (Cambridge, 1908), pp. 530ff.
15. Brian Simon, *The Two Nations*, chapter 1, pp. 17–71; for the Manchester College of Arts and Science and the Manchester Academy, see pp. 58–62. For the Lunar Society, see Robert E. Schofield, *The Lunar Society of Birmingham* (Oxford, 1963).
16. Of the 14 members of the Lunar Society, 4 (Richard Edgeworth, Thomas Day, Erasmus Darwin and Joseph Priestley) published important books on education.
17. Jeremy Bentham, *Chrestomathia* (London, 1816); Brian Simon, *The Two Nations*, pp. 79–82.
18. This movement is interestingly analysed in Ian Inkster and Jack Morrell (eds.), *Metropolis and Province: Science in British Culture, 1780–1850* (London, 1983). See especially the introductory chapter by Inkster and the chapters by Orange (on Newcastle) and Neve (on Bristol).
19. W. D. Rubinstein, 'Wealth, Elites and the Class Structure of Modern Britain', *Past and Present*, no. 76 (August 1977). Rubinstein's thesis concerning the 'two middle classes' is very relevant to this analysis.
20. Gladstone's letter to the Clarendon Commission is reprinted in the *Report of the Public School Commission*, vol. 2, pp. 42–3: 'The materials of what we call classical training were prepared, and we have a right to say were advisedly and providentially prepared, in order that it might become . . . the complement of Christianity in its application to the culture of the human being.'
21. Introduction to the English edition of *Socialism: Utopian and Scientific*, in Karl Marx and Frederick Engels, *Selected Works* (London, 1950), vol. 2, pp. 102–3.
22. Michael Sanderson's *The Universities and British Industry, 1870–1970* (London, 1972), a full specialist study, makes it clear that it was not until the later 1880s or 1890s that the universities, both ancient and modern, began to make any substantial contribution to British industry.
23. Elie Halévy, in *Imperialism and the Rise of Labour* (London, 1961), gives the following figures for British capital invested abroad: 1842, £144 million; 1877, £600 million; 1882, £875 million; 1893, £1698 million; 1905, £2025 million.
24. Though it could be argued that Herbert Spencer's *Education, Intellectual, Moral, and Physical*, first published in 1861, which restated and developed the utilitarian approach, came close to such a statement, while T. H. Huxley also wrote much on education from an advanced liberal–scientific standpoint in the closing decades of the century.
25. Donald Jones, *The Making of the Education System, 1851–81* (London, 1977), includes a useful analysis of this movement in chapter 2, pp. 13–27.

26. David Allsobrook, 'An Investigation of Precedents for the Recommendations of the Schools Inquiry Commission, 1864–1867', unpublished PhD thesis, University of Leicester, 1979. See especially chapter 3, 'Local Authorities and Unilateralism: I, Mid-Century Contrast: Diocesan and County Boards: County Schools'. See also David Allsobrook, *Schools for the Shires* (Manchester, 1986).

27. For the influence of this grouping, the 'academic liberals', see David Reeder (ed.), *Educating Our Masters* (Leicester, 1980), especially the editor's introduction. See also chapter 6 – T. H. Green's 1882 lecture concerning the aspirations of middle-class intellectuals of the 1860s to develop a national system of education based on the reform of middle-class schools.

28. Allsobrook, 'An Investigation', chapters 3 and 7.

29. *First, Second and Third Reports of the Commissioners on the Education of the Poor, 1819–20*.

30. Royal Commission on Oxford University (established 1850); Royal Commission on Cambridge University (1850); Royal Commission on Elementary Education (Newcastle Commission, 1858); Royal Commission on the Public Schools (Clarendon Commission, 1861). The Schools Inquiry Commission (Taunton Commission) was appointed in 1864, reporting in 1868.

31. Schools Inquiry Commission, *Report*, vol. 1, pp. 576, 578.

32. An investigation of a sample of Cambridge students shows that the proportion coming from grammar schools fell from 16 per cent in the period 1752–99 to 7 per cent in the period 1850–99. Of the remaining 93 per cent in the latter period, 82 per cent came from 'public' schools and 11 per cent from private schools. See Hester Jenkins and D. Caradog Jones, 'Social Class of Cambridge Alumni', *British Journal of Sociology*, vol. 1, no. 2 (June 1950).

33. Schools Inquiry Commission, *Report*, vol. 1, pp. 16, 18.

34. *Ibid.*, vol. 1, p. 20.

35. *Ibid.*

36. But see Owen, *English Philanthropy*, chapter 9, 'Remodelling Ancient Trusts: The Endowed Schools'; and Fletcher, *Feminists and Bureaucrats*, for a thorough study of the outcomes of the Commissioners' work for girls' education.

37. G. R. Parkyn, *Life and Letters of Edward Thring* (London, 1900), p. 178.

38. John Honey, 'Tom Brown's Universe: The Nature and Limits of the Victorian Public Schools Community', in Brian Simon and Ian Bradley (eds.), *The Victorian Public School* (Dublin, 1975), pp. 19–33.

39. Rubinstein makes the point that it was the London-based commercial and financial section of the middle class, mainly Anglican, which was 'far readier to send its sons to a major public school and Oxbridge, than were the manufacturers [from the Midlands and the North]'. See Rubinstein, 'Wealth, Elites', pp. 113–14.

40. See Norman Vance, 'The Ideal of Manliness'; and J. A. Mangan, 'Athleticism: A Case Study of the Evolution of an Educational Ideology', in Simon and Bradley (eds.), *The Victorian Public School*, chapters 7 and 9.

41. This position is strongly argued in Martin J. Wiener, *English Culture and the Decline of the Industrial Spirit, 1850–1980* (Cambridge, 1981).

42. For an analysis of Mill's position, see Simon, *The Two Nations*, pp. 74–9.

43. A. Patchett Martin, *Life and Letters of the Right Honourable Robert Lowe Viscount Sherbrooke* (London, 1893), vol. 2, p. 323. To the leading liberals 'this remark was no more than a truism', as James Bryce put it. See Reeder, *Educating Our Masters*, p. 8.

44. L. Althusser, 'Ideology and Ideological State Apparatuses', in L. Althusser, *Lenin and Philosophy and Other Essays* (London, 1971), pp. 121–73. For Antonio Gramsci's position, see his *Prison Notebooks*, ed. and trans. Quintin Hoare and Geoffrey Nowell Smith (London, 1971).

4. Defining institutions: the endowed grammar schools and the systematisation of English secondary education

1. Unpublished letter from Fritz Ringer to Brian Simon.

2. J. M. Compton, in 'Open Competition and the Indian Civil Service 1854–1876', *English*

Historical Review, no. 327 (1968), p. 267, states that the competition scheme was 'drawn up expressly for a high proportion of high honours graduates from the two older universities'.

3. *Return from all schools having an Endowment of more than £500 a year of the number of scholars in regular attendance and the number of hours of study per week*, in continuation of Parl. Paper 393, 14 August 1879, and 121, 23 March 1885. According to this document Eton spent 22 hours per week on classics teaching in the fifth and sixth forms; Harrow spent 30 hours.

4. *Ibid.* Aspiring 'public' schools spent similar amounts of time on classics as did the nine 'great' schools (see note 7): Uppingham 23 hours, Sedbergh 14+ hours, Felsted 24½ hours, Tonbridge 16 hours.

5. J. Lawson, *A Town Grammar School through Six Centuries* (Oxford, 1963). Lawson, in this study of Hull Grammar School, gives a fine example of this process. In 1886, Lawson writes, the school 'was in a constant state of suspended extinction'. In 1890 a school song was written; in 1891 the school acquired a coat of arms, which was soon afterwards worn as a cap badge, marking the beginning of a school uniform. Games were also introduced for the first time at this period.

6. School histories (see below) provide many examples. Chigwell acquired an ex-Lancing master as its head in 1868; Stockport Grammar School appointed a headmaster with Uppingham and Dulwich connections (see note 10).

7. The 'Nine' were Eton, Winchester, Westminster, Charterhouse, St Paul's, Merchant Taylors', Harrow, Rugby and Shrewsbury.

8. *Report of her Majesty's Commissioners appointed to inquire into the Revenues and Management of certain Colleges and Schools and the studies pursued and instruction given therein, 1864.*

9. *Return of pupils in public and private secondary and other schools in England, June 1897*, Education Department, C-8634.

10. The following school histories were consulted: W. E. Brown and F. R. Poskitt, *The History of Bolton School* (Bolton, 1976); H. L. Clarke and W. N. Weech, *A History of Sedbergh School, 1595–1925* (Sedbergh, 1925); M. Cox, *A History of Sir John Deane's Grammar School, Northwich, 1557–1908* (Manchester, 1975); M. R. Craze, *A History of Felsted School, 1564–1947* (Ipswich, 1955); R. E. Davidson, *The History of Truro Grammar and Cathedral School* (Mevagissey, 1970); B. L. Deed, *A History of Stamford School* (Stamford, 1954); M. Eggleshaw, *The History of Wallasey Grammar School Walsall* (Wallasey, [1967]); D. P. J. Fink, *Queen Mary's Grammar School Walsall* (Walsall, 1954); M. A. Fleming, *Witney Grammar School* (Oxford, 1960); L. Fox, *A Country Grammar School: A History of Ashby de la Zouch Grammar School through Four Centuries* (Oxford, 1967); A. D. Grounds, *A History of King Edward VI Grammar School, Retford* (Retford, 1970); J. A. Graham and B. Phythian, *The Manchester Grammar School, 1515–1965* (Manchester, 1965); E. Hinchcliffe, *Appleby Grammar School – from Chantry to Comprehensive* (Appleby, 1974); W. J. Hodgkiss, *The History of Ashton-in-Makerfield Grammar School* (Liverpool, 1953); R. E. Huddleston, J. R. Wilson and J. S. Warbrick, *The History of Bentham Grammar School, 1726–1976* Lancaster, 1976?); R. L. Hudson, *The History of Dartford Grammar School* (Dartford, 1966); D. M. Day, *The History of Lymm Grammar School* (Altrincham, 1960); J. C. V. Kendall and M. P. Jackson, *A History of the Free Grammar School, Chesterfield* (privately roneoed, 1965); J. Lawson, *A Town Grammar School through Six Centuries* (Oxford, 1963); E. Lloyd, *Nantwich and Acton Grammar School, 1560–1960* (Nantwich, 1960); B. Newman, *The Bosworth Story* (London, 1967); R. S. Paul and W. J. Smith, *A History of Middleton Grammar School, 1412–1964* (Middleton, 1965); N. Salmon, *Ilkley Grammar School, 1607–1957* (Ilkley, 1957); W. Serjeant, *A History of Tuxford Grammar School* (Tuxford, 1969?); G. Stott, *A History of Chigwell School* (Ipswich, 1960); A. W. Thomas, *A History of Nottingham High School, 1515–1953* (Nottingham, 1957); W. G. Torrance, *The History of Alleyne's Grammar School, 1558–1958* (Uttoxeter, 1959); B. Varley, *The History of Stockport Grammar School* (Manchester, 1946); L. P. Wenham, *The History of Richmond School* (Richmond, 1958); A. White, *A History of Loughborough Endowed Schools* (Loughborough, 1969).

11. Following the Endowed Schools Act (1869), three Endowed Schools Commissioners were appointed to administer the Act. For reasons which are too lengthy to be mentioned here

the Act was subsequently modified in 1874 and powers of supervision and reorganisation of endowed schools passed to the Charity Commission. From my study of the files of individual schools, it appears that there was very considerable continuity of policy and action between the Endowed Schools Commissioners and the Charity Commissioners. For the purposes of this study, therefore, I have not thought it relevant to distinguish between them, and both Endowed Schools Commissioners and the Charity Commissioners are referred to throughout as 'the Commissioners'.

12. Set B in Figure 4.1 was obtained by listing all those schools which gained at least one open award in 1887 as listed in the *Pall Mall Gazette* for that year on Saturday 15 October. In Figure 4.3 Set B was obtained by listing the 1887 *Pall Mall Gazette* schools together with all the schools listed in the table entitled '77 Schools by Oxford and Cambridge Scholarship Success' in John Honey, *Tom Brown's Universe* (Millington, 1977), p. 245. The term 'awards', which is widely used in this chapter, requires some explanation. Both fees and living expenses at Oxford and Cambridge in the nineteenth century were high and a heavy expense for the middle ranks of the professions and of the administration. Awards varied in size from £50 to £60 per annum and can be roughly grouped under the following headings:

Closed awards	*Open awards*
(a) Given by a particular college and only to pupils of one named school or group of schools.	Given by individual colleges to pupils from any school reaching the required standard of academic performance.
(b) Awards attached to a particular school and given to a pupil from that school to enable him to take up a place at Oxford or Cambridge.	

13. Schools Inquiry Commission, *Report*, vol. 1, pp. 164–8.
14. *Ibid.* pp. 15–16.
15. *Return from all schools having an Endowment of more than £500 a year of the number of scholars in regular attendance and the number of hours of study per week*, in continuation of Parl. Paper 393, 1879, and 121, 23 March 1885.
16. *Return as regards the number of Schemes finally approved and in force in England and Wales under the Endowment Schools Act 1869, 1873, 1874, and 1879*, PF 373 E 1.
17. PRO ED 27/5536.
18. PRO ED 27/1551.
19. PRO ED 27/1555.
20. PRO ED 27/5177.
21. PRO ED 27/5178.
22. PRO ED 27/5536.
23. PRO ED 27/5240.
24. Sources: Schools Inquiry Commission, vol. 1: *Final Summary for Whole of England and Wales; Return of pupils in public and private secondary and other schools, June 1897*.
25. Brown and Poskitt, *History of Bolton School*.
26. Kendall and Jackson, *History of Chesterfield*.
27. Cox, *History of Northwich*.
28. Salmon, *Ilkley Grammar School*.
29. Lawson, *A Town Grammar School*.
30. Grounds, *King Edward VI Grammar School*, pp. 185, 215.
31. Eggleshaw, *History of Wallasey*.
32. I should have liked to include Bampton and Lowther schools since these also figure on the SIC list of Westmorland schools. However, there were no files on Bampton, and Lowther appears to have closed as a grammar school after 1867.
33. PRO ED 27/5127.
34. PRO ED 27/5155.
35. PRO ED 27/5200.
36. *Ibid.*
37. *Ibid.* Emphasis added.
38. PRO ED 27/5240.
39. PRO ED 27/5242. Emphasis added.

5. The reconstruction of secondary education in England, 1869–1920

1. For this feature of English education, see J. Ben David and A. Zloczower, 'Universities and Academic Systems in Modern Societies', *European Journal of Sociology*, vol. 3 (1962), pp. 45–84.
2. See also Gillian Sutherland, 'Secondary Education: The Education of Middle Classes', in Gillian Sutherland (ed.), *Education: Commentaries on British Parliamentary Papers* (London, 1977), pp. 137–66.
3. W. E. Marsden, 'Social Stratification and Nineteenth-Century English Urban Education', in R. Goodenough and W. E. Marsden (eds.), *Urban Educational History in Four Nations* (New York and London, forthcoming). For a survey of ecological adaptation, see his other writings, especially 'Education and the Social Geography of Nineteenth-Century Towns and Cities', in David Reeder (ed.), *Urban Education in the 19th Century* (London, 1977), pp. 49–73; and 'Schools for the Urban Lower Middle Class: Third Grade or Higher Grade?', in Peter Searby (ed.), *Educating the Victorian Middle Class* (Leicester, 1982), pp. 45–56.
4. The most sophisticated exposition of how education became a site of struggle between competing social groups in the cities is contained in the relevant chapters of Dennis Smith, *Conflict and Compromise: Class Formation in English Society 1830–1914. A Comparative Study of Birmingham and Sheffield* (London, 1982).
5. Endowed Schools Commission, *Report, 1872*, XXIV, appendix 2.
6. The Endowed Schools Commission was responsible for establishing schemes relating to 178 grammar schools, and the Charity Commission was responsible for establishing schemes relating to 355 grammar schools. See Endowed Schools Commission *Final Report, 1875*, XXVII, appendices A and B; *Royal Commission on Secondary Education, 1895*, XLIX, vol. 9, appendix A (1), Roby Return.
7. As illustrated in statements cited by Roy Lowe in 'Robert Morant and the Secondary Regulations of 1904', *Journal of Educational Administration and History*, vol. 16, no. 1 (1984), pp. 37–46.
8. Schools Inquiry Commission, *Report, 1867–8*, XXVII, Appendix, pp. 152–5.
9. Frank Musgrove, *School and the Social Order* (London, 1979), p. 103.
10. G. Gomez, 'The Endowed Schools Acts, 1869 – a Middle-Class Conspiracy? The South-West Lancashire Evidence', *Journal of Educational Administration and History*, vol. 6, no. 1 (1974), pp. 9–18. See also the data on Preston Grammar School, which shows that two-thirds of admissions (1859–63 and 1869–73) were drawn from the lower middle class (P. J. Dixon, 'The Lower Middle Class Child in the Grammar School: A Lancashire Industrial Town, 1850–1875', in Searby, *Educating the Victorian Middle Class*, pp. 57–71).
11. Michael Sanderson, 'Literacy and Social Mobility in the Industrial Revolution in England', *Past and Present*, vol. 56 (1972), pp. 75–104.
12. Schools Inquiry Commission, *Assistant Commissioners Report*, vol. 9, pp. 245–460.
13. See the documentation in J. S. Hurt, *Elementary Schooling and the Working Classes, 1860–1918* (London, 1979), pp. 12–16.
14. Schools Inquiry Commission, *Assistant Commissioners Report*, vol. 8, pp. 118–19.
15. W. E. Marsden, basing his analysis on inspectors' reports and reports to the Newcastle Commission on Popular Education (1861), refers to this initiative and the debate on the subsidising of middle-class children through the elementary schools in his forthcoming essay on 'Social Stratification and Nineteenth-Century English Urban Education'.
16. Schools Inquiry Commission, *Report*, vol. 1, appendix, pp. 150–1.
17. T. W. Bamford, 'Public Schools and Social Class, 1800–1850', *British Journal of Sociology*, vol. 12 (1961), table 3, p. 229; J. A. Banks, *Victorian Values* (London, 1981), p. 54 and, in general, chapter 6 on the 'meritocratic emphasis'.
18. W. D. Rubinstein, 'Wealth, Elites and the Class Structure of Modern Britain', *Past and Present*, vol. 76 (1977), pp. 99–126.
19. Schools Inquiry Commission, *Assistant Commissioners Report*, vol. 9, p. 147.
20. Rev. E. H. Giffard, 'Statistics of King Edward's Grammar School, Birmingham', *National Association for the Promotion of Social Science, 1857* (London, 1858), pp. 130–4. The

classical school actually drew more than one half of its pupils from the business class at this date.

21. Rev. J. S. Howson, 'Statistics of the Liverpool Collegiate Institution', *National Association for the Promotion of Social Science, 1858* (London, 1859), pp. 241–9. The upper classical school drew 38 per cent of its 143 boys from parents in finance and merchanting, and 39 per cent from parents in professional occupations.

22. But according to an Assistant Commissioner the lower middle class preferred local schools, and the small centrally placed grammar schools were of poor quality (Schools Inquiry Commission, *Assistant Commissioners Report*, vol. 17, pp. 239–42).

23. See also David Ward, 'The Public Schools and Industry in Britain after 1870', *Journal of Contemporary History*, vol. 2 (1967), pp. 37–52; and, for girls' schools, Joyce S. Pederson, 'The Reform of Women's Secondary and Higher Education: Institutional Change and Social Values in Mid- and Late-Victorian England', *History of Education Quarterly*, vol. 19 (1979), pp. 61–94.

24. See Dennis Smith, 'The Urban Genesis of School Bureaucracy', in Roger Dale *et al.* (eds.), *Schooling and Capitalism* (London, 1976), pp. 66–77.

25. George Griffith, *Going to Markets and Grammar Schools* (London, 1870) is an interesting contemporary survey.

26. For examples, see F. E. Balls, 'The Endowed Schools Act of 1869 and the Development of the British Grammar School', *Durham Research Review*, vol. 19–20 (1967), pp. 207–15, 219–29.

27. F. E. Balls, 'The Endowment of Education in the Nineteenth Century: The Case of the Bedford Harpur Trust', *History of Education*, vol. 6, no. 2 (1977), pp. 103–13.

28. For an example of such a school, see A. D. Ground, *A History of King Edward VI Grammar School Retford* (Retford, 1970), pp. 160–4.

29. C. P. Hill, *The History of Bristol Grammar School* (London, 1951).

30. An earlier return of 1883 showed that no first-grade and only 13 second-grade schools had become third grade. Although there had been 25 new third-grade schools provided and 21 elementary schools had become third grade, this hardly made up the provision needed (Select Committee on the Endowed Schools Act, *Report, 1886*, CIXI, appendix 3). For a comment on the situation as revealed by Bryce (The Royal Commission on Secondary Education), see Harold Perkin, 'Middle-Class Education and Employment in the Nineteenth Century. A Critical Note', *Economic History Review*, vol. 14 (1961–2), esp. p. 130.

31. R. M. Hartwell, 'The Service Revolution: The Growth of Services in the Modern Economy 1700–1914', in C. Cipolla (ed.), *Fontana Economic History of Europe* (Glasgow, 1973), vol. 11, pp. 358–96.

32. See, in general, Geoffrey Crossick, 'The Emergence of a Lower Middle Class in Britain: A Discussion', in Geoffrey Crossick (ed.), *The Lower Middle Class in Britain* (London, 1977), pp. 11–60; and Gregory Anderson, *Victorian Clerks* (Manchester, 1976).

33. Crossick, 'The Emergence of a Lower Middle Class', p. 21.

34. D. C. Coleman, 'Gentlemen and Players', *Economic History Review*, vol. 26 (1973), pp. 92–116.

35. See the discussion in Christine Heward, 'Industry, Cleanliness and Godliness: Sources and Problems in the History of Scientific and Technical Education and the Working Classes, 1850–1910', *Studies in Science Education*, vol. 7 (1980), pp. 87–128.

36. For the distribution of minor scholarships, see Marsden's table in 'Schools for the Urban Lower Middle Class'.

37. A. H. D. Acland and H. L. Smith, *Studies in Secondary Education* (London, 1906), makes this point. In a modern study of pupils winning county junior technical scholarships to attend the Technical School in Leicester, from 1893 to 1899, it was found that one-third entered clerical occupations. See Malcolm Seaborne, 'Education in the Nineties: the work of the Technical Instruction Committees', in Brian Simon (ed.), *Education in Leicestershire, 1540–1940* (Leicester, 1968), p. 190.

38. It must have been disconcerting and demoralising, therefore, when the Board of Education started raising objections to the quality of buildings and facilities after 1900. The two

Bristol schools, for example, cost £14,000 and £24,000 respectively to erect, and in view of the careful planning and financial outlay it can be inferred that the School Board was not thinking of these schools as a short-term or temporary expedient.

39. For Bradford, see the summary and citation of references in Marsden, 'Schools for the Urban Lower Middle Class', and for Sheffield the section on Sheffield in Smith, *Conflict and Compromise*.

40. H. J. Foster, 'Private, Proprietary and Public Elementary Schools in a Lancashire Residential Town: A Contest for the Patronage of the Lower Middle Class', in Searby (ed.), *Educating the Victorian Middle Class*, pp. 71–85.

41. Department of Science and Art, *Returns, 1898–9*.

42. A return of 1883 shows that 42 per cent of awards to 166 endowed schools had gone to children from elementary schools, but only 9 per cent of these were held in first-grade schools. P. Gordon cites the return in 'The Endowed Schools Act and the Education of the Poor, 1860–1900', *Durham Research Review*, vol. 17 (1966), pp. 47–58. A similar distribution has been discerned from analysing returns from the 1890s which show below-average intakes of elementary scholars in those schools with more boarders and university entrants. See K. I. MacDonald, 'The Public Elementary School Pupil within the Secondary School System of the 1890s', *Journal of Educational Administration and History*, vol. 6, no. 1 (1974), pp. 19–26.

43. In addition to works already cited, see Patrick Keane, 'An English County and Education: Somerset 1889–1902', *English Historical Review*, vol. 138 (1973), pp. 286–311; and P. H. J. H. Gosden and P. Sharp, *The Development of an Education Service: The West Riding, 1889–1974* (Oxford, 1978).

44. Intermediate schools were also introduced into Wales.

45. Dennis Smith summarises this situation in 'Social Conflict in Urban Education', in Reeder, *Urban Education in the 19th Century*, pp. 95–114. See also C. Heward, 'Education, Examinations and the Artisans', in Roy Macleod (ed.), *Days of Judgement* (Driffield, 1982), pp. 45–64.

46. *The Times*, 22 September 1897.

47. For the 'organic' relationships between elementary and secondary education with the development of higher-grade and organised science schools, see E. J. R. Eaglesham, *From School Board to Local Authority* (London, 1956), appendices A–E. This also reproduces the first Morant memorandum on the higher-grade schools (1897).

48. Royal Commission on Secondary Education, *Report, 1895*, XLIII, vol. 1, pp. 130–5.

49. Brian Simon, *Education and the Labour Movement* (London, 1965).

50. For this memorandum, see R. C. Lilley, 'Attempts to Implement the Bryce Commission's Recommendations – and its Consequences', *History of Education*, vol. 11, no. 2 (1982), pp. 99–111.

51. K. O. Roberts, 'The Separation of Secondary Education from Technical Education, 1889–1903', *The Vocational Aspect of Education*, vol. 21, no. 49 (1969), pp. 101–5.

52. Board of Education, *Report upon Questions affecting Higher Elementary Schools, 1906*, p. 23. The progress of higher elementary schooling after this date is discussed in Olive Banks, *Parity and Prestige in English Secondary Education* (London, 1955), chapter 4.

53. I am grateful to Brian Simon for this point, as elaborated in his unpublished paper on the 'pedagogy of optimism'.

54. See E. J. R. Eaglesham, 'Implementing the Education Act of 1902', *British Journal of Educational Studies*, vol. 10, no. 2 (1962), pp. 153–75; and the relevant section of Asher Tropp, *The Schoolteachers* (London, 1957).

55. Olive Banks drew attention to this point initially. See also A. Kazamias, *Politics, Society and Secondary Education in England* (Philadelphia, 1966).

56. As pointed out by Roy Lowe in his 'Robert Morant'.

57. E. W. Jenkins, 'Science Education and the Secondary School Regulations, 1902–09', *Journal of Educational Administration and History*, vol. 10, no. 2 (1978), pp. 31–8.

58. N. Whitbread, 'The Early Twentieth-Century Secondary Curriculum Debate in England', *History of Education*, vol. 13, no. 3 (1984), pp. 221–33.

59. J. Roach, 'Examinations and the Secondary Schools 1900–1945', *History of Education*, vol. 8, no. 1 (1979), pp. 45–58; Banks, *Parity and Prestige*, pp. 41–2, 53.

60. In Fritz Ringer, *Education and Society in Modern Europe* (Bloomington and London, 1979), pp. 220, 232.
61. Whitbread, 'Curriculum Debate', p. 231.
62. All statistics from the Board of Education, *Returns*.
63. This kind of reappraisal is being undertaken by Mel Vlaeminke, a PhD research student at the Leicester School of Education, as part of a larger historical study of secondary education in Bristol and other cities. I am grateful for her assistance in making suggestions about the significance of the higher-grade schools and the attitudes of the Board of Education towards them.
64. Lord Eustace Percy, *Education at the Crossroads* (London, *c.* 1930), p. 59.

6. The sinews of society: the public schools as a 'system'

1. Though many of those participating in these campus riots and sit-ins in that period were motivated by heartfelt political concerns, none the less the behaviour which resulted sometimes offered uncanny parallels with that of English 'public' school rebellions. See John Honey, *Tom Brown in South Africa* (Grahamstown, 1972), p. 22; F. A. Y. Brown, *Family Notes* (Genoa, 1917), p. 86; and Philippe Ariès, *Centuries of Childhood* (London, 1962), pp. 315–18.
2. For details, see John Honey, *Tom Brown's Universe* (London and New York, 1977), esp. chapter 3. On preparatory schools, see also Donald Leinster-Mackay, *The Rise of the English Preparatory School* (London, 1984).
3. Honey, *Tom Brown's Universe*, chapter 4; B. Simon and I. Bradley (eds.), *The Victorian Public School* (Dublin, 1975), chapter 2.
4. Honey, *Tom Brown's Universe*, pp. 203–29.
5. *Ibid.*, p. 125.
6. See, for example, Robert Roberts, *The Classic Slum* (Manchester, 1971), chapter 8.
7. J. W. Mackail, *J. L. Strachan-Davidson* (Oxford, 1925), p. 68.
8. Computations by the author from entries in the *Keble College Register, 1870–1925*, ed. O. C. C. Nicolls (Oxford, 1927); and *Balliol College Register, 1833–1933*, ed. I. Elliott (Oxford, 1934). Research by J. Honey and Mark Curthoys on the origins of the Oxford entrants (to be reported in the forthcoming 1800–1914 volumes of the official history of the university) shows that, of all those who received schooling within the United Kingdom and who matriculated in the three academic years 1895–8, three-fifths came from the 50 schools identified as the main schools of the 'public' schools community (Column A in Table 6.1), as did also an exactly similar proportion of the entrants in the three years 1911–14.
9. Michael Sanderson, *The Universities and British Industry, 1850–1970* (London, 1972), pp. 52–9. Some of these issues are dealt with in Martin J. Wiener, *English Society and the Decline of the Industrial Spirit, 1850–1980* (Cambridge, 1981).
10. Sir Ralph Furse, *Aucuparius* (London, 1962); J. A. Mangan, 'The Education of an Elite Imperial Administration: The Sudan Political Service and the British Public School System', *International Journal of African Historical Studies*, vol. 15, no. 2 (May 1982).
11. F. M. L. Thompson, chapter on 'Britain', in David Spring (ed.), *European Landed Elites in the Nineteenth Century* (Baltimore, 1977).
12. Honey, *Tom Brown's Universe*, chapter 5.

7. Structural change in English higher education, 1870–1920

1. *Statement on the Needs of Oxford University, 1907* (Bodleian Library, MS Top Oxon, c. 236).
2. Bodleian Library, MS. LH/Misc/1/1.
3. R. A. Lowe, 'English Elite Education in the Late Nineteenth and Early Twentieth Centuries', in W. Conze and J. Kocka, *Bildungsbürgertum im 19. Jahrhundert* (Stuttgart, 1985), pp. 149–53.
4. *Birmingham University Prospectus* (1904).

5. Letter from John Daw to Joshua Fitch, 2 May 1871 (PRO ED 27/695).
6. Letter from James Bryce to Henry Sidgwick, 4 January 1868 (Bodleian Library, MS Bryce 15).
7. Letter from H. E. Rawlinson (President of the Royal Geographical Society) to the Vice Chancellor, 3 July 1871 (Bodleian Library, MS MR/7/4/1).
8. Letter from W. R. Anson (All Souls) to the Royal Geographical Society, 15 February 1899 (Bodleian Library, MS MR/7/4/4).
9. *Transactions of the National Association for the Promotion of Social Science* (London, 1870), p. 311.
10. *Ibid.*, p. 316.
11. *Trans NAPSS* (London, 1876), p. 44.
12. *Report of a Conference on Secondary Education in England* (Oxford, 1893), p. 11.
13. *Ibid.*
14. *Statement on the Needs of Oxford University, 1907.*
15. Lord Curzon of Kedleston, *Principles and Methods of University Reform* (Oxford, 1909), p. 46.
16. Letter on University Extension (unsigned) (Bodleian Library, MS Eng. Hist. c. 786).
17. R. A. Lowe, 'Some Forerunners of R. H. Tawney's Longton Tutorial Class', *History of Education*, vol. 1, no. 1 (1972), pp. 53–4.
18. Curzon, *Principles and Methods*, p. 49.
19. *Ibid.*, p. 64.
20. See R. A. Lowe, 'The Expansion of Higher Education in England', in K. H. Jarausch (ed.), *The Transformation of Higher Learning, 1860–1930* (Stuttgart, 1982), pp. 37–56.
21. Bryce Report, *Secondary Education* (London, 1895), vol. 1, p. 219.
22. *Ibid.*, vol. 1, p. 234.
23. *Ibid.*, vol. 1, p. 142.
24. Board of Education, *Reports from University Colleges* (London, annually from 1894).
25. Letter from James Bryce to Henry Sidgwick, 21 October 1897 (Bodleian Library, MS Bryce 15).
26. Letter from Henry Sidgwick to James Bryce, 6 November 1899 (*ibid.*).
27. Papers relating to the 1922 Commission on the Reform of the Ancient Universities (Bodleian Library, MSS Top Oxon, b. 104–9, c. 267).
28. *Ibid.*
29. *Ibid.*
30. *Ibid.*
31. Board of Education Consultative Committee, *Interim Report on Scholarships for Higher Education* (London, 1916), p. 66.
32. *Ibid.*, p. 31.
33. G. S. M. Ellis, *The Poor Student and the University* (London, 1942), p. 6.
34. D. V. Glass and J. L. Gray, 'Opportunity and the Older Universities', in L. Hogben, *Political Arithmetic* (London, 1938), pp. 428–33.
35. PRO, ED 12/139.
36. Bryce Report, vol. 1, p. 230.

8. The debate on secondary school reform in France and Germany

1. Antoine Prost, *Histoire de l'enseignement en France, 1800–1967* (Paris, 1969), p. 256.
2. Joseph Moody, *French Education since Napoleon* (Syracuse, 1978), p. 101; Theodore Zeldin, *France: 1848–1945*, vol. 2 (Oxford, 1977), p. 294; Viviane Isambert-Jamati, 'Une réforme des lycées et collèges: Essai d'analyse sociologique de la réforme de 1902', *L'année sociologique*, 3rd series, vol. 20 (1969), pp. 9–60; Patrick Harrigan, *Mobility, Elites, and Education in French Society of the Second Empire* (Waterloo, Ontario, 1980).
3. James Albisetti, *Secondary School Reform in Imperial Germany* (Princeton, 1983).
4. Robert Anderson, *Education in France, 1848–1870* (Oxford, 1975), pp. 56, 67–72, 98–105, 172–3; Nicole Hulin, 'A propos de l'enseignement scientifique: une réforme de l'enseignement secondaire sous le Second Empire, la "bifurcation" (1852–1864)', *Revue d'histoire*

des sciences, vol. 35 (1982), pp. 217–45; Sandra Horvath-Peterson, *Victor Duruy and French Education: Liberal Reform in the Second Empire* (Baton Rouge and London, 1984), pp. 128–31.

5. Anderson, *Education in France*, pp. 180–2; Jules Simon, *La réforme de l'enseignement secondaire* (Paris, 1874), pp. 43, 302–13; Clement Falcucci, *L'humanisme dans l'enseignement secondaire en France an XIXᵉ siècle* (Toulouse and Paris, 1939), pp. 311, 341–2.

6. Fritz Ringer, *Education and Society in Modern Europe* (Bloomington and London, 1979), p. 119; George Weisz, *The Emergence of Modern Universities in France* (Princeton, 1983), p. 178.

7. Albisetti, *Secondary School Reform*, pp. 71–6.

8. Raoul Frary, *La question du latin* (Paris, 1885), pp. 30, 15, 121, 187. See also Robert Gildea, 'Education and the *Classes Moyennes* in the Nineteenth Century', in Donald Baker and Patrick Harrigan (eds.) *The Making of Frenchmen* (Waterloo, Ontario, 1980), p. 293; and Hulin, 'A propos de l'enseignement scientifique', p. 227.

9. Albisetti, *Secondary School Reform*, pp. 62–71, 82–7.

10. Duruy to the Emperor Napoleon III, cited by Horvath–Peterson, *Victor Duruy*, pp. 133–4.

11. C. R. Day, 'Technical and Professional Education in France: The Rise and Fall of *l'enseignement secondaire spécial*, 1865–1902', *Journal of Social History*, vol. 6 (1972–3), pp. 189–90, 186–7; Anderson, *Education in France*, p. 211; Ringer, *Education and Society*, pp. 320, 64–5.

12. Alexandre Ribot, *La réforme de l'enseignement secondaire* (Paris, 1900), p. 18.

13. Zeldin, *France*, vol. 2, p. 294; Day, 'Technical Education', pp. 191–2; Ringer, 'Introduction', p. 7 above.

14. See Léon Bourgeois' comments to the Ribot Commission in Ribot, *La réforme*, p. 285.

15. Frederic Ernest Farrington, *French Secondary Schools* (London, 1910), p. 73; Anderson, *Education in France*, pp. 59–60. I disagree with Moody's assertion (*French Education*, pp. 121–2) that there were few protests about how much pupils had to memorise in the *lycée*.

16. Victor de Laprade, *L'éducation homicide: Plaidoyer pour l'enfance* (Paris, 1868), pp. 30, 45, 19, 133, 81, 71–2, 93.

17. Simon, *La réforme*, pp. 91–2, 84, 302.

18. Falcucci, *L'humanisme*, p. 388; Octave Gréard, *Education et instruction, vol. 3: Enseignement secondaire* (Paris, 1887), p. 1; Paul Bourget, *Outre-Mer: Impressions of America* (New York, 1895), p. 277; Edmond Desmolins, *A quoi tient la supériorité des Anglo-Saxons?* (Paris, 1898), p. 113.

19. Falcucci, *L'humanisme*, p. 377; Alfred Binet and Victor Henri, *La fatigue intellectuelle* (Paris, 1898), p. 7. The Conseil Supérieur was an advisory group of experts linked to the Ministry of Public Instruction. See Weisz, *Modern Universities*, pp. 120–3.

20. Binet and Henri, *La fatigue intellectuelle*, pp. 10–23.

21. See Table 2.4 in Ringer, 'On Segmentation', above.

22. Falcucci, *L'humanisme*, pp. 381, 411–12; Prost, *Histoire de l'enseignement*, p. 251.

23. Viviane Isambert-Jamati, *Crises de la société, crises de l'enseignement: Sociologie de l'enseignement secondaire française* (Paris, 1970), p. 147. I disagree with her argument (p. 145) that there was no link between the reform of the classical track in 1890 and the upgrading of modern secondary education in 1891.

24. Albisetti, *Secondary School Reform*, pp. 208–42.

25. Hippolyte Taine, *Les origines de la France contemporaine* (Paris, 1901), vol. 11, p. 346; Michel Bréal, *Excursions pédagogiques* (Paris, 1882), p. 15; Alfred Fouillée, *L'enseignement au point de vue national* (Paris, 1891), p. 64. On the history of pedagogical training for *lycée* teachers, see Viviane Isambert-Jamati, 'La formation pédagogique des professeurs à la fin du dix-neuvième siècle', *Journal de psychologie normale et pathologique*, vol. 67 (1970), esp. pp. 270–3; on the hostility to 'scientific pedagogy' on the part of the director of the Ecole Normale Supérieure, see Robert Smith, *The Ecole Normale Supérieure and the Third Republic* (Albany, 1982), p. 72.

26. Falcucci, *L'humanisme*, pp. 390, 392; Isambert-Jamati, *Crises*, p. 158.

27. Ribot, *La réforme*, p. 86; Isambert-Jamati, 'La formation pédagogique', pp. 261, 275–91. On the fate of pedagogy in the universities, see Weisz, *Modern Universities*, pp. 280–4.

28. Eugen Weber, 'Gymnastics and Sports in Fin-de-Siècle France', *American Historical Review*, vol. 76 (1971), p. 74; Anderson, *Education in France*, p. 186; Simon, *La réforme*, pp. 138–9; Bréal, *Excursions pédagogiques*, pp. 119, 126.
29. Isambert-Jamati, *Crises*, p. 132; Weber, 'Gymnastics', pp. 79–84; Eugen Weber, 'Pierre de Coubertin and the Introduction of Organized Sport in France', *Journal of Contemporary History*, vol. 5, no. 2 (1970), pp. 7, 13.
30. Farrington, *French Secondary Schools*, pp. 154–8; Weber, 'Gymnastics', p. 76; Weber, 'Coubertin', p. 10; Ribot, *La réforme*, p. 171; Marcel Spivak, 'Le développement de l'éducation physique et du sport français de 1852 à 1914', *Revue d'histoire moderne et contemporaine*, vol. 24 (1977), p. 38.
31. See the comments of two American visitors, James Russell, *German Higher Schools* (New York, 1905), pp. 146–7; and Frederick Bolton, *The Secondary School System of Germany* (New York, 1900), pp. 52–3.
32. Bourgeois, cited in Ribot, *La réforme*, pp. 285–6.
33. Isambert-Jamati, 'Une réforme', p. 50.
34. Frary, *La question du latin*, p. 15; Edouard Maneuvrier, *L'éducation de la bourgeoisie sous la République* (Paris, 1888), p. 24; Taine, *La France contemporaine*, vol. 11, p. 350.
35. Ribot, *La réforme*, p. 72; Ringer, *Education and Society*, p. 320.
36. Georges Fonsegrive, *La question du latin* (Paris, 1898), p. 28; Lavisse cited in Ribot, *La réforme*, p. 215.
37. Gabriel Compayré, 'The Reform in Secondary Education in France', *Educational Review*, vol. 25 (1903), p. 136.
38. Gabriel Compayré, 'Recent Educational Progress in France', *Educational Review*, vol. 27 (1904), p. 28.
39. Albisetti, *Secondary School Reform*, pp. 235–6, 244–7.
40. *Das humanistische Gymnasium*, vol. 11 (1900), pp. 105–24.
41. The Prussian *Gymnasium* regained just 3 hours of Latin after 1900, despite having lost 9 hours in 1882 and 15 in 1892.
42. Fouillée, *L'enseignement*, pp. 63–5, 180, 174–5, 167, 182, 190; Alfred Fouillée, *Les études classiques et la démocratie* (Paris, 1898), pp. 88, 65.
43. Albisetti, *Secondary School Reform*, pp. 91–3, 289.
44. *Ibid.*, p. 283.
45. George Weisz, 'Reform and Conflict in French Medical Education, 1870–1914', in Robert Fox and George Weisz (eds.), *The Organization of Science and Technology in France, 1808–1914* (Cambridge, 1980), p. 88.
46. Albisetti, *Secondary School Reform*, pp. 98–108, 188–9, 244–5.
47. Ringer, *Education and Society*, pp. 316, 335; Weisz, 'French Medical Education', p. 88.
48. Henry Bérenger, *Les prolétaires intellectuelles de France* (Paris, n.d.), pp. 7–14. Fouillée and LeBon cited Bérenger's statistics without comment.
49. Ribot, *La réforme*, p. 74.
50. R. E. Hughes, *The Making of Citizens: A Study in Comparative Education* (London and New York, 1902), p. 223.
51. Simon, *La réforme*, p. 264; Frary, *La question du latin*, pp. 73–5; Gustave LeBon, *The Psychology of Socialism* (New York, 1899), pp. 369, 373. Despite his opposition to classical education, Frary strongly supported elite secondary schools.
52. David Ralston, *The Army of the Republic* (Cambridge, Mass., and London, 1967), pp. 40–2, 104, 303.
53. Fouillée, *Les études classiques*, p. 164; Lavisse cited in Ribot, *La réforme*, p. 214.
54. Frary, *La question du Latin*, p. 67; Bérenger, *Prolétaires*, p. 29; Bourget, *Outre-Mer*, p. 277; Gustave LeBon, *Psychologie de l'éducation* (Paris, 1907), p. 47; LeBon, *Psychology of Socialism*, pp. 126, 150, 369.
55. Weisz, *Modern Universities*, pp. 232–3.
56. Isambert-Jamati, 'Une réforme', p. 50.
57. Ringer, *Education and Society*, pp. 272, 291; Albisetti, *Secondary School Reform*, pp. 288–9.
58. Albisetti, *Secondary School Reform*, pp. 140–58, 178–85, 210–11.

59. Simon, *La réforme*, pp. 313–15; Zeldin, *France*, vol. 2, p. 230.
60. Bréal, *Excursions pédagogiques*, pp. 108–9; Frary, *La question du latin*, p. 158.
61. Anderson, *Education in France*, p. 72; Falcucci, *L'humanisme*, pp. 306, 311; William Keylor, *Academy and Community: The Foundation of the French Historical Profession* (Cambridge, Mass., 1975), p. 20; Moody, *French Education*, pp. 79, 114; Simon, *La réforme*, p. 305.
62. Malet cited in Suzanne Citron, 'Enseignement secondaire et idéologie élitiste entre 1880 et 1914', *Le mouvement social*, vol. 96 (1976), p. 97.
63. Carlton J. H. Hayes, *France: A Nation of Patriots* (New York, 1930), pp. 43–55; Pierre Nora, 'Ernest Lavisse: Son rôle dans la formation du sentiment national', *Revue historique*, vol. 228 (1962), pp. 99–104.
64. Ch. V. Langlois and Charles Seignobos, *Introduction to the Study of History*, trans. G. G. Berry (London, 1898), p. 331; Keylor, *Academy and Community*, pp. 98–9.
65. John Scott, *Republican Ideas and the Liberal Tradition* (New York, 1951), p. 103; J. E. S. Hayward, 'The Official Social Philosophy of the French Third Republic: Léon Bourgeois and Solidarism', *International Review of Social History*, vol. 6 (1961), p. 26; Léon Bourgeois, *L'éducation de la démocratie française* (Paris, n.d.), pp. 53, 184.
66. Falcucci, *L'humanisme*, p. 354; Fouillée, *Les études classiques*, p. 130; Alfred Croiset in Ernest Lavisse *et al.*, *L'éducation de la démocratie* (Paris, 1903), p. 54.
67. Citron, 'Enseignement secondaire'.
68. Isambert-Jamati, 'Une réforme', p. 24; Victor Friedel, 'Problems of Secondary Education in France', *School Review*, vol. 15 (1907), p. 179.

9. On 'systems' of education and their comparability: methodological comments and theoretical alternatives

1. Manning Nash, 'The Role of Village Schools in the Process of Cultural Modernisation', in T. La Belle (ed.), *Education and Development* (Los Angeles, 1972), p. 491.
2. Fritz Ringer, *Education and Society in Modern Europe* (Bloomington and London, 1979), p. 1; Margaret Archer, *Social Origins of Educational Systems* (London and Beverly Hills, 1979), p. 1; Konrad Jarausch (ed.), *The Transformation of Higher Learning, 1860–1930* (Stuttgart, 1983), pp. 7f. Some of the methodological and theoretical problems involved in the comparative approach to the social history of education are discussed in Jürgen Schriewer, 'Vergleichend-historische Bildungsforschung: Gesamttableau oder Forschungsansatz', *Zeitschrift für Pädagogik*, vol. 30, no. 3 (1984), pp. 323–42.
3. Adam Przeworski and Henry Teune, *The Logic of Comparative Social Enquiry* (New York and London, 1970). On the rather inconsistent and controversial transference of the 'logic of comparative inquiry' into the field of comparative education, see the discussion in Jürgen Schriewer, '*Erziehung* und *Kultur*: Zur Theorie und Methodik vergleichender Erziehungswissenschaft', in W. Brinkmann and K. Renner (eds.), *Die Pädagogik und ihre Bereiche* (Paderborn and Munich, 1982), pp. 185–236.
4. Hilary Steedman in an earlier draft of her contribution to this volume, in Willem Frijhoff (ed.), *L'Offre d'Ecole: The Supply of Schooling* (Paris, 1983), p. 165.
5. For an analogous contrasting of predominantly 'endogenous' and 'exogenous' approaches to explaining structural change in modern educational systems, see Mohamed Cherkaoui, *Les changements du système éducatif en France, 1950–1980* (Paris, 1982), pp. 27f.
6. The specific ways of coping with the general economic crisis in late nineteenth-century Europe by restrictive social–protectionist policies in Germany became especially clear in comparative studies. See Commission Internationale d'Histoire des Mouvements Sociaux et des Structures Sociales, *Petite entreprise et croissance industrielle dans le monde aux XIXe et XXe siècles* (Paris, 1981), esp. the Rapport Général. See also Heinrich August Winkler, *Liberalismus und Antiliberalismus* (Göttingen, 1979).
7. Ringer, *Education and Society*, pp. 231–47.
8. Niklas Luhmann, *Soziologische Aufklärung* (3 vols., Opladen, 1970–81); Niklas Luhmann, 'Differentiation of Society', *Canadian Journal of Sociology*, vol. 2 (1977), pp. 29–53; Niklas Luhmann and Karl-Eberhard Schorr, *Reflexionsprobleme im Erziehungssystem* (Stuttgart, 1979); Niklas Luhmann, *The Differentiation of Society* (New York, 1982).

9. Luhmann, 'Differentiation of Society', p. 35.
10. Emile Durkheim, *Education et sociologie* (Paris, 1973), pp. 47ff.
11. Karl Mannheim, *Wissenssoziologie: Auswahl aus dem Werk*, ed. Kurt Wolff (Berlin and Neuwied, 1964), p. 652.

10. Systematisation: a critique

1. Detlef Müller, 'The Qualifications Crisis and School Reform in the Late Nineteenth Century', *History of Education*, vol. 9 (1980), p. 315. I had to complete this essay without having a copy of the final version of Müller's contribution to this volume, so that my comments are based on earlier drafts.
2. Müller, 'The Qualifications Crisis', p. 315.
3. Matthew Arnold, *Higher Schools and Universities in Germany* (London, 1874), p. 5.
4. Müller, 'The Qualifications Crisis', p. 326.
5. Even historians who speak of an absolute oversupply of students in the last years of the Weimar Republic usually do not suggest that in principle too large a percentage of the age cohort was attending the universities.
6. Müller, 'The Qualifications Crisis', p. 331.
7. Hartmut Titze, 'Enrollment Expansion and Academic Overcrowding in Germany', in Konrad Jarausch (ed.), *The Transformation of Higher Learning, 1860–1930* (Stuttgart and Chicago, 1983), pp. 66–8.
8. Fritz Ringer, *Education and Society in Modern Europe* (Bloomington and London, 1979), pp. 272, 291. For a more thorough statement of this thesis, see James Albisetti, *Secondary School Reform in Imperial Germany* (Princeton, 1983), especially pp. 287–90.
9. For Germany, see especially Konrad Jarausch, *Students, Society, and Politics in Imperial Germany* (Princeton, 1982).
10. For a more detailed critique of Müller's views about the 'comprehensive' *Gymnasium* before 1870, see Peter Lundgreen, 'Die Bildungschancen beim Übergang von der 'Gesamtschule' zum Schulsystem der Klassengesellschaft im 19. Jahrhundert', *Zeitschrift für Pädagogik*, vol. 24 (1978), pp. 101–15.
11. Robert Anderson, 'Secondary Education in Mid-Nineteenth-Century France: Some Social Aspects', *Past and Present*, vol. 53 (1971), p. 134; Patrick Harrigan, *Mobility, Elites, and Education in French Society of the Second Empire* (Waterloo, Ontario, 1980), pp. 18, 21–2; Robert Anderson, *Education in France, 1848–1870* (Oxford, 1975), pp. 60, 71; Robert Gildea, 'Education and the *Classes Moyennes* in the Nineteenth Century', in Donald Baker and Patrick Harrigan (eds.), *The Making of Frenchmen* (Waterloo, Ontario, 1980), pp. 279–84.
12. Titze, 'Enrollment Expansion', p. 78.
13. For the effects of the Endowed Schools Act on girls' education, see Sheila Fletcher, *Feminists and Bureaucrats: A Study of the Development of Girls' Education in the Nineteenth Century* (Cambridge, 1980).

11. Segmentation: a critique

1. P. Steinbach, 'Alltagsleben und Landesgeschichte', *Hessisches Jahrbuch für Landesgeschichte*, vol. 29 (1979), pp. 225–305; p. 259 is critical of the analyses of Lundgreen and others.
2. See, for example, H. Kaelble, 'Chancengleichheit und akademische Ausbildung in Deutschland, 1910–1960', *Geschichte und Gesellschaft*, vol. 1 (1975), pp. 121–49; and K. Hammerich, *Aspekte einer Soziologie der Schule* (Düsseldorf, 1975).
3. Fritz Ringer, *Education and Society in Modern Europe* (Bloomington and London, 1979), pp. 22–31.
4. *Ibid.*, p. 30. See also the controversy with Lundgreen in P. Lundgreen, 'Bildung und Besitz – Einheit oder Inkongruenz in der europäischen Sozialgeschichte', *Geschichte und Gesellschaft*, vol. 7 (1981), pp. 262–75; and Fritz Ringer, 'Bestimmung und Messung von Segmentierung', *Geschichte und Gesellschaft*, vol. 8 (1982), pp. 280–5.
5. Ringer, *Education and Society*, pp. 29f.

6. Fritz Ringer, 'Education and the Middle Classes in Modern France', in W. Conze and J. Kocka (eds.), *Bildungsbürgertum in 19. Jahrhundert, Teil I: Bildungssystem und Professionalisierung im internationalen Vergleich* (Stuttgart, 1985), pp. 109–46.

7. P. Bourdieu, *Die feinen Unterschiede* (Frankfurt a.M., 1982); Ringer, 'Education and the Middle Classes', p. 109, note 1.

8. Ringer, 'Education and the Middle Classes', p. 109.

9. Fritz Ringer, 'Differences and Cross-National Similarities among Mandarins', *Comparative Studies in Society and History* (January 1986).

10. P. Drewek and K. Harney, 'Relative Autonomie: Selektivität und Expansion im modernen Schulsystem', *Zeitschrift für Pädagogik*, vol. 28 (1982), pp. 591–608.

11. E. Kästner, *Das fliegende Klassenzimmer: Ein Roman für Kinder* (Zürich, 1933).

12. M. R. Lepsius, *Extremer Nationalismus: Strukturbedingungen vor der nationalsozialistischen Machtergreifung* (Stuttgart, 1966).

13. Fritz Ringer, *The Decline of the German Mandarins: The German Academic Community, 1890–1933* (Cambridge, Mass., 1969).

Index

DATE LOANED

GAYLORD 3563			PRINTED IN U.S.A.